Andreas Storkenmaier

Financial Markets and Public Information

Financial Markets and Public Information

by

Andreas Storkenmaier

KIT Scientific Publishing

Dissertation, Karlsruher Institut für Technologie
Fakultät für Wirtschaftswissenschaften
Tag der mündlichen Prüfung: 26. Mai 2011
Referenten: Prof. Dr. Ryan Riordan, Prof. Dr. Rudi Studer

Impressum

Karlsruher Institut für Technologie (KIT)
KIT Scientific Publishing
Straße am Forum 2
D-76131 Karlsruhe
www.ksp.kit.edu

KIT – Universität des Landes Baden-Württemberg und nationales
Forschungszentrum in der Helmholtz-Gemeinschaft

KIT Scientific Publishing 2011
Print on Demand

ISBN 978-3-86644-694-6

Contents

List of Figures

List of Tables

List of Abbreviations

AEX	Amsterdam Exchange Index
AMEX	American Stock Exchange
CAC	Cotation Assistée en Continu
CPI	Corruption Perceptions Index
DAX	Deutscher Aktien Index
ECN	Electronic Communication Network
FSA	Financial Services Authority
GDP	Gross Domestic Product
GMM	General Method of Moments
ICT	Information and Communication Technology
IME	Information and Market Engineering
IPO	Initial Public Offering
IT	Information Technology
KIT	Karlsruhe Institute of Technology
LSE	London Stock Exchange
MiFID	Markets in Financial Instruments Directive
MRR	Madhavan, Richardson, and Roomans
MTF	Multilateral Trading Facility
NIST	National Institute of Standards and Technology
NMS	National Market System
NYSE	New York Stock Exchange
OLS	Ordinary Least Squares
PNAC	Primary News Access Code
RIC	Reuters Instrument Code
RNSE	Reuters NewsScope Sentiment Engine
SEC	US Securities and Exchange Commission
SIRCA	Securities Industry Research Centre of Asia-Pacific
SVM	Support Vector Machine
TAQ	Trade and Quote
TRBC	Thomson Reuters Business Classification
TSX	Toronto Stock Exchange
VAR	Vector Autoregression
VMA	Vector Moving Average
WFE	World Federation of Exchanges
WSJ	Wall Street Journal

Chapter 1

Introduction

1.1 Motivation

> "Markets function only through the transmission of information – both good and bad. It used to be that the fast horse, the clipper ship, or Mister Reuter's land telegraph brought the news by which fortunes were made and lost. Today it is the electron."[1]

This quote, given almost thirty years ago, posits a long history of interaction between news and financial markets while also addressing the dramatic increase in the speed of news dissemination since the early days of large news organizations. Finance literature includes studies that analyze news events even back in the mid 19th century. Willard et al. (1996) use prices from financial markets to find important events as perceived by the public during the American civil war based on reactions of asset prices to war news. The 19th century financial markets already incorporated new information from news into security prices. The study by Willard et al. (1996) analyzes financial markets and public information during the early days of modern financial markets when information was indeed still transmitted on a "fast horse, the clipper ship, or Mister Reuter's land telegraph".

To make informed decisions on the basis of public information, market participants have always requested expeditious and accurate news. In a world without seamless electronic communication news providers already put great effort into delivering business news as fast as possible. One example is, as already pointed out, the fierce competition for war

[1]Walter B. Wriston, "The Information Society: From Gutenberg to SWIFT", speech given at the SWIFT Conference SIBOS '82 on 23 September 1982 in Washington, D.C., Permanent URL: http://hdl.handle.net/10427/36045. Walter B. Wriston was CEO of Citicorp. from 1967 to 1984.

news during the American civil war which could have had a profound effect on financial markets. To speed up the delivery of American news to England, Paul Julius Reuter, the founder of Thomson Reuters[2], had a telegraph line built from the south-west corner of Ireland to Cork which already had a telegraph connection to London. Selected American news were put into water-proofed canisters on mail steamers arriving from the United States and then thrown into to the water close to the south-west Irish coast. A Reuters steam-tender would then pick up those canisters and the news would be cabled to London, delivering news substantially faster than other news providers (Read, 1999, p. 40).

As communication technology advanced, financial market participants requested the same improvement from news delivery. Once the transatlantic telegraph cable was operational, the speed of news between North America and England had dramatically increased. A long delay of news "had become unacceptable. From now onwards the business community [in London] expected to receive American stock market and commodity information via Reuters in hours instead of days" (Read, 1999, p. 94). This trend has continued until today dramatically driven by the recent advancements in communication and information technology.

The last decades have seen drastic changes in trading technology and the way that financial markets operate. Starting with the computerization of tasks on exchange floors, over the introduction of completely electronic markets, up to algorithmic trading which now makes up more than half of equity trading by recent estimates, trading has become almost completely computerized (Hendershott and Riordan, 2009). Technology and computers have also revolutionized financial news dissemination and created demanding requirements to financial news products from the customer side. As trading technology has advanced, news providers like Thomson Reuters, Bloomberg, and Dow Jones have kept pace and deliver news to market participants around the world within fractions of a second through electronic systems. News that could have taken substantial time to reach financial market centers only a few decades ago is now globally available at the click of a button. Global data networks and satellites even reach to the remotest places on earth. In the quote at the beginning of this chapter, Walter B. Wriston talks about "the electron" as the major mode of news dissemination. Currently, most news is still interpreted by humans but news providers have started to offer newswire products with machine learning

[2]Today, Thomson Reuters in one of the major companies for professional financial information and general professional news dissemination. The company is publicly listed at the Toronto Stock Exchange and the New York Stock Exchange with 2009 revenues of $12.9 Billion and more than 55,000 employees worldwide (see 2009 annual report and http://thomsonreuters.com/).

systems that specifically cater to algorithmic traders. The electron now is not only the basis for news dissemination but it is also in the process of taking over the analysis of news. Computer systems drastically facilitate the information processing capabilities of market participants and the speed of information processing.

News has come a long way since Paul Julius Reuter founded Reuters more than 150 years ago. However, the basic requirements to providers of news, which is relevant for financial markets, remain the same: accuracy, speed, and impartial distribution. News messages are one major part of the public information set available to traders and investors in financial markets. News and information in general have a profound impact on the functioning of financial markets and price dynamics. Despite news' long history of importance for financial markets, the relation of news to financial markets and how this set of public information translates into prices still lacks understanding. This thesis sheds light on the question how newswire messages, specifically machine-readable newswire messages as one form of public information, influence modern computerized equity markets. More generally, this thesis studies how markets process information and translate it into security prices. How information is incorporated into security prices is a key issue in financial markets research and essential for the understanding of financial markets.

1.2 Structure of the Thesis

The main part of this thesis[3] is structured into three chapters. Chapter 2 is based on a joint working paper with Ryan Riordan and Martin Wagener (cf. Riordan, Storkenmaier, and Wagener, 2010b). Chapter 3 is based on a working paper with my co-authors Martin Wagener and Christof Weinhardt (cf. Storkenmaier, Wagener, and Weinhardt, 2010) whereas Chapter 4 is based on a joint working paper with Markus Höchstötter and Ryan Riordan (cf. Höchstötter, Riordan, and Storkenmaier, 2011). Each chapter focuses on a different aspect of public information in modern equity markets and on how information is processed through markets. All chapters base on the same news data set as their proxy for public information. The news data set comprises of Thomson Reuters newswire messages which additionally feature tags for an automatic processing in empirical analyses based on

[3]Financial support by the IME Graduate School at the Karlsruhe Institute of Technology (KIT) funded by Deutsche Forschungsgemeinschaft (DFG) and financial support by the Karlsruhe House of Young Scientists (KHYS) is gratefully acknowledged.

machine learning techniques.[4] Tags include information on the tone of a news message, its relevance, and its novelty.

Chapter 2 studies the impact of intraday firm specific public information on intraday price discovery, liquidity, and trading intensity in a pure electronic limit order market. The analysis is based on trading at the Toronto Stock Exchange since it operates a pure electronic limit order book which is same market model operated by many international exchanges. Additionally, the Canadian equity market has a low degree of fragmentation of order flow during the observation period. The reaction to news is studied separately for novel positive, negative, and neutral news messages which arrive during normal trading hours. Most existing empirical research is not able to ex-ante differentiate newswire messages by their tone (cf. Ranaldo, 2006). Theoretical models suggest varying pre-news information gathering and post-news information processing capabilities of market participants (Kim and Verrecchia, 1991, 1994). Chapter 2 specifically addresses the following research questions:

- How do firm specific newswire messages separated into positive, negative, and neutral messages affect high-frequency price discovery, liquidity, and trading intensity in an electronic limit order market?
- How do firm specific newswire messages in such a setting impact the high-frequency interaction between price discovery, liquidity, and trading intensity?

Chapter 3 studies the impact of firm specific public information on trading in fragmented markets and particularly on the price discovery process, liquidity, and trading intensity. The analysis is based on a sample of FTSE 100 stocks traded on the London Stock Exchange and on Chi-X, the largest multilateral trading facility in Europe. Daily aggregate values for both trading characteristics and newswire messages are used. The impact of public information on trading is based on a comparison between positive, negative, and neutral news days. FTSE 100 stocks are suitable for this study since they exhibit a high degree of fragmentation during the observation period with one large multilateral trading facility, Chi-X, as the major second trading venue after the LSE. In fragmented markets, public information has multiple opportunities to translate into prices which leads to the following research questions:

[4] I am grateful to Thomson Reuters for providing access to Thomson Reuters NewsScope Sentiment Engine archive data.

- How does positive or negative firm specific news impact the price discovery process, liquidity, and trading intensity of individual markets in a fragmented environment?
- How does firm specific news in this setting influence characteristics of market fragmentation and shifts in price discovery, liquidity, and trading intensity between trading venues?

Chapter 4 shifts the focus from high-frequency, intraday, and daily analyses to international equity markets and comovement measured on a monthly level. It studies the influence of the flow of firm specific public information on stock market comovement, thus also on idiosyncratic stock price variability. Existing literature suggests that time-varying characteristics of stock return comovement are influenced by information production (Brockman et al., 2010). The stock return comovement measure in Chapter 4 is based on a common measure developed by Campbell et al. (2001). I use a direct measure of firm specific information based on Thomson Reuters newswire messages. Existing literature also suggests that stock return comovement is heavily influenced by a country's institutional setting (Morck et al., 2000) which might also influence the association of firm specific information and stock return comovement. To clarify the influence of firm specific public information on the time-varying characteristics of stock return comovement, Chapter 4 addresses the following research questions:

- How does the relative firm specific public information flow in an entire market drive the time-varying component of stock return comovement?
- How do country specific financial development and transparency characteristics influence the association of firm specific public information and stock return comovement?

Chapter 2

High-Frequency Market Dynamics and Public Information

2.1 Introduction

Most professional traders observe newswires like Thomson Reuters, Bloomberg, or Dow Jones. They spend a considerable amount of money on such information sources and emphasize the importance of speed and accuracy of news. Newswire messages represent much of the real-time information traders receive. In general, information is central to efficient financial markets and the formation of prices. The intraday high-frequency impact of newswire messages, especially in today's automated equity markets, is however still little understood. It its unclear whether newswire messages contain new information, whether traders act in advance of or after such messages, and how such newswire messages impact the price dynamics in modern electronic limit order markets.

This chapter studies the impact of Thomson Reuters newswire messages on the intraday price dynamics of stocks traded at the Toronto Stock Exchange, a modern electronic exchange. The Toronto Stock Exchange is specifically suitable for such an analysis. First, it represents a pure limit order book market comparable to most continental European Exchanges. Second, in contrast to the German or French market, there is no major second language news stream which reduces potential side effects. Third, during this study's observation period the Canadian market has a very low level of fragmentation.

To my knowledge this is the first market microstructure analysis to cluster newswire messages based on content into positive, negative, and neutral messages. The differentiation between positive, negative, and neutral news enables an investigation of asymmetric reactions to newswire messages based on sentiment. I find higher adverse selection costs around news messages. Negative messages induce significantly higher adverse selection costs than positive news messages. Liquidity increases around positive and neutral messages whereas liquidity slightly decreases around negative messages. Trading intensity increases around all types of news messages. Summing up, the results suggest different information gathering and information processing capabilities of market participants and show asymmetric reactions to good and bad news.

The remainder of this chapter is structured as follows. Section 2.2 introduces related literature. Section 2.3 gives an overview on the institutional structure of the Toronto Stock Exchange. Section 2.4 provides a detailed explanation of the used newswire messages, trade and order book data, and the sample selection process. Section 2.5 introduces the research design and methodology. Section 2.6 provides results and interpretation and Section 2.7 finally concludes this chapter.

2.2 Related Work

Literature that is related to this chapter can be characterized on two dimensions. The first dimension is the type of an information event. Information events might be scheduled macroeconomic news, earnings announcements, or relate to media content which is highly ambiguous and harder to quantify. The Thomson Reuters newswire messages used in this analysis are somewhat in-between those extremes. They are not as widespread and ambiguous as arbitrary media content but are rather ambiguous and hard to interpret in comparison to earnings announcements or macroeconomic news. The second dimension on which related literature can be classified is the temporal scope of the analysis, i.e. whether an analysis focuses on intraday high-frequency effects or daily impacts. Additionally, literature that relates to information processing in trading is highly relevant for my analysis. The notion of information in markets, its impact, and its relevance have had a startling effect on market microstructure research. Since Bagehot (Pseud.) (1971) challenged existing views on the functioning of financial markets and following the seminal works of Glosten and Milgrom (1985) and Kyle (1985), information has been a central theme in many market microstructure papers.

The Bagehot (Pseud.) (1971) paper is not a particularly scientific paper, it was published in a practitioners' journal under a pseudonym without any empirical or theoretical modelling. It has been later revealed that the author was Jack Treynor, a practitioner in the financial services industry (Treynor, 1995). Just by reasoning without mathematical models Bagehot (Pseud.) (1971) introduces the notion of information asymmetry, the role of information in trading, and the relation of both to bid-ask spreads. The author postulates the idea that a spread has to exist without exogenous influences solely based on the fact that some market participants have private information and that specifically the size of the spread also depends on information asymmetry, new ideas back in 1971. Although the article is by no means theoretical or empirical, its basic ideas have inspired much of information-based market microstructure research in the following years and even decades. Traditional economics often argue for the irrelavance of the price setting mechanism or use the fiction of a walrasian auctioneer. However, such assumptions require that trading is irrelevant for a resulting equilibrium. In situations with asymetrically informed market participants such assumptions are unlikely to hold and the price setting and information processing mechanisms matter for the economic outcomes of markets. Glosten and Milgrom (1985) present a theoretical model, formalizing Bagehot (Pseud.) (1971), that explains how informed market participants reveal information to the market only through trading and how as a result a bid-ask spread exists purely based on differential information without exogenous transaction costs. Kyle (1985) introduces one of the first models to examine strategic trading behavior of informed traders. Both theoretical models explain behavior that can be observed in reality and which could not be explained by previous market microstructure models.

As one of the recent papers closest to my analysis, Ranaldo (2006) analyzes the market dynamics of firm specific news at the Paris Bourse from an intraday perspective. His six months news data is based on the Reuters alert system. Additionally, he also analyzes earnings announcements as a comparison. However, in contrast to my data, he is not able to differentiate between news messages based on ex-ante news sentiment (i.e. positive, negative, or neutral). Ranaldo (2006) sorts news data into return bins depending on market reactions to ex-post differentiate between results but he does not use a measure that is exogenous to the market. Also my data spans four years instead of only 6 months. He finds a marginally significant increase in liquidity and slightly lower adverse selection costs around news arrivals for all types of news. Order books are sufficiently liquid around news arrivals which shows strong competition for liquidity supply catering an increase in liquidty demand. Ranaldo (2006) also concludes that "the whole information flow, and not just earnings announcements, has a significant market impact". One paper by Groß-Klußmann and Hautsch (2011) which uses the same news data that I use, has only appeared when I was in the process of finalizing this thesis. While I focus in this chapter on high-frequency market microstructure effects, Groß-Klußmann and Hautsch (2011) focus on high-frequency returns, profitability, and as a consequence on the validity of the news data set. They find that "high-frequency trading activity indeed significantly reacts to intraday company-specific news items". Their paper also reveals a general increase of the bid-ask spread and an increase in trading volume around news messages. However, they do not differentiate between positive, negative, and neutral news items for market microstructure changes around news messages.

Krinsky and Lee (1996) analyze the impact of scheduled earnings announcements on trading at the NYSE and AMEX. They find that the adverse selection component of the spread increases around earnings announcements while at the same time the order processing and inventory holding costs significantly decline. They attribute this effect to temporary information advantages of informed investors and to faster news processing capabilities of public information processors. The authors use intraday data for their analysis and cluster a trading day into half-hour intervals. Additional to information asymmetry, they find an increase in trading volume before and after earnings announcements as well as an increase in volatility around earnings announcements. In an analysis of the impact of scheduled macroeconomic announcements on U.S. government bond trading (Green, 2004), results show higher adverse selection costs around macroeconomic news releases as a consequence of private information impounded through order flow. In contrast to the Toronto Stock Exchange, US government bond trading is organized as a dealer market which might yield different results than a public limit order market. Green (2004) controls for surprise in the empirical model which can be easily done for macroeconomic news since forecasts are available. In contrast, I cannot control for surprise with firm specific newswire messages as no forecast or expected value for comparison is available.[1] Berry

[1] A range of additional studies analyzes the impact of macroeconomic news announcements on financial markets. Niessen (2007) researches into the effect of media coverage on macroeconomic news processing in the futures market for government bonds. Her paper provides evidence that there is macroeconomic information processing prior to economic indicator releases induced through media coverage. Higher pre-announcement media coverage increases investor attention and leads to stronger post-announcement market reactions. Evans and Lyons (2008) investigate the effect of macroeconomic news on foreign exchange markets. They analyze a broad spectrum of macroeconomic news and study the direct influence on prices through order flow. They find that after the announcement of macro economic news there is more information impounded into the market through order flow than during normal times. This finding translates into higher adverse selection after macro news than normal and is not consistent with the hypothesis that public information is directly impounded into the market and directly causes price changes. Andersen et al. (2007) analyze different futures markets with respect to the release of macroeconomic information. They find quick significant responses also in non-US government bond futures

and Howe (1994) also analyze the intraday impact of public information arrivals. Their proxy for public information is the number of news releases by Thomson Reuters' news service per unit of time. They argue that "Reuter's News is selected as [their] data source for public information flow because it provides market participants with a timely source of information on news stories that impact financial markets. [...] Market participants use this news service on a regular basis, along with Dow Jones News Service and perhaps a few other newswires, as a prime news source for economic decision making". This is essentially the same reason why I use Reuters news for the analysis in this chapter. One caveat of their study is the relatively noisy proxy for public information. Berry and Howe (1994) only count the number of Reuters news per half-hour interval and additionally focus on market activity not firm specific trading. Their "results suggest a positive, moderate relationship between public information and trading volume, but an insignificant relationship with price volatility" (Berry and Howe, 1994).

Little evidence exists on the use of news messages by algorithmic traders. Algorithmic trading is defined as "the use of computer algorithms to automatically make certain trading decisions, submit orders, and manage those orders after submission" (Hendershott et al., 2011). Since algorithmic trading data is usually proprietary, researcher often need to fall back on heuristics. Hendershott and Riordan (2009) present one study that uses direct proprietary data which enables them to differentiate between algorithmic traders and human traders. Algorithmic traders in their analysis comprise of both algorithmic traders implementing human investment decisions and high frequency traders. They find that algorithmic traders contribute more to price discovery than human traders. Chaboud et al. (2009) find that algorithmic traders in the foreign exchange market monitor macroeconomic news and pull out of the market for a short time after economic news arrivals to safeguard themselves against higher adverse selection costs. However, after a short time of retreat from the market, they provide more liquidity than non-algorithmic traders the

markets. This finding indicates a quick and thus efficient price discovery process. Fleming and Remolona (1999) find a reduction in trading volume and sharp price reactions with higher volatility after the publication of macroeconomic news in the US Treasury market. In their study, the quoted spread increases around macroeconomic news announcements and then slowly reverts to normal. They also find highly significant cross-market linkages between trading venues in different countries. Hess et al. (2008) focus their analysis on the liquidity provision around macrocenomic news announcements in the German Bund Futures market. They measure liquidity supply through the quoted spread and volume at the best bid and ask. However, they lack order book data to analyze liquidity at order book levels beyond the best bid and ask. In their paper, they find that bid and ask volume decreases around macroeconomic news announcements while the quoted spread increases. This footnote is based on Storkenmaier, Riordan, Weinhardt, and Studer (2010).

hour after macroeconomic news announcements. This result is robust for not only US nonfarm payroll but also for other US macroeconomic news announcements. Chaboud et al. (2009) show that at least some news is monitored automatically by computers.

Ederington and Lee (1993) investigate effects of scheduled macroeconomic news on interest rate and foreign exchange futures markets and find higher volatility after news announcements. They study fast reactions with five-minute intervals after the announcement of macroeconomic information like US nonfarm payroll or the consumer price index. Empirical evidence also suggests that firms assume intraday effects of their announcements and thus time their information releases (Patell and Wolfson, 1982). Firms release good earnings and dividend announcements intraday and bad ones after trading hours. It seems that firms which release information assume that the intraday response of trading to good or bad news matters to the eventual price of their shares. This hints to potential asymmetric responses of traders to good and bad news.

From a theoretical perspective, Kim and Verrecchia (1991) formulate a model which explains higher adverse selection costs prior to an anticipated announcement such as earnings announcements. Traders acquire costly private information to trade in advance of a public announcement. The model also shows what is intuitively clear, the costs for information gathering influence the magnitude of private information gathering negatively. Higher marginal costs to aquire information reduce asymmetric information since less private information is gathered pre-announcement. Finally, Kim and Verrecchia (1991) relax the assumption that an announcement needs to be anticipated. They find that anticipated announcements provide stronger incentives to aquire private information than unanticipated announcements. Their model "also confirms the intuition that [...] volume arises due to differential belief revision" (Kim and Verrecchia, 1991). Put into a short sentence, the Kim and Verrecchia (1991) model shows that pre-announcement information gathering induces information asymmetry. Kim and Verrecchia (1994) introduce in their model the notion that different traders have varying capabilities to interpret earnings announcements. The evaluation of announcements and news depends on a trader's ability to interpret news but it might also depend on the support a trader has in analyzing news announcements. In reality, computers might help to significantly increase the speed of news analysis or staff that connects announcement information with other information sources enables certain traders to aquire superior private information from public information sources. Also, traders have different intellectual capabilities to process information and to process it fast. All this might lead to an increase in adverse selection costs after earnings announcements due to higher information asymmetry. The Kim and Verrecchia (1994) model predicts a reduction in liquidity. However, trading volume might still increase despite a decrease in liquidity around earnings announcements. Another theoretical model developed by Harris and Raviv (1993) attributes effects around the announcement of public information to speculative trading. Traders disagree as result of differential private information or different information processing capabilities which leads to a surge in market activity. The Kandel and Pearson (1995) model is another framework that includes the notion of differential interpretation of public signals which explains high volumes around public announcements.

One challenge in the analysis of public information is the transformation of ambiguous news and media content into variables that can be used in econometric models. Several papers analyze such ambiguous content and study its impact on financial markets. However, those studies usually base their analyses on daily data, often driven by the nature of their public information sources. Newspaper content is one of the most frequently studied types of media content. Niederhoffer (1971) provides one of the earliest papers that analyzes media content. He investigates world events which are defined as having appeared as a five- to eight column headline in the New York Times. One of his stated objectives is to "illustrate and suggest specific applications of some techniques for measuring meaning" (Niederhoffer, 1971). One interesting aspect is that he has the headlines manually classified by untrained observers based on classifying guidelines; something which is done through algorithms in more recent research. The paper shows that world events are followed by larger price changes than normal.

Analyzing Wall Street Journal content seems to be quite popular with financial researchers. Liu et al. (1990) analyze the "Heard-on-the-Street" column in the Wall Street Journal (WSJ) and find abnormal returns on announcement days in combination with higher trading volume. The "Heard-on-the-Street" column is a daily column that is supposed to inform readers about developments and news that could potentially have an effect on stock prices (Liu et al., 1990). The observation period covers more than three years and comprises of more than 1,000 columns which were all classified manually into buy or sell recommendations excluding ambiguous columns. The WSJ "Dartboard" column is analyzed by Barber and Loeffler (1993). The column is called "Dartboard" column because four stocks are randomly chosen by throwing a dart and compared against four stocks recommended by professional investment analysts. Stock market reactions include also positive abnormal returns and higher trading volume. As in the previous study by Liu et al.

(1990), Barber and Loeffler (1993) also manually classify the content of the WSJ column.

Tetlock (2007) analyzes the effect of the WSJ column "Abreast of the Market" on the American stock market and the effect of the market on the column. He finds that high pessimism in the WSJ column is followed by lower market prices and thereafter by a reversal to fundamentals. He extracts the pessimism factor using computer based content analysis techniques. The content analysis technique that he applies is based on counting words that belong to different categories such as positive and negative or active and passive. The automated analysis of content has two advantages. First, manually classifying 4,000 WSJ articles would not be feasible. Second, using a straight forward content analysis technique does not run the risk to introduce a personal bias in contrast to a manual classification. Tetlock et al. (2008) analyze whether linguistic content comprises information relevant for financial markets. They find that relevant information that would be hard to quantify is contained within such content. Their whole paper is focused on quantifying language in financial news stories. In contrast to Tetlock (2007), they "extend that analysis to address the impact of negative words in all Wall Street Journal (WSJ) and Dow Jones News Service (DJNS) stories about individual S&P 500 firms from 1980 to 2004" (Tetlock et al., 2008). Such an amount of news data would be impossible to classify manually. Tetlock et al. (2008) state that "by quantifying language, researchers can examine and judge the directional impact of a limitless variety of events, whereas most studies focus on one particular event type, such as earnings announcements, mergers, or analysts' recommendations. Analyzing a more complete set of events that affects firms' fundamental values allows researchers to identify common patterns in firm responses and market reactions to events". This description is comparable to the news data set that I apply in this thesis which allows for a differentiation between good news and bad news and is available for the overall firm specific information flow. Tetlock (2008) shows in an analysis of the reaction of investors to stale information about S&P 500 firms that markets react to stale news through individual overreacting investors but then show subsequent return reversals.

Antweiler and Frank (2004) investigate the link between the information content of Internet stock message boards and financial markets. They use naive bayesian analysis and support vector machines to classify message board stories. Support vector machines is a method borrowed from machine learning in computer science where it is often applied to linguistic content (cf. Joachims, 1998; Tong and Koller, 2001; Leopold and Kindermann, 2002). Antweiler and Frank (2004) find that stock message board postings support the predicition of market volatility. Disagreement among users of the Internet message boards relates to higher trading volume in line with existing literature that shows that disagreement among traders increases trading activity. One interesting aspect of their work is that they classify linguistic information which does not follow any styleguides or basic structural principles like newspaper articles and nevertheless still retrieve valuable information.

News media also effects individual buyers' perception of and their attention towards specific stocks (Barber and Odean, 2008). Individual buyers are more prone to buy stocks which have drawn their attention through media outlets because individual investors have limited resources to consider stock picks. Individual investors can usually choose from many stocks to buy but mostly sell only stocks which they already have in their portfolios. Traditional theoretical models assume that investors "are equally likely to sell securities with negative signals as they are to buy those with positive signals" (Barber and Odean, 2008), in reality however "for actual investors, the decisions to buy and sell are fundamentally different". In short, the authors find asymmetric investor behavior which is affected by news media. Their proxy for news is the Dow Jones News Service. For individual stocks, Barber and Odean (2008) only discriminate between days with news and days without news. Also the breadth of information dissemination has an influence on stock returns (Fang and Peress, 2009). Fang and Peress (2009) find that firms without news have higher returns than firms that are covered by media even when controls are included in the analysis. To study the relation between mass media and returns, Fang and Peress (2009) count how many articles are published about a specific firm in the New York Times, USA Today, the Wall Street Journal, and the Washington Post.

All these studies[2] have in common that they quantify ambiguous media content or otherwise derive quantitative information from linguistic messages. Analysis techniques range from only counting news to sophisticated content analysis methodologies. What I study in this chapter is similar in terms of the content analyzed. The nature of Thomson Reuters newswire messages is close to newspaper or message board content since it needs some form of transformation of linguistic messages into variables for econometric analyses. In my analysis, pre-transformed, already quantified, news messages from Thomson Reuters are used.

First, this chapter examines how newswire messages separated by their tone affect trading intensity, liquidity, and price discovery. Theory and empirical results suggest that I find

[2]There is a range of other studies with daily data concerning public information arrival that provide insight into information processing and liquidity provision. Among those are Thompson et al. (1987), Fleming and Remolona (1999), and Ryan and Taffler (2007). Veronesi (1999) provides a theory of asymmetric influences of good or bad news depending on the prevailing market sentiment.

an increase in trading activity around news arrivals. Evidence for liquidity and adverse selection, or more broadly speaking price discovery, is mixed. Financial theory however suggests an increase in adverse selection costs and a reduction of liquidity. Second, this chapter investigates how trading activity, liquidity, and adverse selection interact around news messages. Literature suggests that competition in the limit order book might have an influence on liquidity supply catering liquidity demand and existing studies also find a rise in trading activity around news messages (Ranaldo, 2006).

2.3 Institutional Details

The Toronto Stock Exchange (TSX) is Canada's most important equity exchange operated by the TMX Group.[3] The TSX offers trading in equities and equity linked products. TMX Group also operates the Montréal Exchange which provides futures and derivatives trading. The historically fragmented Canadian financial exchange sector was reorganized in 1999. The TSX became Canada's only senior equities exchange whereas options and derivates trading was consolidated on the Montréal Exchange. The Alberta and Vancouver exchanges were merged to form the Canadian Venture Exchange[4] also operated by TMX Group[5]. In 1997, the TSX closed its floor operations and moved trading to a completely electronic market. The TSX is North America's third largest equity exchange by trading volume after Nasdaq and the New York Stock Exchange.[6] Canadian exchanges are regulated on a regional level. The TSX is regulated through the Ontario Securities Commision[7] and through the Investment Industry Regulatory Organization of Canada, a self-regulatory organization. Prices on the TSX are used to calculate the S&P/TSX 60 index, Canada's most important stock market index maintained by Standard & Poors. The index comprises of 60 Canadian incorporated constituents of different industry sectors, currently representing approximatly 73% of Canadian market capitalization.[8]

The TSX operates an entirely electronic market with a centralized public limit order

[3] Alternative trading systems do not play an important role during the observation period of this analysis. The TSX's market share by trading volume was still 94.2% in January 2009, directly after the end of the observation period, and close to 100% one year earlier. source: Financial Times, 20 November 2009, "Toronto's trading platforms draw regulatory scrutiny".

[4] Department of Finance Canada, http://www.fin.gc.ca/toc/2002/cansec_-eng.asp.

[5] TMX Group Inc., http://www.tmx.com/.

[6] World Federation of Exchanges, 2008, http://www.world-exchanges.org/statistics/.

[7] OSC, http://www.osc.gov.on.ca/.

[8] Standard & Poors, http://www.standardandpoors.com/.

book. The market features basic limit and market orders. The TSX market model is based on price and time priority. Iceberg orders that display only a portion of their total size are available for a minimum of 500 shares. They sacrifice time priority on the non-displayed portion of the order. In a centralized limit order book, incoming orders are compared to existing orders stored in the book. If the price of the incoming order crosses the price of an existing order, they are matched. The market model also features on-close orders. Market-on-close orders can be entered until twenty minutes before market closing. Afterwards only contra imbalance side limit-on-close orders are accepted. Order parameters consist of expiration parameters as well as immediate-or-cancel and fill-or-kill flags. Market makers, who are essentially liquidity providers, operate within the electronic public limit order book without proprietary information. Liquidity is solely provided by limit orders displayed in the order book. TSX market makers are similar to designated sponsors on Xetra, the electronic limit order market of Deutsche Börse, described by Klar and van den Bongard (2008).

The TSX's continuous trading sessions start at 9:30 a.m. and last until 4:00 p.m. local time equivalent to the New York Stock Exchange. In a pre-opening session, traders can enter orders but they are not executed until the market opening when continuous trading starts. Orders cannot be modified at the opening for 20 to 30 seconds before the start of trading. The TSX co-ordinates the innvocation of circuit breakers that interrupt trading due to highly volatile markets with US financial markets. However, this chapter focuses on continuous trading periods.

2.4 Data and Sample Selection

2.4.1 Stock Market Data

Trade and quote as well as order book data are retrieved from the Thomson Reuters DataScope Tick History archive through SIRCA[9]. Specifically, I retrieve trade prices and volumes, best bid and ask including associated volumes, and order book data three levels into the book from 1 January 2005 to 31 December 2008 for S&P/TSX 60 constituents.[10] All data entries additionally include Thomson Reuters qualifying codes to identify special trades, quotes, or specific trading sessions. Trades and quotes are timestamped to the

[9]Securities Industry Research Centre of Asia-Pacific, I thank SIRCA for providing access to the Thomson Reuters DataScope Tick History archive, http://www.sirca.org.au/.

[10]The analysis also includes a control period with data from 1 January 2003 to 31 December 2006.

millisecond. All prices are reported in Canadian dollars. Since the analysis is restricted to continuous trading, the first and last five minutes of a trading day as well as non-continuous trading sessions, i.e. curcuit breakers, are removed from the data. This avoids biases associated with the information processing and inventory management processes at those times. I also delete crossing trades and on-close orders. Thomson Reuters trading data and RNSE data are timestamped based on the same clock such that timestamps are directly comparable. Tables B.1 and B.2 in Appendix B depict samples of raw trade and quote and raw depth data for the Toronto Stock Exchange.

2.4.2 News Data

To analyze high-frequency news data, I have access to Thomson Reuters newswire messages. The real-time commercial product is called Thomson Reuters NewsScope Real-time while I have access to archive data. The Thomson Reuters NewsScope Real-time data stream is disseminated to approximately 370,000 Reuters screens worldwide. According to Thomson Reuters, they "deliver over 500,000 alerts and over two million unique stories a year"[11]. These numbers show that Thomson Reuters newswire messages are widely disseminated and read by traders all over the world. Thomson Reuters – also Dow Jones, or other professional financial news providers – is most probably perceived as more trustworthy by traders and other financial market professionals than rumors on Internet message boards or television shows. newswire messages provide much of the real-time information flow available to traders. Thomson Reuters specifically advertises their news streams for use by algorithmic traders. However, the bulk of newswire readers should still be human. My data not only comprises normal Thomson Reuters NewsScope Content but is additionally tagged through data generated by the Thomson Reuters NewsScope Sentiment Engine (RNSE). RNSE allows for a transformation of ambiguous news signals into quantitative computer-readable scores. The Thomson Reuters NewsScope Sentiment Engine processes news data on three dimensions: sentiment, relevance, and novelty (Thomson Reuters, 2008a,b). Sentiment reflects the stock specific tone of one news item and is either positive, negative, or neutral. The relevance measure is a stock specific score for a news item indicating the relevance of a certain news message. Finally, novelty indicates whether news with the same content has been released prior to a certain news message.

[11]Thomson Reuters, http://thomsonreuters.com/products_services/financial/financial_products/a-z/newsscope_application_license/.

News messages are tagged for each stock separately. For example, a news message that is positive for Google might be negative for Yahoo while it might be much more relevant for Google than Yahoo. The RNSE analysis is based on machine-learning techniques and computer linguistics without human interaction. Groß-Klußmann and Hautsch (2011) also base their analysis on RNSE news data and find that "news engines [in their paper RNSE] have the potential to successfully pre-structure news".

Thomson Reuters also provides newswire data that has become an acadamic standard in the machine learning community for testing text categorization algorithms. Two data sets are available. One widely used collection of newswire messages is the 'Reuters-21578' text categorization test collection which comprises of 21,578 newswire messages from 1987 (cf. Joachims, 1998; Tong and Koller, 2001; Leopold and Kindermann, 2002; Blöhdorn and Hotho, 2009; Debole and Sebastiani, 2005).[12] In the year 2000, this data collection has been superceded by a new collection of newswire messages called 'Reuters Corpus, Volume 1' (RCV1) which includes 810,000 newswire messages from the years 1996 and 1997 (cf. Lewis et al., 2004; De Melo and Siersdorfer, 2007).[13] In addition, multilingual messages called 'Reuters Corpus, Volume 2' (RCV2) are also available. The National Institute of Standards and Technology[14] (NIST), a US government research agency, took over the distribution of RCV1 and RCV2 in 2004.

While I have access to Thomson Reuters NewsScope Sentiment Engine archive data, professional traders can also purchase the Thomson Reuters NewsScope Sentiment Engine for real-time news content processing. In contrast to prior research, this unique data set allows to cluster news based on content and novelty, and also directly associate relevant news with individual stocks. Table 2.1 reports one sample RNSE news message. An in depth description of data fields in RNSE data is available in Appendix C.

Newswire data are cleaned by reproducible criteria. First of all, I delete all news that links to a news message with similar content during the previous twenty-four hours. This criterium ensures that news messages have a certain novelty and that exactly the same content has not yet been disseminated over Thomson Reuters newswires. Still, I sometimes find double news in the data which have the same PNAC. PNAC is short for primary news access code and identifies one story as it develops. This might be a result of technical irregularities. I keep the first entry and delete all subsequent news messages with the same

[12] http://www.daviddlewis.com/resources/testcollections/reuters21578/.
[13] RCV1 and RCV2, http://trec.nist.gov/data/reuters/reuters.html.
[14] NIST, http://www.nist.gov/.

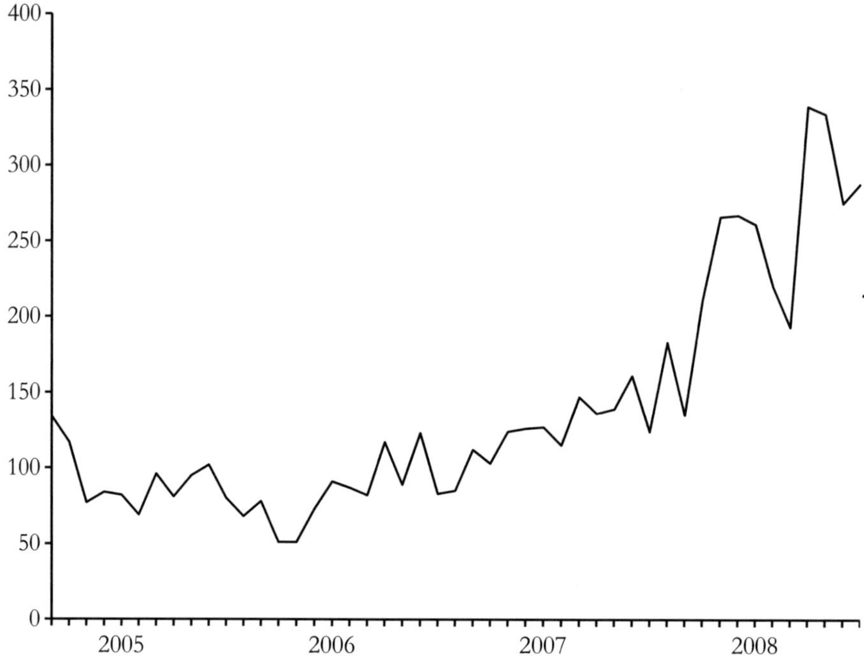

Figure 2.1: **Novel Intraday News Per Year and Month on the TSX 2005 to 2008**. The figure shows the number of novel intraday news messages per year and month for the 2005 to 2008 sample.

PNAC within the same day.[15] After those initial cleaning procedures, only news messages that arrive during continuous trading hours on trading days are kept. Overall, I have 6,625 novel intraday news messages for my analysis. Figure 2.1 shows the development of the number of news over the observation period. The increase in news at the end of 2007 and in 2008 might be a result of the financial crisis during which more newsworthy events happend than during the previous years. Figure 2.2 shows the distribution of news over weekdays. Figure 2.3 depicts the number of news for all half-hour intraday periods, also seperated by news sentiment. The number of neutral news increases sharply during the last half-hour while before, the overall number of news slightly falls from the beginning of the trading day. I control in the analysis for potential side effects with time of day dummy variables and also day of the week dummy variables.

[15]Since PNACs are reused by Thomson Reuters' editorial publishing system, the restriction to the same PNAC within one day ensures that some completely unrelated news messages are not accidentally deleted.

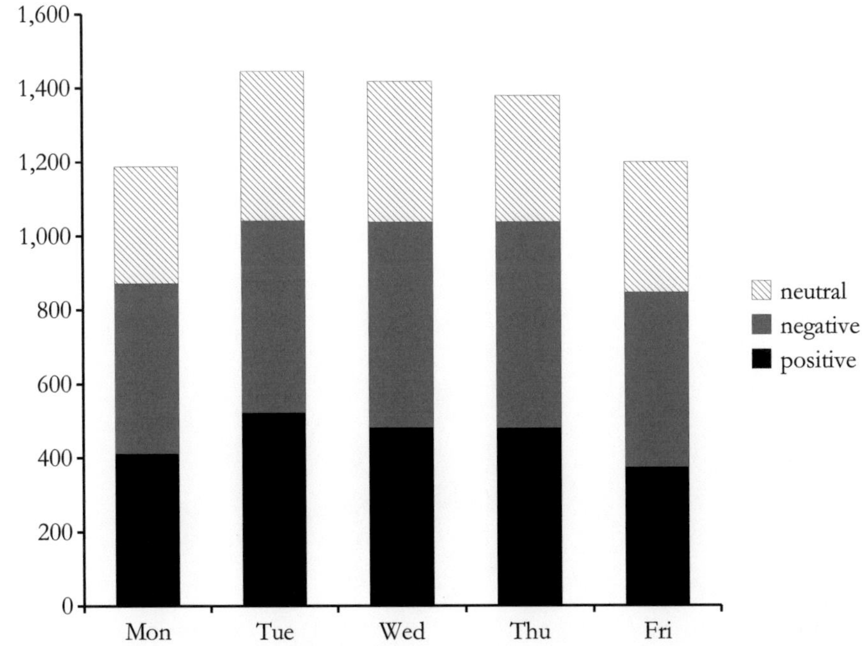

Figure 2.2: **Novel Intraday News Per Weekday on the TSX 2005 to 2008.** The figure shows the number of novel intraday news messages per day of the week for the 2005 to 2008 sample.

2.4.3 Sample Selection

The firm sample is based on S&P/TSX 60 index constituents from 2005 to 2008. The securities represented in this index are the most actively traded and highest quality publicly traded Canadian companies and present a broad cross-section of industries. Index constituents are liquid, often and regularly traded, and a considerable portion of a company's market capitalization is based on free floating securities. The S&P/TSX 60 currently represents approximately 73% of Canadian equity market capitalization.[16] Cleaning the sample, I additionally require that instruments have to be continuously traded over the years 2005 to 2008.

Then the number of news per company and the number of news per company for each sentiment category are used to create the sample. To ensure stable estimation results, one requirement is that the companies in the S&P/TSX 60 index have a minimum amount of

[16]Standard & Poors, http://www.standardandpoors.com/.

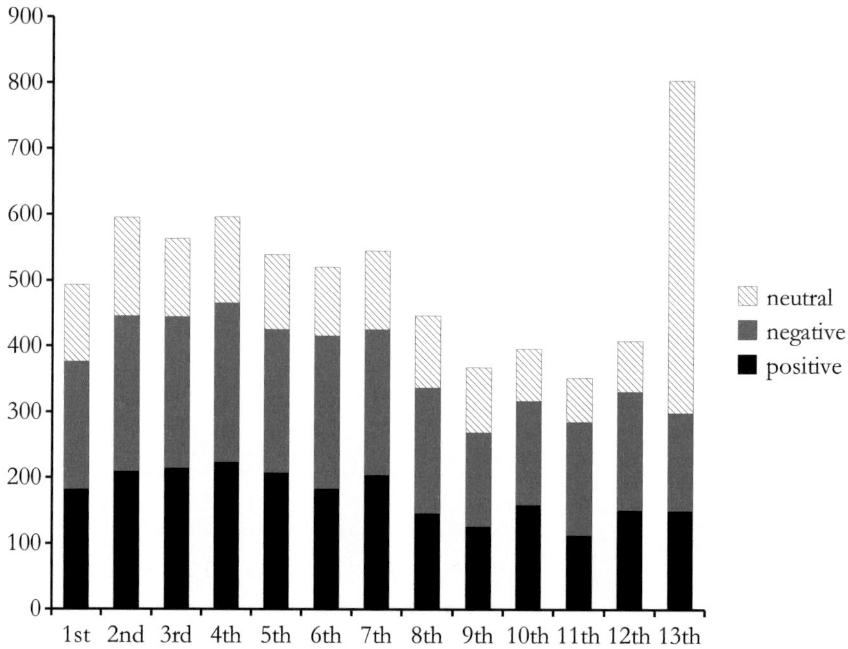

Figure 2.3: **Novel Intraday News Per Time of Day (half-hours) on the TSX 2005 to 2008.** The figure shows the number of novel intraday news messages for time of day half-hour intervals for the 2005 to 2008 sample.

overall news messages and a minimum amount of news messages per sentiment category after all cleaning procedures. Sample companies are require to have at least 80 distinct news messages over the years 2005 to 2008 and at least 10 news messages per sentiment category over the years 2005 to 2008 for stable estimation results. As a result, I have a sample of 33 highly liquid, actively traded S&P/TSX 60 constituents. Table 2.2 provides an overview of the sample and descriptive statistics for each firm in the sample.

2.5 Research Design

2.5.1 Information

To measure information impounded through order flow, I adopt the MRR model introduced by Madhavan, Richardson, and Roomans (1997). I extend the model in the spirit of

Green (2004) to include variables for thirty minute intervals around a firm specific news arrival. The MRR model is a common market microstructure model to approximate the adverse selection component of the bid-ask spread, the information revealed through trades. The authors test their model with data from the New York Stock Exchange. However, they do not limit their model to markets with specialists or dealers but specifically state that liquidity providers may also be traders that post limit orders. When informed traders trade, prices tend to follow their trades which constitutes a risk for market participants that post limit orders. The adverse selection component measures the part of the bid-ask spread that is required as a compensation for liquidity suppliers' risk of losing against informed traders. Hence, the adverse selection component of the bid-ask spread can be interpreted as private information that is impounded into prices through the order flow. The MRR model estimates an adverse selection component as well as an inventory and order processing cost component of the bid-ask spread.

The MRR model is only based on the trade process and analyzes transaction price changes and their relation to the trade direction of order flow. I use the standard Lee and Ready (1991) algorithm to sign trades with contemporaneous quotes as proposed by Bessembinder (2003a). Bessembinder (2003a) compares different heuristics to infer trade direction with proprietary data and finds that a comparison of a trade with the respective contemporaneous quote using Lee and Ready's heuristic provides the best results. In a limit order market without execution inside the spread, this algorithm signs trades without ambiguity if trade and quote timestamps match.

Let x_i be the trade direction, 1 for a market buy order and -1 for a market sell order, at time i and p_i denotes the transaction price. Specifically, i denotes a single observation in the trade process. Then, the original Madhavan et al. (1997) model formulates

$$p_i - p_{i-1} = (\phi + \theta)x_i - (\phi + \rho\theta)x_{i-1} + \epsilon_i \tag{2.1}$$

as its core concept. Let ρ be the first-order autocorrelation, θ denotes the asymmetric information component, and ϕ captures inventory and order processing costs. The original estimation of the model also includes λ in its moment conditions, the probability of an inside the spread execution which is identified through a trade direction of zero. This component is not estimated for the TSX. The TSX features a completely electronic limit order book without inside the the spread executions. The fundamental concept to measure asymmetric information in this model is that only the deviation from expected order flow comprises information. Expected order flow ρx_{i-1} is based on order flow autocorrelation ρ. θ measures "the degree of information asymmetry or the so-called permanent impact of the order flow innovation" (Madhavan et al., 1997). Beliefs about asset values might change through new public information without trade and through information impounded by the order flow whereas the change in belief is positively correlated with order flow innovation. Inventory and order processing costs represent the transitory effect of order flow on prices. The inventory and order processing cost component of the bid-ask spread is not dependent on whether a trade is a buy or sell. Bid and ask quotes that reflect the inventory and order processing cost component are ex-post rational independent of the trade direction. Accordingly, ϕ is not dependent on the trade process' autocorrelation ρ. The model assumes a fixed order size and does not consider trading volume. Madhavan et al. (1997) address this issue and find that trade direction is better suited to estimate their model than signed volume.

To analyze information around news, I extend the original MRR model based on Green (2004). I introduce three dummy variables for thirty minute intervals around a Thomson Reuters news message arrival and for trading periods not close to newswire messages. One dummy variable specifies the thirty minutes of trading prior to a Thomson Reuters news arrival, another dummy variable specifies the thirty minutes after a news arrival, and a third dummy variable specifies trading periods further away from news releases than thirty minutes. A dummy variable takes 1 if the observation is within its assigned period around news releases and 0 otherwise. Let i denote a single observation in the trade point process and t denotes the distance to a news message in minutes, i.e. $t \in \{-30, -29, \ldots, 30\}$, then dummy variables are assigned values as follows:

$$\begin{aligned} D_{1,i} &= 1 \quad \text{if} \quad -30 \leq t < 0 \\ D_{2,i} &= 1 \quad \text{if} \quad 0 \leq t \leq 30 \\ D_{3,i} &= 1 \quad \text{if} \quad t > 30 \vee t < -30 \end{aligned} \tag{2.2}$$

Dummy variables are assigned for news depending on their RNSE news sentiment similar to dummy variables for intervals around news and no-news periods. One dummy variable represents positive news, one represents negative news, and one represents neutral news.[17] Periods not close to any news are assigned no sentiment dummy variable. Let again i

[17] I also test clustering news by relevance. However, price discovery results are essentially the same such that I do not include the relevance measure into the price discovery and liquidity analysis.

denote single observations in the trade point process then sentiment dummy variables are assigned as follows:

$$\begin{aligned} I_{1,i} &= 1 \quad \text{if sentiment } = +1 \\ I_{2,i} &= 1 \quad \text{if sentiment } = -1 \\ I_{3,i} &= 1 \quad \text{if sentiment } = \ 0 \end{aligned} \tag{2.3}$$

If variables do not take 1 then they take 0. Since I hypothesize that bid-ask spread components change around news announcements also depending on the sentiment of a news message, the following extended model with dummy variables for different time intervals and different news types emerges:

$$\begin{aligned} p_i - p_{i-1} = \sum_{n=1}^{2}\sum_{m=1}^{3}\left[(\phi_{n,m}+\theta_{n,m})x_i D_{n,i} I_{m,i} - (\phi_{n,m}+\rho_{n,m}\theta_{n,m})x_{i-1}D_{n,i-1}I_{m,i-1}\right] + \\ (\phi_3+\theta_3)x_i D_{3,i} - (\phi_3+\rho_3\theta_3)x_{i-1}D_{3,i-1} + \epsilon_i \end{aligned} \tag{2.4}$$

Madhavan et al. (1997) use absolute price changes to estimate the model. To support the interpretation of results, I use relative price changes in basis points to estimate Equation 2.4 excluding overnight returns. However, results are robust to using absolute or relative price changes. The model is estimated using the generalized methods of moments (GMM) with the Newey and West (1987) procedure as proposed in the original paper by Madhavan et al. (1997). The Newey-West procedure is robust to autocorrelation and heteroskedasticity. I apply the Newey-West estimator with five lags. Using more lags does not change the significance of the results. Let r_i denote the relative price change which is calculated as $r_i = 10{,}000 \times \ln\left(p_i/p_{i-1}\right)$ then the model can be estimated as

$$\begin{aligned} u_i = r_i + \sum_{n=1}^{2}\sum_{m=1}^{3}\left[-(\phi_{n,m}+\theta_{n,m})x_i D_{n,i} I_{m,i} + (\phi_{n,m}+\rho_{n,m}\theta_{n,m})x_{i-1}D_{n,i-1}I_{m,i-1}\right] - \\ (\phi_3+\theta_3)x_i D_{3,i} + (\phi_3+\rho_3\theta_3)x_{i-1}D_{3,i-1} - \sum_{td=1}^{12}\tau_{td}T_{td} - \sum_{wd=1}^{4}\omega_{wd}W_{wd} \end{aligned} \tag{2.5}$$

including half-hour dummy variables T_{td} for the time of day and dummy variables for the day of the week W_{wd}. Green (2004) also includes external variables in his analysis, however, to account for the surprise in macroeconomic news. Excluding the control variables T_{td}

and W_{wd} from the analysis does not significantly change the results. The constant α and the parameter vector

$$\begin{aligned}\beta = {} & (\theta_{1,1}, \theta_{1,2}, \theta_{1,3}, \theta_{2,1}, \theta_{2,2}, \theta_{2,3}, \theta_3, \\ & \phi_{1,1}, \phi_{1,2}, \phi_{1,3}, \phi_{2,1}, \phi_{2,2}, \phi_{2,3}, \phi_3, \\ & \rho_{1,1}, \rho_{1,2}, \rho_{1,3}, \rho_{2,1}, \rho_{2,2}, \rho_{2,3}, \rho_3)\end{aligned}$$

are exactly identified by the ordinary least squares (OLS) normal conditions and the following additional moment conditions:

$$E\begin{pmatrix} x_i x_{i-1} D_{1,i-1} I_{1,i-1} - \left(x_{i-1} D_{1,i-1} I_{1,i-1}\right)^2 \rho_{1,1} \\ x_i x_{i-1} D_{1,i-1} I_{2,i-1} - \left(x_{i-1} D_{1,i-1} I_{2,i-1}\right)^2 \rho_{1,2} \\ x_i x_{i-1} D_{1,i-1} I_{3,i-1} - \left(x_{i-1} D_{1,i-1} I_{3,i-1}\right)^2 \rho_{1,3} \\ x_i x_{i-1} D_{2,i-1} I_{1,i-1} - \left(x_{i-1} D_{2,i-1} I_{1,i-1}\right)^2 \rho_{2,1} \\ x_i x_{i-1} D_{2,i-1} I_{2,i-1} - \left(x_{i-1} D_{2,i-1} I_{2,i-1}\right)^2 \rho_{2,2} \\ x_i x_{i-1} D_{2,i-1} I_{3,i-1} - \left(x_{i-1} D_{2,i-1} I_{3,i-1}\right)^2 \rho_{2,3} \\ x_i x_{i-1} D_{3,i-1} - \left(x_{i-1} D_{3,i-1}\right)^2 \rho_3 \end{pmatrix} = 0 \tag{2.6}$$

The moment conditions in Equation 2.6 represent autocorrelations of the trade direction indicator. The estimation of Equation 2.5 provides results for asymmetric information θ, the inventory and order processing cost or cost of supplying liquidity ϕ, and the autocorrelation of order flow ρ for each single interval.

To assess the model's statistical significance, likelihood ratio tests as in Green (2004) are applied. These tests compare the GMM criterion function of the unrestricted model with restricted models. Here, the restricted models posit that only one coefficient is needed for each model to capture adverse selection and costs of supplying liquidity without the option for those measures to vary around news arrivals. To consider robustness, I also compare model implied spreads with actual quoted spreads from the data. Since model implied spreads are solely based on the order flow they do not necessarily need to be exactly the same as data based quoted spreads. However, they should be roughly similar in their order of magnitude. The medians of the differences of individual model coefficients of the thirty-three stock specific models are compared with Wilcoxon signed rank tests.

2.5.2 Trading Intensity, Liquidity, and Volatility

To measure trading intensity, I transform the trade process into a process with one observation per minute and calculate the number of trades per minute, number of shares traded per minute, and traded dollar volume per minute. For estimation purposes, the natural logarithms of the number of shares traded per minute and traded dollar volume per minute are used. For the news dummy variable definition, I resort to the MRR information model definition of dummy variables and use exactly the same. The no-news dummy variable does not need to be included, it is the basis of comparison and coefficients capture the difference to no-news periods. I include time dummy variables to account for market trends. Time dummy variables γ_{qy} are included for each quarter for a specific year into all regressions. In this chapter's data, 16 year quarter combinations are found. I also include firm dummy variables F_x with $x \in \{1,2,\ldots,33\}$ where x denotes a single firm. In the regression model, one firm serves as the base category which results in 32 firm dummy variables. Additionally, the equation includes half-hour dummy variables T_{td} for the time of day and dummy variables for the day of the week W_{wd}. Let l denote the minutes in the data and $tm_{x,l}$ denotes the respective trading intensity measure on a minute and per firm basis then the following model is used to assess trading intensity around news messages:

$$tm_{x,l} = a + \sum_{n=1}^{2}\sum_{m=1}^{3} \psi_{n,m} D_{n,x,l} I_{m,x,l} + \sum_{x=1}^{32} \iota_x F_x + \sum_{qy=1}^{15} \zeta_{qy}\gamma_{qy} + \sum_{td=1}^{12} \tau_{td} T_{td} + \sum_{wd=1}^{4} \omega_{wd} W_{wd} + e_{x,l} \tag{2.7}$$

To estimate the linear model in Equation 2.7, Newey and West (1987) standard errors based on five lags are used.[18]

Quote based, ex-ante observable, liquidity is measured based on three different indicators: quoted half spread, the volume at the best bid and ask, and the volume at three depth levels. All three liquidity measures are based on a quote-to-quote process which is then aggregated to minute averages for estimation purposes. Let a_i denote the best ask and b_i the best bid at time i, then quoted half spreads qs_i based on Bessembinder and Kaufman

[18] Compare Cai et al. (2004) who also use the Newey and West (1987) standard errors for an intraday analysis.

(1997) are calculated as follows in basis points:

$$qs_i = \left(\frac{a_i - b_i}{(a_i + b_i)/2}\right) /2 \times 10{,}000 \tag{2.8}$$

Then quoted spreads qs_i are aggregated to per firm and minute average quoted spreads $qs_{x,l}$. Quoted spreads are also calculated as trade-time quoted spreads for which I need the trade process. Those quoted spreads capture liquidity represented through the best bid and ask at the time of trades. Quoted spreads, however, only capture liquidity independent of trade size. To further analyze liquidity, I consider Canadian dollar volume at the best bid and ask (Depth0). Let again be a_i the best ask, b_i the best bid, an_i the number of shares available at the ask, and bn_i the number of shares available at the bid then the Canadian dollar volume at the best bid and ask ev_i is calculated as

$$ev_i = bn_i \times b_i + an_i \times a_i. \tag{2.9}$$

Then Depth0 ev_i is aggregated to per firm and minute average Depth0 $ev_{x,l}$. For estimation purposes, the natural logarithm of Canadian dollar volume at the best bid and ask is used ($lev_{x,l} = \ln ev_{x,l}$). Depth0 only provides information about volume directly at the spread. Order book data allows to analyze available volume deeper into the book and liquidity which is used and needed for larger trades. In combination with the other liquidity measures, depth at three levels (Depth3) allows for a much more precise analysis of liquidity than quoted spreads and bid-ask volume alone. Let $a_{i,dl}$ be the ask at time i on depth level dl, $b_{i,dl}$ denotes the bid on depth level dl, $an_{i,dl}$ is the Canadian dollar volume on a certain depth level at the ask, and $bn_{i,dl}$ denotes the volume at depth level dl on the bid. Then the depth measure d_i for three depth levels is calculated as

$$d_i = \sum_{dl=1}^{3} bn_{i,dl} \times b_{i,dl} + \sum_{dl=1}^{3} an_{i,dl} \times a_{i,dl}. \tag{2.10}$$

Again, Depth3 d_i is aggregated to per firm and minute average Depth3 $d_{x,l}$. As for volume at the best bid and ask the natural logarithm of Depth3 is used for the estmation ($ld_{x,l} = \ln d_{x,l}$).

The effective spread, a trade process based liquidity measure, is the spread paid when a market order is executed against a limit order in the order book and as a trade based measure takes into account available depth. The effective spread also captures institutional features of a market such as iceberg orders. Let p_i be the execution price and D_i the trade direction then the effective spread es_i is defined as

$$es_i = D_i \times \frac{p_i - (a_i + b_i)/2}{(a_i + b_i)/2} \times 10{,}000. \tag{2.11}$$

The model to estimate the impact on liquidity measures is comparable to the one for trading intensity (Equation 2.7). Before I estimate the models, all liquidity measures are aggregated to minute data to have approximately the same number of observations as for trading intensity. Let l be the indicator for one minute, x for a firm, and $lm_{x,l}$ the liquidity measure under consideration for a firm and minute. Using the same definition for dummy variables as for trading intensity, the following model emerges:

$$\begin{aligned} lm_{x,l} = a + \sum_{n=1}^{2}\sum_{m=1}^{3}\psi_{n,m}D_{n,x,l}I_{m,x,l} + \sum_{x=1}^{32}\iota_x F_x + \sum_{qy=1}^{15}\zeta_{qy}Y_{qy} + \\ \sum_{td=1}^{12}\tau_{td}T_{td} + \sum_{wd=1}^{4}\omega_{wd}W_{wd} + e_{x,l} \end{aligned} \tag{2.12}$$

I estimate the model exactly like the one for trading intensity with Newey and West (1987) standard errors.

To estimate realized volatility, also known as realized variance (cf. Hansen and Lunde, 2005), I construct one minute midpoint to midpoint returns from quote data. With realized volatility, I assess high-frequency volatility changes around newswire messages depending on the news sentiment (negative, positive, or neutral). To calculate the square of returns for the realized volatility, logarithmic midpoint returns are used. Let mp_l denote a one minute midpoint then the one minute realized volatility is defined as

$$rv_l = \left(ln \frac{mp_l}{mp_{l-1}} \right)^2 \times 10{,}000. \tag{2.13}$$

The original realized volatility measure is multiplied by 10,000 to enhance readability of the numbers.[19] Scaling realized volatility by 10,000 does not change its statistical properties. The same regressions as above are used to analyze realized volatility around newswire

[19]Usually, one minute returns are quite small in magnitude which would lead to very small numbers in the result tables.

messages for news with different sentiments. All measures are winsorized at 0.1% and 99.9% to account for potential extreme values through technical data recording errors.

2.5.3 Returns and Profitability

To assess basic profitability, I calculate excess returns for different intervals g around a news announcement. Returns are calculated from thirty minutes before news arrivals up to the news arrival, from a news arrival to thirty minutes after a news arrival, and from thirty minutes before to thirty minutes after news arrive through the Thomson Reuters system. Ten minute returns around news arrivals are calculated equivalently to returns thirty minutes around news arrivals. Let $r_{x,g}$ be the simple stock specific return, v_g denotes the TSX/S&P 60 return over the same time intervall, $p_{x,g}$ denotes a stock specific price whereas p^s_g denotes the index price then excess returns are defined as

$$z_{x,g} = r_{x,g} - v_g = \ln \frac{p_{x,g}}{p_{x,g-1}} - \ln \frac{p^s_g}{p^s_{g-1}}. \tag{2.14}$$

Let $S_{x,g}$ denote sentiment for a return and $W_{x,g}$ denotes relevance. I regress returns on sentiment multiplied by relevance since I hypothesize that, for profits, news with higher relevance should somehow correlate with higher price jumps. Then the following regression with firm dummy variables emerges:

$$z_{x,g} = a + f(S_{x,g} \times W_{x,g}) + \sum_{x=1}^{32} F_x + e_{x,g} \tag{2.15}$$

I perform regressions on all news and on groups of news each missing either positive, negative, or neutral news. Standard errors are White (1980) heteroskedasticity consistent standard errors. Durbin-Watson tests show little autocorrelation in the residuals of regressions with news based returns as the dependent variable, which is something one would expect given the fact that there is no certain time interval between different unscheduled news.

2.6 Results and Interpretation

For each stock in this chapter's data set, I collect information on the number of news items and average sentiment. The descriptive statistics to the sample are contained in Table 2.2. The average firm has 201 distinct news items, and an average sentiment of -0.0356 which is marginally negative. A firm specific sentiment of 0 for a single news item indicates that sentiment for this news item in combination with the specific firm is neutral. The average sentiment is in line with studies that report a bias of news media to report more on negative than on positive events (Soroka, 2006). In total, I observe 6,625 information events derived from firm specific news messages over a period of four years. The average firm market capitalization over the years 2005 to 2008 is approximatly C$24bn. Market capitalization ranges from C$5.5bn to C$63bn with an accumulated market capitalization of C$791bn. The overall domestic market capitalization of firms traded on the TSX was C$1,256bn at the end of 2008, comparable to the market capitalization at Deutsche Börse in Germany.[20] This is an indication that the firm sample comprises a large share of Canadian market capitalization. Table 2.2 also shows that the sample represents a broad cross-section of industries.

The focus of the analysis lies on intraday price dynamics and I calculate a number of appropriate descriptive measures. In Table 2.3, summary statistics are presented for periods without news, before and after news for positive, negative, and neutral news separately. Descriptives in this table are not yet adjusted for the year and quarter and for firm specific effects. I present results for each 'setting' for quoted spreads over all quote changes and for quoted spreads only at trade-time, effective spreads, volume at the best (Depth0), depth at three levels into the order book (Depth3), trading intensity (number of trades per minute), numbers of shares traded per minute, volume per minute, and share price volatility (realized volatility).

[20] World Federation of Exchanges, http://www.world-exchanges.org/statistics/.

Table 2.1: **Sample News.** Table 2.1 shows one novel intraday RNSE news message for the firm 'Research in Motion' (RIM.TO).

Sample RNSE News Item - TSX	
timestamp	24 OCT 2007 16:30:02.064
bcast_ref	RIM.TO
stock_ric	RIM.TO
item_id	2007-10-24_16.30.01.nN24487523.T1.8da5a8b6
relevance	0.150756
sentiment	1
sent_pos	0.559651
sent_neut	0.358283
sent_neg	0.0820664
lnkd_cnt1	0
lnkd_cnt2	0
lnkd_cnt3	0
lnkd_cnt4	0
lnkd_cnt5	0
lnkd_id1	.
lnkd_id2	.
lnkd_id3	.
lnkd_id4	.
lnkd_id5	.
lnkd_idpv1	.
lnkd_idpv2	.
lnkd_idpv3	.
lnkd_idpv4	.
lnkd_idpv5	.
item_type	ARTICLE
item_genre	NOT DEFINED
bcast_text	RIM rolls out Facebook software for BlackBerry
dsply_name	2
pnac	nN24487523
story_type	S
cross_ref	.
proc_date	24-OCT-2007
take_time	16:30:01
story_date	24-OCT-2007
story_time	16:30:01
named_item	.
take_seqno	1
attribtn	RTRS
prod_code	E U CAN G PSC RNP DNP PGE PCO PCU EMK
topic_code	BUS CA US DE INV TEL WWW SFWR HDWR ENT LEI TEEQ TECH COMS ELC CEEU EUROPE WEU LEN RTRS
co_ids	RIMM.O RIM.TO DT.N
lang_ind	EN

Table 2.2: **Descriptive Statistics for Sample Companies.** The sample is based on stocks continuously listed in the S&P/TSX 60 index between 2005 and 2008. 33 stocks qualify for the sample after filtering based on newswire data. Table 2.2 reports descriptive statistics for the number of news, news sentiment and relevance, market value, and economic sector. News measures are derived from Thomson Reuters RNSE data whereas market value and economic sector are based on Compustat data. The average per company sentiment is denoted 'Sent'. The overall number of news (#) as well as the number of news differentiated by sentiment are reported. 'MVal' stands for the average market value in Million Candian dollars. The table is sorted by the descending number of news per company in the analysis.

Company Name	#News	#+	#-	#o	Sent	MVal	Economic Sector
Barrick Gold	518	156	169	193	-0.0251	30,944	Materials
Research in Motion	366	112	181	71	-0.1896	32,982	Info. Tech.
Royal Bank of Canada	361	125	134	102	-0.0249	62,805	Financials
EnCana	302	102	129	71	-0.0894	45,014	Energy
Toronto-Dominion Bank	290	103	135	52	-0.1103	45,919	Financials
Nortel Networks	287	86	116	85	-0.1045	8,922	Info. Tech.
Bank of Nova Scotia	270	119	83	68	0.1333	45,957	Financials
Goldcorp	252	68	67	117	0.0040	21,011	Materials
Canadian Imperial Bank	247	59	135	53	-0.3077	27,133	Financials
BCE	239	92	100	47	-0.0335	25,807	TelCo Services
Petro-Canada	215	74	75	66	-0.0047	21,602	Energy
Bank of Montreal	205	70	84	51	-0.0683	29,202	Financials
Suncor Energy	205	68	89	48	-0.1024	36,976	Energy
Cameco	201	87	41	73	0.2289	21,713	Energy
Potash Corp. of Sask.	193	69	89	35	-0.1036	24,745	Materials
Can. Natural Resources	179	59	83	37	-0.1341	32,472	Energy
Can. National Railway	178	52	94	32	-0.2360	23,564	Industrials
Bombardier	175	69	58	48	0.0629	7,030	Industrials
Teck Resources	175	70	67	38	0.0171	12,575	Materials
Imperial Oil	162	57	54	51	0.0185	40,966	Energy
Enbridge	158	51	69	38	-0.1139	14,086	Energy
Telus	145	52	68	25	-0.1103	15,428	TelCo Services
TransCanada	143	87	39	17	0.3357	20,011	Energy
Agrium	139	53	46	40	0.0504	6,510	Materials
Kinross Gold	134	30	39	65	-0.0672	8,689	Materials
Nexen	133	37	52	44	-0.1128	14,857	Energy
Talisman Energy	131	44	36	51	0.0611	18,680	Energy
Manulife Financial	118	43	44	31	-0.0085	52,332	Financials
National Bank of Canada	118	40	52	26	-0.1017	8,876	Financials
Magna International	114	40	50	24	-0.0877	8,233	Consumer Discr.
Rogers Communications	96	38	38	20	0.0000	22,898	TelCo Services
Yamana Gold	91	29	13	49	0.1758	5,573	Materials
Agnico-Eagle Mines	87	26	37	24	-0.1264	6,385	Materials
Mean	201	69	78	54	-0.0356	23,967	
Standard Deviation	93	31	41	34	0.1278	14,965	
Median	178	68	68	48	-0.0672	21,620	
Minimum	87	26	13	17	-0.3077	5,573	
Maximum	518	156	181	193	0.3357	62,805	
Sum	6,625	2,267	2,566	1,792		790,914	

Table 2.3: **Descriptive Statistics Market Measures.** Table 2.3 provides descriptive statistics for the market measures over all companies in the sample. Descriptives are shown overall and for different news periods and no-news periods. 'QSpread' denotes the average quoted spread per minute whereas 'QSpreadT' denotes the average quoted spread per minute at trades. 'ESpread' denotes the average effective spread per minute. 'Depth0' is the average Canadian dollar volume at the best bid and ask and 'Depth3' is the dollar volume three levels into the order book. '#TradesMin' is the average number of trades per minute, '#SharesMin' the average numbers of shares traded per minute and 'VolumeMin' the average Canadian dollar volume traded per minute. 'RV' represents realized volatility based on minute-to-minute midpoint returns. Spread measures are in basis points (bps). Measures are calculated for the years 2005 to 2008 over the whole sample.

	QSpread (in bps)	QSpreadT (in bps)	ESpread (in bps)	Depth0 (in C$1,000)	Depth3 (in C$1,000)	#TradesMin	#SharesMin	VolumeMin (in C$1,000)	RV
Overall									
Mean	4.7422	3.7639	3.8118	132	416	9.70	5,746	234	0.01196
StdDev	4.7786	4.3977	4.4004	116	404	11.97	17,197	352	0.11027
No news									
Mean	4.7480	3.7681	3.8159	132	415	9.53	5,667	230	0.01183
StdDev	4.7808	4.3926	4.3960	116	401	11.73	17,025	345	0.11035
Before News (positive)									
Mean	4.4162	3.5294	3.5746	142	458	13.55	8,188	343	0.01710
StdDev	4.0826	3.8690	3.8552	143	523	15.99	23,887	498	0.13380
After News (positive)									
Mean	4.3673	3.4886	3.5362	143	461	13.16	7,906	335	0.01117
StdDev	3.9593	3.7472	3.7556	135	488	15.73	21,781	516	0.05413
Before News (negative)									
Mean	4.7265	3.7557	3.8097	121	399	16.93	8,343	357	0.02277
StdDev	5.5519	5.4426	5.4032	115	465	19.16	21,407	490	0.14118
After News (negative)									
Mean	4.6377	3.7116	3.7622	126	411	15.97	8,090	341	0.01628
StdDev	5.5925	5.5496	5.5166	122	522	17.89	21,126	484	0.09143
Before News (neutral)									
Mean	4.5722	3.6538	3.7091	145	476	15.57	8,744	330	0.01759
StdDev	4.1409	3.9847	3.9928	127	537	17.76	22,770	441	0.11895
After News (neutral)									
Mean	4.4957	3.6117	3.6653	148	476	16.08	9,503	373	0.01517
StdDev	3.7754	3.5745	3.5820	134	516	18.90	21,084	487	0.07905

The overall average quoted spread is 4.7422 basis points (bps), the average quoted spread at trade-time is 3.7639 bps, and the average effective spread is 3.8118 bps. Spreads on the TSX are very small, thus they are evidence for a generally highly liquid market. Since the TSX does neither feature hidden liquidity inside the spread nor inside the spread executions, effective spreads are on average slightly smaller than quoted spreads at trade-time. However, general quoted spreads are significantly larger than effective spreads which indicates that market monitoring occurs and market participants trade when it is comparably cheap to trade. Market participants are able to monitor quoted spreads, Depth0, and Depth3 ex-ante. Effective spreads and exact timestamps for quoted spreads at trade-time can only be observed ex-post. The small difference between quoted spreads at trade-time and effective spreads indicates that there is often sufficient liquidity at Depth0, even during news periods. Depth3 (avg. C$416k) is approximately three times higher than Depth0 (avg. C$132k) which shows in combination with quoted spreads at trade-time and effective spreads that sufficient liquidity exists on average on the first three levels of the order book. Trading intensity measures also show that the sample is actively traded with an average of ten trades per minute and firm. Descriptive statistics provide some evidence that liquidity increases around positive and neutral news. The average effective spread during no news periods is 3.8159 bps, for positive news it is slightly lower before news with 3.5746 bps and 3.5362 bps after news. Effective spreads before neutral news are on average 3.7091 bps and they are 3.6653 bps after neutral news. The values are inconclusive for negative news. In line with existing literature, I find that each of the measures of trading activity is larger around news announments (cf. Green, 2004; Berry and Howe, 1994; Liu et al., 1990). To further investigate and estimate information, liquidity, trading intensity, and volatility, the regression models presented in Section 2.5 are applied.

Table 2.4: **Information Estimations Around News.** Table 2.4 provides the results of the MRR model for no-news and news periods. Results comprise of the adverse selection components θ, order processing costs ϕ, and trade autocorrelations ρ. The terms positive, negative, and neutral relate to the RNSE news sentiment. 'Before news' and 'after news' describe thirty minute intervals before and thirty minute intervals after a news message is disseminated over Thomson Reuters' news wire systems. The MMR model is estimated on a per company basis for the years 2005 to 2008. By-company estimation results in Panel A consist of the medians and means of GMM estimation results for each single company in the sample. Robust median t-statistics can be found below estimates in parantheses. Panel B provides differences between different intervals and no-news periods and between pre- and post-news periods. The medians of the differences ΔEst are compared with Wilcoxcon Signed Rank tests. 'a' denotes significance at the 0.1% level, 'b' at the 1% level, and 'c' at the 5% level.

Panel A: By-Company Information Estimations - MRR Model

			positive		negative		neutral	
		no news (nn)	before news	after news	before news	after news	before news	after news
Adv. Selection	Median Est.	1.4741	1.7630	1.5632	1.5574	1.6086	1.6194	1.3884
θ	Mean Est.	1.4282	1.6808	1.6478	1.8309	1.9807	1.8085	1.7461
	Median t-stat	(270.50)	(25.71)	(26.20)	(28.88)	(28.09)	(23.81)	(20.65)
Order Proc.	Median Est.	1.1374	1.0011	0.8889	1.0131	0.8777	0.7810	1.0036
ϕ	Mean Est.	1.5922	1.3123	1.2335	1.5121	1.1915	1.1322	1.2462
	Median t-stat	(198.81)	(17.37)	(13.37)	(16.72)	(13.19)	(11.95)	(16.81)
Autocorr.	Median Est.	0.3500	0.3948	0.3996	0.4176	0.4050	0.4270	0.3998
ρ	Mean Est.	0.3585	0.4326	0.4443	0.4229	0.4401	0.4646	0.4231
	Median t-stat	(565.91)	(46.68)	(54.75)	(60.01)	(66.81)	(50.65)	(42.57)

continued on next page ...

...continued from Table 2.4

Panel B: By-Company Information Estimation Differences - MRR Model

		positive		negative		neutral		positive	negative	neutral
		before - nn	after - nn	before - nn	after - nn	before - nn	after - nn	before - after	before - after	before - after
Adv. Selection	Median ΔEst	0.1524[b]	0.0861[b]	0.2000[a]	0.2140[a]	0.1965[b]	0.0368	0.0649	0.0178	0.0749
θ	p-value	0.0015	0.0098	< .0001	< .0001	0.0043	0.3655	0.5815	0.6812	0.1813
	(Wilcoxon T.)									
Order Proc.	Median ΔEst	-0.0606[c]	-0.1524[a]	0.0298	-0.1215[c]	-0.2142[a]	-0.0669[c]	-0.0081	0.1155	-0.1015
ϕ	p-value	0.0116	0.0007	0.4888	0.0445	< .0001	0.0262	0.5576	0.1754	0.0980
	(Wilcoxon T.)									
Autocorr.	Median ΔEst	0.0432[b]	0.0594[a]	0.0312[a]	0.0440[a]	0.0690[a]	0.0289[c]	-0.0204	0.0023	0.0217
ρ	p-value	0.0015	0.0004	0.0002	0.0006	< .0001	0.0192	0.4778	0.7071	0.2947
	(Wilcoxon T.)									

2.6.1 Information

To understand information processing around news announcements, I present the results of the extended MRR model. Theory (cf. Kim and Verrecchia, 1994) suggests that informed trading after information events should increase. Depending on the type of an event, scheduled versus unscheduled, and the instrument traded, informed trading may also increase before an event (cf. Kim and Verrecchia, 1991). Differential pre-news announcement information gathering capabilities of market participants and varying post-news information processing capabilities lead to differential news interpretation.

In general, the MRR estimation is quite consistent with quoted and effective spreads calculated from the trade and quote data. Since spread components are estimated based on the trade point process in the MRR model, they do not necessarily need to exactly compare to quoted spreads. However, they should be comparable in magnitude. Panel A of Table 2.4 provides the estimates for the adverse selection component of the spread, the order processing cost component, and the trade autocorrelations. The sum of adverse selection costs and order processing costs during no-news periods based on the mean estimate is 2.6115 bps (1.4741 + 1.1374) which is not too far off the quoted spread at trade-time of 3.7639 bps. The adverse selection component of the spread is 1.4741 bps during no-news periods and increases for all settings around news announcements except after neutral news. I find consistent with intuition, and in contrast to Green (2004) who analyzes a dealer market, a positive order processing cost component of spreads for all news settings. Order processing costs fall as adverse selection costs increase. In comparsion, adverse selection is the larger of the two spread components.

Median t-statistics of all MRR coefficients are highly significant. Table 2.7 provides statistics of the likelihood ratio tests for the MRR models. I report mean and median χ^2 statistics as well as the number of significant individual models at the 0.1% level out of the 33 sample firms. The χ^2 statistics for the likelihood tests for adverse selection and order processing costs are highly significant with median χ^2 values of 194 and 189. I find that out of 33 individual models, 32 models are highly significant at the 0.1% level for adverse selection costs and 32 are also highly significant for order processing costs.

Panel B of Table 2.4 provides information on the difference between no-news periods and news periods before and after news arrivals for positive, negative, and neutral news. As one would expect, adverse selection costs are higher after positive and negative news than in periods without news. The only period around news messages in which adverse selection is not statistically different to no-news periods, is after neutral news. The differences for positive news of 0.1524 bps and 0.0861 bps are significant at the 1% level. The values for negative news at 0.2000 bps and 0.2140 bps are higher than the values for positive news and also highly significant at the 0.1% level. Neutral news messages show a significant increase in adverse selection pre-news arrival and no statistically significant effect after arrival in comparison to no-news periods.

Interesting is the highly significant increase in adverse selection around negative news in comparison to positive news. As described above, the theoretical models of Kim and Verrecchia (1991, 1994) predict higher adverse selection costs around information events. Market participants put different levels of effort into information gathering. Consequently, some market participants are better informed than others pre-announcement. Differential levels of private information raise the level of information asymmetry in a market pre-news which induces higher adverse selection costs. In general, it does not matter how the pre-announcement information is acquired. It might be that this information is driven by insider trading (information leakage) or it could be more innocuous such as news announcements before the Reuters' release by a competitor or other information sources, e.g. rumors. Krinsky and Lee (1996) provide empirical evidence for Kim and Verrecchia (1991, 1994) and find higher adverse selection costs around announcements comparable to my results for positive and negative news. Before neutral news arrive at a market, adverse selection costs are higher than normal but although being higher post-news arrival the difference is not statistically significant. One possible explanation in the light of existing models is that information gatherers cannot agree pre-news whether information is positive or negative which induces higher adverse selection costs. What exactly happens post neutral news arrivals is however not entirely clear.

The main differences between my study and those of others are that Thomson Reuters' firm specific newswire messages are generally unscheduled and that I have an ex-ante exogenous tone (positive, negative, or neutral) for news messages. Ranaldo (2006) attempts to solve this problem ex-post by sorting events into return bins after the arrival of a news message. However, my data is potentially better suited to reflect traders' impression of news. It is interesting that there are significant differences between positive, negative, and neutral news and the positive and negative ones in particular. Traditional finance theory does not differentiate between positive and negative public information. However, psychological studies from the field of impression formation show that humans react stronger to bad news than to good news, they react asymmetrically (Soroka, 2006; Ronis and Lipinski, 1985). As one example from the finance literature, Tetlock (2007) only finds significant market reactions to bad news in a Wall Street Journal column. There is additional finance literature that finds asymmetric reactions of market participants to good and bad information in general. Akhtar et al. (2011) study the effect that the monthly release of the Australian consumer sentiment has on the Australian stock market. They find a significant impact of bad information while good information does not have a statistically significant effect on the stock market. They attribute this result to the 'negativity effect' found in psychology literature. Stock markets react stronger to monetary policy decisions that are bad for stock markets than to those that are good for stock markets on an intraday level (Chuliá et al., 2010). Chen et al. (2003) find that "negative news from the US market will cause a larger decline in a national stock return [i.e. non-US market returns] than an equal magnitude of good news".

A concept that provides additional insights into the different results for positive and negative news may be found in the literature on ambiguity and ambiguity aversion.[21] People, and as such also market participants, do not like ambiguity and prefer known over unknown risk. Ambiguity aversion has been further developed within financial models (cf. Epstein and Schneider, 2008, 2010; Leippold et al., 2008; Gagliardini et al., 2009). Text can generally be classified as ambigous information, in that the information content is more difficult to interpret than the price signals generated in markets (trades and quotes). Ambiguity averse traders react asymmetrically to ambiguous information (Epstein and Schneider, 2008), if the information is positive they act as if they are unsure of the precision of the information, and if information is negative they act as if it is precise. If the market is composed of a proportion of investors that exhibit ambiguity aversion, this may help to explain the fact that the adverse selection costs around negative news are higher than around positive news. Both, the more psychological view of asymmetric reaction and the more economics oriented model of ambiguity aversion, base on the same understanding of human nature and provide explanations to observed trader behavior in this chapter.

[21]The fundamental concept of ambiguity aversion is based on a hypothetical experiment by Ellsberg (1961). In an experiment, there are two boxes with red and blue balls. Both boxes contain 100 balls. One box contains 50 blue and 50 red balls whereas the distribution of balls in the other box is unknown to participants. Subjects are now asked to draw a ball. They play the game twice and receive a payoff of e.g. 100 if they draw a red ball the first time and they receive the same payoff if they draw a blue ball the second time they play the game. Although it violates expected and subjective expected utility, on average participants draw both times from the box of which they know that it contains 50 blue and 50 red balls. They strictly prefer drawing from the risky box of which they know that it represents a fair coin toss over the box with the unkown distribution of balls.

Table 2.5: **Trading Intensity and Liquidity Estimations Around News.** Table 2.5 provides results for trading intensity and liquidity measures around news in contrast to no-news periods over the years 2005 to 2008. The terms positive, negative, and neutral relate to the RNSE news sentiment. The terms 'before news' and 'after news' describe thirty minute intervals before and thirty minute intervals after a news message is disseminated over Thomson Reuters' news wire systems. Overall GMM estimation results for liquidity measures are reported in Panel A and for trading intensity in Panel B. All estimations are calculated with firm and year/quarter dummy variables. Robust t-statistics can be found below estimates in parantheses. Quoted spreads and effective spreads are measured in basis points and 'lnDepth0' represents the natural logarithm of the available volume at the best bid and ask in Canadian Dollars. 'lnDepth3' is the natural logarithm of available volume in Canadian Dollars at the top three order book levels. Liquidity measures are aggregated to minute averages prior to estimation. The number of shares traded per minute and the traded dollar volume per minute are transformed through the natural logarithm for the regressions. I omit estimates for firm and time dummy variables. 'a' denotes significance at the 0.1% level, 'b' at the 1% level, and 'c' at the 5% level.

Panel A: Liquidity Estimations

		positive		negative		neutral		positive	negative	neutral
		before news	after news	before news	after news	before news	after news	before - after	before - after	before - after
Quoted Spread	Estimate	-0.0526^c	-0.0257	0.0794^c	0.0835^c	-0.0841^b	-0.0463	-0.0269	-0.0041	-0.0379
	t-stat	(-2.09)	(-1.08)	(2.22)	(2.31)	(-3.10)	(-1.82)			
lnDepth0	Estimate	0.0404^a	0.0378^a	-0.0117^b	-0.0037	0.0743^a	0.0577^a	0.0026	-0.0080	0.0167
	t-stat	(8.98)	(8.39)	(-2.95)	(-0.92)	(14.52)	(10.59)			
lnDepth3	Estimate	0.0497^a	0.0497^a	-0.0025	0.0067	0.0886^a	0.0688^a	0.0000	-0.0092	0.0198
	t-stat	(11.41)	(11.44)	(-0.65)	(1.71)	(17.21)	(12.69)			
Effective Spread	Estimate	-0.0323	-0.0140	0.0811^c	0.0947^c	-0.0487^b	-0.0208	-0.0183	-0.0136	-0.0278
	t-stat	(-1.39)	(-0.63)	(2.28)	(2.59)	(-1.87)	(-0.92)			

continued on next page ...

...continued from Table 2.5

Panel B: Trading Intensity Estimations										
		positive		negative		neutral		positive	negative	neutral
		before news	after news	before news	after news	before news	after news	before - after	before - after	before - after
#Trades per Min.	Estimate	1.8201[a]	1.6631[a]	2.8623[a]	2.2139[a]	2.2551[a]	3.5241[a]	0.1570	0.6484	-1.2690
	t-stat	(18.09)	(16.62)	(25.48)	(20.90)	(18.56)	(24.99)			
ln #Shares per Min.	Estimate	0.1890[a]	0.1809[a]	0.2015[a]	0.2956[a]	0.1555[a]	0.2769[a]	0.0081	-0.0042	-0.1214
	t-stat	(22.84)	(21.90)	(26.43)	(26.80)	(17.39)	(28.15)			
ln Volume per Min.	Estimate	0.2053[a]	0.1983[a]	0.1860[a]	0.1885[a]	0.1614[a]	0.2787[a]	0.0070	-0.0025	-0.1172
	t-stat	(24.49)	(23.72)	(23.73)	(24.13)	(17.77)	(27.64)			

2.6.2 Trading Intensity, Liquidity, and Volatility

To understand liquidity around news and to further understand the price dynamics around news arrivals, it is important to bear in mind that liquidity, information, and trading intensity are inherently related. Table 2.5 provides regression results (Equation 2.12) on liquidity and trading activity. Results for liquidity are more mixed than for information. However, compared with each other, all liquidity measures provide consistent results. I find that before and after positive news liquidity increases. For negative news liquidity generally falls, more so before than after news. Theory would suggest a consistent reduction in liquidity over all news types which is at odds with my empirical findings (cf. Kim and Verrecchia, 1994). Consistent with existing literature (Berry and Howe, 1994), trading intensity increases around all different types of news.

All coefficients in Table 2.5 represent the difference of the respective period to no-news periods. Panel A shows that liquidity increases significantly around positive and around neutral news. Liquidity increases if spreads tighten and depth increases. In this analysis quoted spreads decrease 0.0526 bps before positive news and decrease 0.0257 bps after positive news, however not statistically significant after positive news. A decrease in quoted spreads corresponds to an increase in liquidity. The liquidity enhancing effect is generally stronger for neutral news than for positive. The increase in liquidity for neutral news is almost double the increase for positive news. The quoted spread increases, corresponding to to a decrease in liquidity, before negative news by 0.0794 bps and 0.0835 bps after negative news.

Results for Depth0, Depth3, and effective spreads are similar to those for quoted spreads. All four measures combined paint a picture of increasing liquidity around positive and neutral news and decreasing liquidity around negative news. Not all measures are statistically significant for all news types but when they are, values are highly coherent. For each news type and each period before or after news at least two liquidity measures are statistically significant and never contradictory. Comparing negative and positive news messages, the former seem to have a stronger influence on spreads while the latter more strongly affect available depth.

Panel B of Table 2.5 provides results for trading intensity. Trading intensity increases around all types of news. It increases a bit more for negative than for positive news if measured in the number of trades per minute and it increases stronger for positive news if measured in Canadian dollar volume. However, trading intensity increases even more around neutral news compared to both positive and negative news. Substantial differential interpretation by market participants can be observed which is in line with the neutrality of such news messages; traders might not aggree on the meaning of neutral messages.

Table 2.7 provides in Panel A likelihood ratio (LR) tests and χ^2 statistics for all liquidity and trading intensity estimations. All LR tests are highly significant which implies that all models are better specified than the restricted models from the LR tests.

Since theory (cf. Kim and Verrecchia, 1991, 1994) predicts a reduction of liquidity around information events my results for positive and neutral news may at first seem contradictory. However, the types of news that I analyze are different to the mostly studied scheduled macroceconomic announcements or earnings announcements. On average, newswire messages surely have a lower impact than earnings or macroeconomic announcements and also their implications are on average much lower than those of major world events. Trading intensity increases around news announcements which reflects changes in expectations of individual investors who adjust to their new expectations through trade. Liquidity suppliers in electronic limit order markets operate in a highly competitive environment (Biais et al., 1995). With higher trading intensity around positive and neutral news announcements, liquidity suppliers compete for liquidity supply. They try to cater the increase in liquidity demand. As explained above, traders potentially react differently to positive and negative news messages. Reactions to positive and neutral news are weaker than to negative news. Positive and neutral news might not be considered overly ambiguous by market participants such that competition for liquidity supply generally persists around such news. Ranaldo (2006) also finds a slight increase in liquidity around news arrivals. Ambiguity aversion may help to explain the liquidity results around negative news. If investors are expecting negative and ambiguous news, they will adjust their limit order to include the 'worst-case' scenario that the negative news is precise. After negative news, investors only slowly re-adjust their limit orders to the new information and no statistical difference in liquidity to the no-news period can be found. Liquidity has also been found to usually decrease around macroeconomic announcements (Fleming and Remolona, 1999; Green, 2004). A single negative news has on average still much less impact and importance in comparison to e.g. macroeconomic news. However, in terms of a trader's perception of the strenght of impact, negative news might be potentially closer to macroeconomic news or earnings announcements than positive news such that they are considered more important and reactions are stronger (asymmetric reaction). As a result, competition for liquidity supply might not increase around negative news messages but even slightly falls.

Additionally, I find that realized volatility is slightly higher around arrivals than during no news periods consistent over all types of news: positive, negative, and neutral. Table 2.6 provides the exact coefficients for realized volatility around news arrivals including robust t-statistics. The LR test χ^2 statistic for the realized volatility estimation is 34 which is highly significant at the 0.01% level (Table 2.7). The results for realized volatility pre- and post-news arrival are also consistent with the MRR information results. Around news, adverse selection costs are higher than during no-news periods for all three different news sentiments (cf. Table 2.4, Panel B) which indicates higher private information flow around news. French and Roll (1986) find that a major determinant of return volatility is trading of informed market participants, i.e. private information flow revealed to the market through trades. I find this pattern in the data of this chapter with higher realized volatility around news.

Table 2.6: **Realized Volatility Estimations Around News.** Table 2.6 provides estimates for realized volatility measures around news in contrast to no-news periods over the years 2005 to 2008. The terms positive, negative, and neutral relate to the RNSE news sentiment. The terms 'before news' and 'after news' describe thirty minute intervals before and thirty minute intervals after a news message is disseminated over Thomson Reuters' news wire systems. All estimations are calculated with firm and year/quarter dummy variables. Robust t-statistics can be found below estimates in parantheses. Realized Volatility is based on one-minute returns. I omit estimates for firm and time dummy variables. 'a' denotes significance at the 0.1% level, 'b' at the 1% level, and 'c' at the 5% level.

Realized Volatility Estimations										
		positive		negative		neutral		positive	negative	neutral
		before news	after news	before news	after news	before news	after news	before - after	before - after	before - after
Realized Vola.	Estimate	0.0016^{a}	0.0014^{a}	0.0031^{a}	0.0015^{a}	0.0018^{a}	0.0032^{a}	0.0003	0.0017	-0.0014
	t-stat	(6.21)	(5.99)	(9.50)	(4.78)	(5.04)	(8.65)			

Table 2.7: **Likelihood Ratio Tests.** Table 2.7 provides likelihood ratio (LR) test statistics for the estimations for liquidity, trading intensity, realized volatility, and the MRR model. The likelihood test results provide statistics for the restricted model with all pre- and post-news intervals captured by one coefficent. Panel A provides χ^2 statistics for the liquidity, trading intensity, and realized volatility models and p-values. Panel B provides likelihood ratio test statistics for the MRR model. The likelihood test results provide statistics for the restricted MRR model with all pre-, post- and no-news periods captured by one coefficent.

Panel A: LR Tests		
	χ^2-stat	p-value
Liquidity		
Quoted Spread	28	0.0002
lnDepth0	290	$<.0001$
lnDepth3	310	$<.0001$
Effective Spread	18	0.0029
Trading Intensity		
#Trades per Min.	161	$<.0001$
ln #Shares per Min.	93	$<.0001$
ln Volume per Min.	84	$<.0001$
Realized Volatility	34	$<.0001$

Panel B: LR Tests for MRR Estimations			
	Mean χ^2-stat	Median χ^2-stat	# of significant out of 33 (0.1% level)
Adverse Selection θ	240	194	32
Order Processing ϕ	260	189	32
Autocorrelation ρ	281,331	111,977	33

2.6.3 Robustness

Since the main sample period includes the financial crisis period in 2008, I also perform an analysis on a control data set. The control sample comprises of the same firms as the main sample. Only for the MRR estimations, the number of firms reduces from 33 to 26 since I apply the same rules for a minimum number of news as in the main sample.[22] A minimum number of news messages is required to receive stable MRR estimation results. My control data observation period comprises the years 2003 to 2006, four years comparable to the main observation period. The year 2003 is the first year with RNSE archive data available. The years 2003 to 2006 encompass a financially stable period. Figures 2.4, 2.5, and 2.6 de-

[22]The following firms are removed from the original sample for the robustness check MRR sample as a result of an insufficient number of news messages: Agnico-Eagle Mines Ltd. (AEM.TO), Agrium Inc. (AGU.TO), Magna International Inc. (MGa.TO), Potash Corporation of Saskatchewan Inc. (POT.TO), and Rogers Communications Inc. (RCIb.TO).

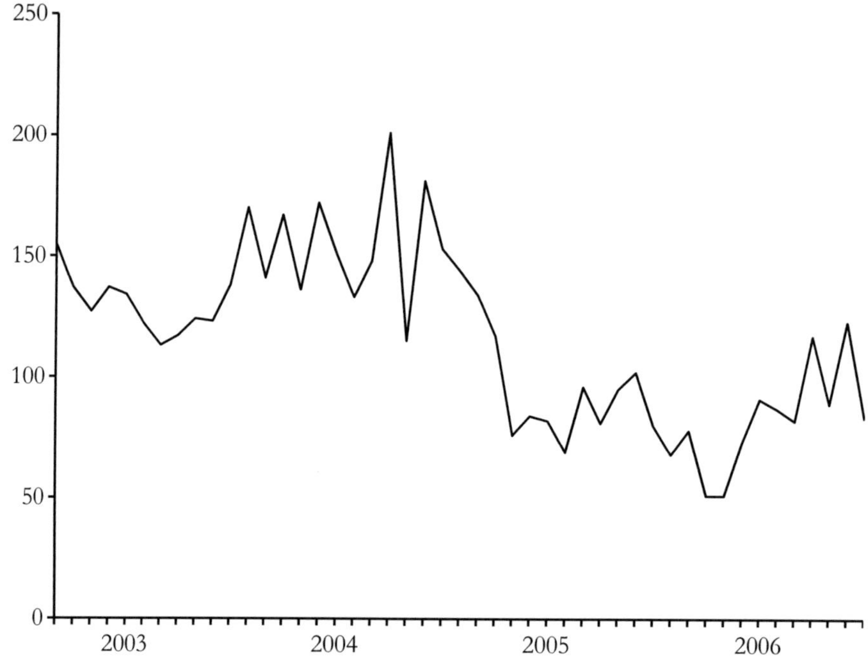

Figure 2.4: **Novel Intraday News Per Year and Month on the TSX 2003 to 2006.** The figure shows the number of novel intraday news messages per year and month for the 2003 to 2006 sample.

pict the number of news per month of a year, the number of news per weekday, and the number of news per time of day. The number of news over the robustness period is not dramatically different from the main sample period with 5,590 news messages and 6,625 news messages respectively. The estimations for information, liquidity, and trading intensity are performed exactly like the estimations for the 2005 to 2008 period. Estimations also include dummies for day of the week and time of day effects. Tables 2.8 and 2.9 show the estimation results.

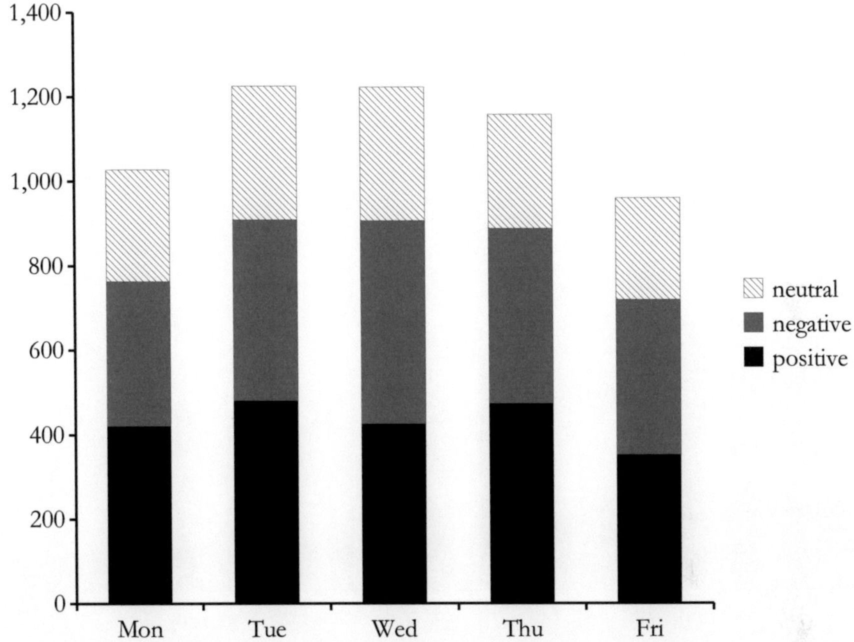

Figure 2.5: **Novel Intraday News Per Weekday on the TSX 2003 to 2006.** The figure shows the number of novel intraday news messages per day of the week for the 2003 to 2006 sample.

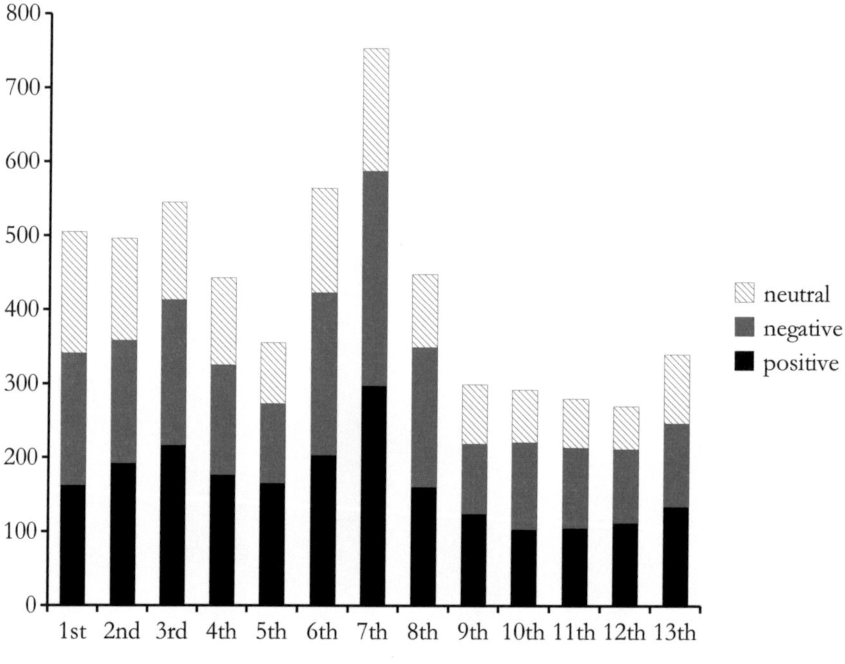

Figure 2.6: **Novel Intraday News Per Time of Day (half-hours) on the TSX 2003 to 2006.** The figure shows the number of novel intraday news messages for time of day half-hour intervals for the 2003 to 2006 sample.

Table 2.8: **Information Estimations Around News – Control Period**. Table 2.8 provides the results of the MRR model for no-news and news periods. Results comprise of the adverse selection components θ, order processing costs ϕ, and trade autocorrelations ρ. The terms positive, negative, and neutral relate to the RNSE news sentiment. 'Before news' and 'after news' describe thirty minute intervals before and thirty minute intervals after a news message is disseminated over Thomson Reuters' news wire systems. The MMR model is estimated on a per company basis for the years 2003 to 2006. By-company estimation results in Panel A consist of the medians and means of GMM estimation results for each single company in the sample. Robust median t-statistics can be found below estimates in parantheses. Panel B provides differences between different intervals and no-news periods and between pre- and post-news periods. The medians of the differences ΔEst are compared with Wilcoxcon Signed Rank tests. 'a' denotes significance at the 0.1% level, 'b' at the 1% level, and 'c' at the 5% level.

Panel A: By-Company Information Estimations - MRR Model

			positive		negative		neutral	
		no news (nn)	before news	after news	before news	after news	before news	after news
Adv. Selection	Median Est.	1.2855	1.9038	1.9451	2.4117	2.3536	1.8432	2.1576
θ	Median t-stat	(200.37)	(13.18)	(14.73)	(11.93)	(12.72)	(13.55)	(12.77)
Order Proc.	Median Est.	1.5190	1.2682	1.2844	1.1947	0.7202	1.2626	0.7705
ϕ	Median t-stat	(177.60)	(8.76)	(8.55)	(5.98)	(2.99)	(8.01)	(6.36)
Autocorr.	Median Est.	0.3286	0.4212	0.4579	0.4972	0.3463	0.4124	0.5313
ρ	Median t-stat	(367.71)	(34.76)	(32.49)	(39.11)	(43.92)	(25.58)	(29.84)

continued on next page ...

. . . continued from Table 2.8

Panel B: By-Company Information Estimation Differences - MRR Model

		positive		negative		neutral		positive	negative	neutral
		before - nn	after - nn	before - nn	after - nn	before - nn	after - nn	before - after	before - after	before - after
Adv. Selection	Median ΔEst	0.2578[a]	0.2677[a]	0.7150[a]	0.7269[a]	0.3500[a]	0.6248[a]	0.0840	-0.0490	-0.2353
θ	p-value	< .0001	< .0001	< .0001	< .0001	< .0001	< .0001	0.3641	0.3776	0.1403
	(Wilcoxon T.)									
Order Proc.	Median ΔEst	-0.2965[b]	-0.1338[c]	-0.3429[c]	-0.5504[b]	-0.3396[b]	-0.5054[a]	0.0276	0.2484	0.2542
ϕ	p-value	0.0071	0.0112	0.0156	0.0011	0.049	< .0001	0.9508	0.1791	0.2056
	(Wilcoxon T.)									
Autocorr.	Median ΔEst	0.0810[a]	0.1092[a]	0.1680[a]	0.2445[a]	0.0649[a]	0.2006[a]	-0.0027	-0.0064	-0.0593
ρ	p-value	< .0001	< .0001	< .0001	< .0001	0.0004	< .0001	0.8726	0.5116	0.0816
	(Wilcoxon T.)									

Table 2.9: **Trading Intensity and Liquidity Estimations Around News – Control Period.** Table 2.9 provides results for trading intensity and liquidity measures around news in contrast to no-news periods over the years 2003 to 2006. The terms positive, negative, and neutral relate to the RNSE news sentiment. The terms 'before news' and 'after news' describe thirty minute intervals before and thirty minute intervals after a news message is disseminated over Thomson Reuters' news wire systems. Overall GMM estimation results for liquidity measures are reported in Panel A and for trading intensity in Panel B. All estimations are calculated with firm and year/quarter dummy variables. Robust t-statistics can be found below estimates in parantheses. Quoted spreads and effective spreads are measured in basis points and 'lnDepth0' represents the natural logarithm of the available volume at the best bid and ask in Canadian Dollars. 'lnDepth3' is the natural logarithm of available volume in Canadian Dollars at the top three order book levels. Liquidity measures are aggregated to minute averages prior to estimation. The number of shares traded per minute and the traded dollar volume per minute are transformed through the natural logarithm for the regressions. I omit estimates for firm and time dummy variables. 'a' denotes significance at the 0.1% level, 'b' at the 1% level, and 'c' at the 5% level.

Panel A: Liquidity Estimations

		positive		negative		neutral		positive	negative	neutral
		before news	after news	before news	after news	before news	after news	before - after	before - after	before - after
Quoted Spread	Estimate	-0.2939^{a}	-0.2908^{a}	-0.4712^{a}	-0.3810^{a}	-0.1609^{c}	-0.1462	-0.0031	-0.0903	-0.0147
	t-stat	(-9.25)	(-9.44)	(-14.61)	(-12.08)	(-3.02)	(-1.85)			
lnDepth0	Estimate	0.0199^{a}	0.0077	-0.0187^{a}	-0.0215^{a}	-0.0013	0.0084	0.0122	0.0028	-0.0097
	t-stat	(4.29)	(1.65)	(-3.87)	(-4.49)	(-0.22)	(1.40)			
lnDepth3	Estimate	0.0287^{a}	0.0281^{a}	-0.0100^{c}	-0.0076	0.0094	0.0128^{c}	0.0007	-0.0023	-0.0035
	t-stat	(7.14)	(7.10)	(-2.36)	(-1.87)	(1.79)	(2.43)			
Effective Spread	Estimate	-0.2397^{a}	-0.2487^{a}	-0.3769^{a}	-0.3175^{a}	-0.1129^{c}	-0.2128^{a}	0.0090	-0.0594	0.1000
	t-stat	(-8.30)	(-8.88)	(-12.64)	(-10.66)	(-2.21)	(-5.32)			

continued on next page ...

. . . continued from Table 2.9

Panel B: Trading Intensity Estimations										
		positive		negative		neutral		positive	negative	neutral
		before news	after news	before news	after news	before news	after news	before - after	before - after	before - after
#Trades per Min.	Estimate	0.9364^{a}	0.9213^{a}	1.5297^{a}	1.4126^{a}	0.8925^{a}	1.3618^{a}	0.0151	0.1170	-0.4693
	t-stat	(14.17)	(12.67)	(18.30)	(18.35)	(9.62)	(13.95)			
ln #Shares per Min.	Estimate	0.2074^{a}	0.1892^{a}	0.2552^{a}	0.2405^{a}	0.1373^{a}	0.2718^{a}	0.0182	0.0147	-0.1346
	t-stat	(20.66)	(18.94)	(23.10)	(22.45)	(10.77)	(20.64)			
ln Volume per Min.	Estimate	0.2242^{a}	0.2107^{a}	0.2776^{a}	0.2623^{a}	0.1460^{a}	0.2908^{a}	0.0134	0.0153	-0.1449
	t-stat	(21.46)	(20.25)	(23.83)	(23.21)	(10.91)	(21.17)			

Comparable to the main observation period, adverse selection costs increase significantly around news arrivals. The increase around negative news is much stronger than around positive news. The only differencc is a strong increase after the arrival of neutral news. An increase in adverse selection costs after neutral news is generally consistent with the main observation period but the magnitude of the increase is much higher in comparison to other news types and periods. However, it is also not entirely clear what drives the results for adverse selection after neutral news during the main observation period.

Liquidity results are more mixed than in the main observation period. While results are very consistent for positive and neutral news with a liquidity enhancing effect, results are more ambiguous around negative news messages. One can see a clear indication of a reduction of liquidity around negative news in the main observation period from 2005 to 2008. In the control period, one cannot say whether liquidity increases or decreases around negative news messages. Spreads decrease while depth also decreases. What can be said about negative news, again consistent with the main observation period, is that I do not find a clear increase in liquidity in contrast to positive and neutral news. A possible explanation for the differences might be that liquidity suppliers react more sensitive to negative news during the financial crisis period. Trading intensity results in the control period are consistent with the main observation period. Trading intensity increases around all types of news. Table 2.10 provides LR tests for the control period which show that the models are better specified than the restricted models.

2.6.4 Returns and Profitability

The previous sections provide evidence that there is a significant difference between positive, negative, and neutral news in terms of price discovery and liquidity. In this section, I provide a simple profitability analysis based on groups of news with different sentiments. All returns z_g in this section are calculated against the market index, the TSX 60. I calculate the 10 minute returns pre- and post-news arrivals and the return from 10 minutes before a news message is released to 10 minutes after a news message arrives. The same analysis is performed for thirty minute intervals. From a profitability perspective post-news returns are most interesting. The independent variable in the regression (see subsection 2.5.3) is the sentiment of a news message multiplied with the relevance of a news message. I hypothesize that the impact on returns is stronger if a news message is more relevant for an instrument. For each time interval (10 minutes or 30 minutes), four different groups of

Table 2.10: **Likelihood Ratio Tests – Control Period.** Table 2.10 provides likelihood ratio (LR) test statistics for the estimations for liquidity, trading intensity, realized volatility, and the MRR model. The likelihood test results provide statistics for the restricted model with all pre- and post-news intervals captured by one coefficent. Panel A provides χ^2 statistics for the liquidity, trading intensity, and realized volatility models and p-values. Panel B provides likelihood ratio test statistics for the MRR model. The likelihood test results provide statistics for the restricted MRR model with all pre, post and no-news periods captured by one coefficent.

Panel A: LR Tests		
	χ^2-stat	p-value
Liquidity		
Quoted Spread	38	$<.0001$
lnDepth0	59	$<.0001$
lnDepth3	82	$<.0001$
Effective Spread	28	$<.0001$
Trading Intensity		
#Trades per Min.	64	$<.0001$
ln #Shares per Min.	82	$<.0001$
ln Volume per Min.	87	$<.0001$

Panel B: LR Tests for MRR Estimations			
	Mean χ^2-stat	Median χ^2-stat	# of significant out of 26 (0.1% level)
Adverse Selection θ	266	128	26
Order Processing ϕ	328	166	24
Autocorrelation ρ	93,954	28,585	26

messages are analyzed to isolate the group with the highest effect on returns. I examine all news, all news without positive news, all news without negative news, and all news without neutral news. Table 2.11 reports all regression results on returns. There are no significant coefficients for the 10 minute intervals around news. The picture changes for 30 minute intervals. Results show that excess returns are driven by negative messages. I find significant coefficients at the 10% level in all groups except the one without negative news. Significant returns only exist for time intervals that include the post-news period. These results provide some evidence that returns are indeed driven by news messages, i.e. public information. If accounted for transaction costs, returns based on the simple strategie to buy and sell solely based on the product of sentiment and relevance are not high enough to sustain a profitable business. However, highly sophisticated automated trading strategies based on news might have the potential to generate sustainable positive returns which are profitable from a business perspective.

2.7 Conclusion

In this chapter, I analyze the impact of Thomson Reuters newswire messages on intraday price discovery, liquidity, and trading intensity at the Toronto Stock Exchange. In contrast to existing literature, I am able to cluster news based on message content. News data are split into groups of news messages with positive, negative, and neutral sentiment which gives me the opportunity to study asymmetric reactions to news messages. News messages are not sorted based on ex-post return measures but on ex-ante message content based measures. The adverse selection component of the spread is estimated with an extension of the Madhavan et al. (1997) model.

Results provide evidence of asymmetric reactions to news. In general, I find higher adverse selection costs around news messages which can be explained through information gathering prior to news arrivals and differential information processing capabilities of market participants after news arrivals. On the the sentiment level, negative news messages induce significantly higher adverse selection costs than positive news messages. Liquidity increases around positive and neutral messages whereas it decreases around negative messages. Trading intensity increases around all types of news messages. A possible explanation for the difference between news messages with different sentiment could be ambiguity aversion and asymmetric reaction to news. Ambiguity averse traders react asymmetrically to ambiguous information such as news messages. If the market is composed of a proportion of ambiguity averse traders, this provides a possible explanation for my results. The main contribution of this chapter is that I show that traders react asymmetrically to intraday news arrivals. I find that newswire messages as one form of public information generally have a significant impact on intraday trading in an electronic limit order market.

The next chapter studies the impact of news in a different institutional setting with high market fragmentation and public information's impact on fragmentation characteristics. In contrast to this chapter, information, liquidity, and trading activity measures are aggregated to daily averages to facilitate the comparison of different markets.

Table 2.11: **Profitability Analysis.** Table 2.11 provides basic profitability analyses. Excess returns are calculated for each stock with the TSX/S&P 60 index returns for 10 and 30 minute intervals around news arrivals. I regress returns on sentiment multiplied by relevance and include company dummy variables. Regressions are performed on all news and on groups of news each missing either positive, negative, or neutral news messages. Robust t-statistics are provided in parentheses. 'a' denotes significance at the 1% level, 'b' at the 5% level, and 'c' at the 10% level.

	Excess Returns (z_g) All News			
	10 min. around news		30 min. around news	
	Estimate	t-stat	Estimate	t-stat
Pre News	-0.000030	(-0.26)	0.001235	(1.10)
Post News	-0.001200	(-0.82)	0.002701[c]	(1.88)
Pre and Post	-0.001140	(-0.83)	0.000753[c]	(1.69)
	Excess Returns (z_g) No Positive News			
	10 min. around news		30 min. around news	
	Estimate	t-stat	Estimate	t-stat
Pre News	0.000154	(0.70)	0.005476	(1.46)
Post News	-0.002170	(0.79)	0.005933[c]	(1.75)
Pre and Post	-0.002030	(-0.73)	0.001104[c]	(2.40)
	Excess Returns (z_g) No Negative News			
	10 min. around news		30 min. around news	
	Estimate	t-stat	Estimate	t-stat
Pre News	-0.000050	(-0.31)	-0.001960	(-0.92)
Post News	-0.000080	(-0.55)	-0.001280	(-0.97)
Pre and Post	-0.000100	(-0.42)	0.000239	(0.66)
	Excess Returns (z_g) No Neutral News			
	10 min. around news		30 min. around news	
	Estimate	t-stat	Estimate	t-stat
Pre News	-0.000020	(-0.20)	0.001052	(0.98)
Post News	-0.001080	(-0.81)	0.002410[c]	(1.77)
Pre and Post	-0.001100	(-0.82)	0.000737[c]	(1.66)

Chapter 3

Fragmented Markets and Public Information

3.1 Introduction

Both, technology and regulation, have radically changed trading in equities. The dramatic advancement of information and communication technology has enabled providers of trading venues to operate their markets entirely electronically in computing centers without any floor interaction. The competitive barriers of entering the market as a trading venue operator have significantly decreased as a result of technology. Additionally, regulation in Europe[1] and the United States[2] has allowed for new regulated trading venues in addition to incumbent exchanges. Such alternative trading venues are called multilateral trading facilities (MTF) in Europe and electronic communication networks (ECN) in the United States. Incumbent exchanges have lost signficant market shares to such alternative trading venues. As a consequence, specifically in Europe, trading in blue chip stocks is no longer concentrated on one national exchange.

In such a dynamic trading landscape, new information has multiple opportunities to translate into prices. In this chapter, I analyze the impact of the tone found in firm specific public information proxied through Thomson Reuters newswire messages on trading in fragmented markets in FTSE 100 constituents listed on the London Stock Exchange (LSE). Within the scope of the analysis, two fundamental research questions arise. First, what is

[1]In Europe, the Markets in Financial Instruments Directive (MiFID) allows for additional regulated trading venues.

[2]In the United States, Regulation NMS determines how orders are handeled between regulated exchanges and alternative trading venues with the goal to foster competition.

the impact of positive or negative firm specific public information on trading, specifically liquidity and information, in individual electronic securities markets in a fragmented market environment. Second, how does positive or negative firm specific public information influence characteristics of market fragementation and traders' preferences for different markets. In contrast to much of the existing public information literature, I use an ex-ante measure for the tone of public information. My data set of newswire messages includes, since it is the same as in Chapter 2, a computed sentiment measure which is either positive, negative, or neutral for a single news item with respect to a specific firm. In contrast to Chapter 2, the final regression framework analyzes measures on a daily basis to enable a comparison of different trading venues. However, daily averages are still compiled from intraday trading data to capture market microstructure effects.

The main results of this chapter are that I find on negative public information days lower liquidity, an increase in trading activity especially in mid-sized trades on the LSE, and a small growth in private information. I also observe a shift in private information processing to the LSE as a result of negative public information. On days with positive public information, no significant change in liquidity is discovered, again a strong rise in trading activity, and overall less private information impounded into markets but a significant shift of the remaining private information from Chi-X to the LSE. One key finding is that negative and positive public information have an asymmetric impact on trading. Also, informed trading resorts to the LSE during times of high levels of public information consistent with Chowdhry and Nanda (1991). This result is consistent with literature which shows that market participants trade off factors such as execution speed for liquidity and flexibility under uncertain market conditions (Goldstein and Kavajecz, 2004).

The remainder of this chapter is structured as follows. Section 3.2 introduces related work. Section 3.3 gives an overview of the institutional structures of the LSE and Chi-X. Section 3.4 provides a description of the newswire data set, trading data, and the sample while Section 3.5 presents market measures used in this chapter. Section 3.6 introduces the regression framework and provides results and Section 3.7 finally concludes this chapter.

3.2 Related Work

Existing public information literature considers different types of public information ranging from media content to scheduled earnings announcements. Thomson Reuters newswire messages are somewhat in-between those extrems. In addition, in the securities trading industry, newswire messages represent a large portion of the real-time information traders receive.

Many papers that investigate the effect of public information or ambiguous linguistic news content on financial markets are already presented in Chapter 2 Section 2.2. One study by Ryan and Taffler (2007) specifically analyzes trading and public information at the LSE. The authors find that firm specific news releases drive trading activity in the British market especially in FTSE 100 trading. The major news source that drives trading volume in their study is analyst activity measured through analyst reports in news data. They argue that analyst activity also represents "sell-side analysts possessing superior information processing skills and/or having access to 'private' information". In general, an increase in trading volume reflects differential interpretation of information by investors (Kim and Verrecchia, 1991). Traders disagree and as a result shift to their new expectation level, which is based on the additional information, through trade. The relation of trading volume and public information is a well described phenomenon, also in papers presented in Chapter 2. Morse (1981) provides one very early study based on daily data. He shows that earnings announcements significantly increase daily trading volume. Mitchell and Mulherin (1994) examine the number of daily news announcements of Dow Jones & Company. They find a direct, however small, relation between trading activity and the number of Dow Jones messages. Empirical evidence for the price discovery process and liquidity is not as clear as it is for trading volume and existing studies report sometimes conflicting results (cf. Chapter 2 Section 2.2). In contrast to existing studies that focus on returns, this chapter focuses on the influence of firm specific public information on explicit market microstructure characteristics, i.e. liquidity, trading activity, and information.

From a theoretical perspective the, in Chapter 2 presented, Kim and Verrecchia (1991, 1994) models provide predictions about adverse selection costs, trading activity, and liquidity for a single market. Pre-announcement information gatherers have superior private information which increases the adverse selection component of the spread while the same effect is observed post-announcement as a result of different information processing capabilities of market participants. Additionally, the models predict an increase of trading volume and a decrease in liquidity around public information announcements. However, the Kim and Verrecchia (1991, 1994) models do not provide predictions about what should happen between markets if an instrument is traded on several trading venues. For my analysis, existing empirical evidence and financial theory suggest for an individual market that

I find an increase in trading activity on days with a high level of public information. Empirical evidence for liquidity and adverse selection is mixed while financial theory suggests an increase in adverse selection costs and a reduction of liquidity.

On 1 November 2007, MiFID, the Markets in Financial Instruments Directive[3], passed by the European Union, came into effect. The stated "objective of MiFID is to foster a fair, competitive, transparent, efficient, and integrated European financial market" (Degryse, 2009). Market fragmentation in Europe is a relatively new phenomenon. Prior to MiFID, a single incumbent exchange existed in most European countries with little competition to fear. EU countries had the possibility to employ a concentration rule which required that all orders had to be executed on a regulated market.

MiFID has enabled alternative trading venues, MFTs, to compete against regulated exchanges. Specifically, an MTF is defined as "a multilateral system, operated by an investment firm or a market operator, which brings together multiple third-party buying and selling interests in financial instruments - in the system and in accordance with non-discretionary rules - in a way that results in a contract..."[4]. Under MiFID, MTFs are regulated by the national regulatory authorities. MTFs challenge incumbent exchanges with fast trading platforms, innovative order types, and innovative fee systems. In contrast to US regulation[5], markets are not formally linked and best execution obligations are not primarily focused on the best price principle but include multiple dimensions. Investment firms must "take all reasonable steps to obtain, when executing orders, the best possible result for their clients taking into account price, costs, speed, likelihood of execution and settlement, size, nature or any other consideration relevant to the execution of the order"[6]. Within MiFID, best execution obligations have to be met by financial intermediaries not exchanges. Often, incumbent exchanges stress that investors enjoy less protection when trading on an MTF than they do on incumbent regulated markets. But under MiFID, both, MTFs and regulated markets, are regulated by national regulatory authorities and need adhere to similar rules such as "transparent and non-discretionary rules

[3]Directive 2004/39/EC.

[4]Article 4(1) 2004/39/EC.

[5]Rule 611 of Regulation NMS, the order protection rule, defines that national US markets are protected against trade-throughs. A trade-through occurs when a trade is executed on one market despite the fact that another national market offers a better quote. The SEC's rationale behind the order protection rule is that a protection against trade-throughs would incentivize market participants to post limit orders and thus supply liquidity. The order protection rule only protects the top of the book not the depth of the book.

[6]Article 21(1) 2004/39/EC.

and procedures for fair and orderly trading"[7]. As fast and technologically reliable platforms with competitive pricing, MTFs have been especially successful in attracting order flow for trading in FTSE 100 stocks. On some days in the the first quarter of 2010, the LSE had a market share of less than 50% in its blue chip segment.

To my knowledge there is currently no study that directly investigates the effect of public information specifically in fragmented markets and on characteristics of market fragmentation. With the recent developments in regulation[8], I am interested in how firm specific public information influences trading in fragmented markets. With high market shares, alternative markets are important to be included in empirical analyses.

A recent study by Riordan et al. (2010a) examines market fragmentation in FTSE 100 stocks with an analysis of the LSE and the three largest MTFs (Chi-X, Turqoise, and BATS). They find that the major markets are the LSE and Chi-X with Turquoise and BATS having little influence on price discovery. Chi-X leads in quote based price discovery whereas the LSE leads in trade based price discovery. Both, the LSE and Chi-X, are highly liquid and contribute significantly to total price discovery in FTSE 100 stocks.

Other evidence on market fragmentation is mixed. Mendelson (1987) and Bennett and Wei (2006) find lower liquidity and less efficient markets as a result of the fragmentation of order flow. Mendelson (1987) provides a theoretical model to assess the influence of market fragmentation on price discovery in different market microstructure settings. The author also provides a concise definition of market fragmentation. "We say that the market mechanism is consolidated if all the order data are available when this transformation [of orders to transactions] takes place, e.g., when all orders are channeled to a central trading post. We say that the market is fragmented when orders are decomposed into a number of disjoint subsets, and the transformation is applied to each subset separately, e.g., when an asset is traded in a number of secluded locations" (Mendelson, 1987). He finds that fragmentation can reduce trading volume and increase volatility. However, he concludes that there is no per se optimal solution. "The diversity of exchange mechanisms that prevail around the world as well as across assets reflects the dependence of the appropriate market design on specific circumstances and on factors that are probably not captured by the stylized facts of the market microstructure literature" (Mendelson, 1987). His study calls for a careful analysis of the effects of fragmentation in a specific market setting before jumping

[7] Article 14(1) 2004/39/EC.

[8] MiFID is currently under review and the European Commission has opened consultation on the MiFID review. After the consultation period, the European Commission will propose a MiFID amandement in spring 2011 (http://ec.europa.eu/internal_market/consultations/2010/mifid_en.htm).

to conclusions, for instance with policy decisions. Bennett and Wei (2006) observe liquidity and price discovery for stocks that switch from Nasdaq to the NYSE in the years 2002 and 2003. In those years, order flow of Nasdaq listed stocks was substantially more fragmented than order flow of NYSE listed stocks. The authors attribute a liquidity and price discovery enhancing effect to the increase in order flow consolidation after the switch to the NYSE.

Boehmer and Boehmer (2003), Barclay et al. (2003), and Goldstein et al. (2008) ascertain that competition for order flow has positive effects on price discovery and liquidity. Boehmer and Boehmer (2003) study a natural experiment in 2001 and 2002 when AMEX listed ETFs start trading on the NYSE which results in a higher fragmentation of the order flow. Within the first month of trading, the NYSE has gained a market share of 10%. The ETFs previously traded on AMEX, Nasdaq, and Island ECN, with AMEX having a very similar market structure as the NYSE. Both measured in spreads and depth, market specific liquidity as well as consolidated liquidity strongly increase after the ETFs start trading on the NYSE. Barclay et al. (2003) investigate the interaction of price discovery and liquidity of stocks which are listed on Nasdaq and traded on both Nasdaq and Electronic Communication Networks (ECN). Their data is from the year 2000 when ECNs already executed a major share of order flow of Nasdaq listed stocks. They find that a higher fraction of informed trading is executed on ECNs than on Nasdaq. Those results should counter the often raised concern that ECNs only cream skim order flow when in fact they contribute substantially to price discovery. Goldstein et al. (2008) study Nasdaq listed stocks in a more recent period than Barclay et al. (2003) with data from 2003. In their paper "quote competitiveness is found to increase the probability of executions on all four venues[, Nasdaq, Archipelago, Instinet, and Island ECN,]" (Goldstein et al., 2008) however they conclude that extreme competition among trading venues could be harmful in the long run especially for small cap stocks.

Foucault and Menkveld (2008) combine a theoretical model and empirical analysis in one paper. Their model predicts that market fragmentation and competition result in higher consolidated liquidity and that the liquidity supply of the new trading venue increases with smart order routing. They approximate smart order routing in their empirical analysis with the fraction of trades that do not violate price priority. In the empirical part, they confirm their model with an analysis of the Dutch stock market after the 2004 introduction of EuroSETS, an alternative trading venue which competes against the Euronext system. First, they find more liquidity in the consolidated order book. They also find that trade throughs, the violation of price priority across order books, discourage limit orders. With a higher fraction of traders using smart order routing, trade throughs occur less and EuroSETS provides more liquidity. As a policy implication, Foucault and Menkveld (2008) conclude that is is important to have some protection against trade throughs.

In finance theory, models exists that predict that investors have incentives to concentrate order flow on one market. Pagano (1989) develops a multimarket model in which identical execution costs lead to a concentration on one market. However, investors' preferences might differ in real market environments which could lead to a sustainable multi-market solution. One example could be large liquidity traders that trade on special trading venues to circumvent larger adverse price movements. In this chapter, I am specifically interested in how information is processed and how characteristics of fragmented markets vary with high levels of public information. From a theoretical point of view, Chowdhry and Nanda (1991) model that informed trading gravitates to the most liquid market. Informed traders have the opportunity to use their private information in multiple markets, however, they are attracted by liquidity. If public information processors have higher levels of private information as a result of public information, one would expect that trading volume and price discovery shifts to the more liquid market. Since most trading in FTSE 100 stocks is still executed on the LSE and the LSE's daily trading volume is much larger than that of Chi-X, I anticipate that volume and price discovery shifts to the LSE in times of high levels of public information.

3.3 Institutional Details

In this analysis, I study two markets that offer trading in FTSE 100 stocks: the LSE and Chi-X. The LSE is the incumbent exchange on which FTSE 100 constituents are listed. It is one of the world's largest equity exchanges with an annual value of share trading of 2,796,077 mGBP[9] whereas Chi-X is a multilateral trading facility (MTF) which has emerged only recently but has increased its market share steadily. Both, the LSE and Chi-X, are regulated through the Financial Services Authority (FSA) which is the British regulator of the financial services industry, the LSE as a regulated exchange under MiFID and Chi-X as an MTF. Chi-X started trading about six month ahead of MiFID at the end of March 2007. The full list of FTSE 100 constituents became available on Chi-X on 13

[9] World Federation of Exchanges,
http://www.world-exchanges.org/statistics/annual/2009/equity-markets/total-value-share-trading/.

July 2007. Currently, Chi-X is owned by Instinet, a subsidiary of Nomura Holding, and a number of international investment banks. Its market share in UK equity trading has increased from 9% in March 2008 to 15% when it celebrated its second anniversary in March 2009[10], and finally to 26% in in the first quarter of 2010[11]. Currently, Chi-X is the largest among all existing MTFs.[12] Chi-X not only offers trading in British FTSE 100 constituents but also trades, for instance, stocks listed in the French CAC 40, the German DAX 30, and the Dutch AEX 25.

Chi-X and the LSE compete predominantly on technology and trading costs which translates into different fee structures, network latencies, and IT system service levels. FTSE 100 constituents are traded on the SETS[13] system at the LSE which provides a combination of an electronic limit order market with liquidity provision through market makers. Market makers operate within the electronic public limit order book without proprietary information. Liquidity for non-crossing orders is solely provided by limit orders displayed in the order book. Orders are executed with price-time priority. Iceberg orders that display only a portion of their total size sacrifice time priority on the non-displayed portion of the order such that the priority rule could more precisely be called price-visibility-time priority. The LSE introduced hidden liquidity only on 14 December 2009 to match MTFs. Such orders have to meet the Large-In-Scale considerations of MiFID.[14] These types of orders add liquidity to an order book and are primarily used by informed investors to avoid adverse selection costs.

Chi-X also operates an entirely electronic limit order book with a combination of visible and hidden liquidity based on price-time priority. Comparable to the LSE, hidden orders sacrifice their time priority and have to meet MiFID's Large-In-Scale requirements. In addition to limit orders, market orders, iceberg orders, and hidden orders, Chi-X offers pegged orders. The trading price for such orders is determined based on a reference price, for instance the European Best Bid and Offer (EBBO). Orders on Chi-X are subject to a price check to ensure investors that orders are not executed far away from prices above or below the European Best Bid and Offer. Technically, Chi-X has, on average, ten times lower latencies with 0.4 ms than the LSE.

[10]http://www.chi-x.com/chi-x-press-releases/Chi-X-Europe-Second-Year-Anniversary.pdf.

[11]http://www.chi-x.com/chi-x-press-releases/chi-x-europe-q1-2010-trading-stats-final.pdf.

[12]Other MTFs are, for instance, Turquoise and BATS.

[13]Stock Exchange Electronic Trading Service, http://www.londonstockexchange.com/traders-and-brokers/products-services/trading-services/sets/sets.htm.

[14]MiFID, Directive 2004/39/EC Article 22(2).

During most of the observation period, the LSE and Chi-X both feature a maker-taker pricing scheme. At the LSE an investor is charged between 0.45 basis points (bps) to 0.75 bps for an aggressive order, an incoming order which hits an existing order in the order book. Executed passive orders receive a rebate of up to 0.40 bps. The maker-taker fees and rebates depend on monthly executed order volume. The highest rebate is received above a monthly trading volume of 25 bnGBP, the minimum fee of 0.45 bps per trade is charged with a monthly trading volume above 30 bnGBP. The minimum fee per trade is 25 pence. However, on 1 September 2009 the LSE switched back to their traditional fee schedule with the same pricing scheme for both sides of the market. Chi-X features a maker-taker pricing scheme with a rebate of 0.20 bps for passive orders and a fee of 0.30 bps for aggressive orders. The LSE and Chi-X feature dynamic tick sizes based on the price of a specific stock. Since tick size is found to have an influence on market characteristics (cf. Harris, 1994; Goldstein and Kavajecz, 2000; Jones and Lipson, 2001; Bessembinder, 2003b), I control for tick size differences between the LSE and Chi-X in the regression framework. Such changes, however, only influence a minor part of the sample (13 firms) for a very limited period of time with the longest time period being 31 trading days. Both markets' continuous trading sessions start at 8:00 a.m. GMT and last until 16:30 p.m. GMT which is equivalent to most major continental European exchanges which start at 9:00 a.m. GMT-1 and stop trading at 17:30 p.m. GMT-1.

3.4 Data and Sample Selection

3.4.1 Stock Market Data

Again, trade and quote data are retrieved from the Thomson Reuters DataScope Tick History archive through SIRCA for both, the LSE and the multilateral trading facility Chi-X. I specifically retrieve trade prices, volumes, and best bid and ask including associated volumes from 1 December 2009 to 31 December 2009. Data entries also include qualifying codes to identify special trades and quotes. Trades and quotes are timestamped to the millisecond. All prices in the data are reported in British pence. I restrict the analysis to continuous trading and delete the first and last fiveteen minutes of a trading day. Cutting the first and last fiveteen minutes avoids biases associated with opening and closing procedures. I also delete all crossing trades from the data. Trades within the spread at the LSE are also deleted prior to the introduction of hidden liquidity at the LSE. However, those trades only constitute 0.5% of all trades and regression results do not change if those trades are left in the data. Table B.3 in Appendix B depicts a sample of raw trade and quote data.

The LSE and Chi-X have individual order books which I retrieve both. For additional analyses, a consolidated order book is constructed that includes all quotes and trades from both markets which are then matched based on the Reuters Instrument Code and timestamps. The construction of the consolidated order book is explained in more detail in Section 3.5. Thomson Reuters also provides an xbo-data stream, a consolidated European data feed, that merges data of all regulated trading in FTSE 100 stocks. Since this chapter focuses on the LSE and Chi-X, I construct my own consolidated order book which also allows for an easy attribution of data entries to either the LSE or Chi-X. In a test with the four major markets in FTSE 100 trading (LSE, Chi-X, Turquoise, and BATS), only marginal differences between the constructed consolidated order book and the Thomson Reuters xbo-stream are found. The analysis focuses on the LSE and Chi-X. With a combined market share in FTSE 100 trading of approximately 85% during 2009, they account for the major share of trading in those firms. Also, Riordan et al. (2010a) find that the LSE and Chi-X contribute the major share to price formation.

3.4.2 News Data

This chapter's analysis is based on the same news data as presented in Chapter 2 Section 2.4, the news data which are also used throughout this thesis. This chapter specifically uses news data for firms listed on the LSE. It is important to recall that one news item is scored separately for different firms and its sentiment can either be positive, negative, or neutral. A news message that is positive for Vodafone could be negative for British Telecom (both firms compete in the telecommunications sector) while it might be much more relevant for British Telecom than for Vodafone. Imagine both companies bid for a large contract which is eventually awarded to one company. News about this is clearly positive for the company that won the contract and clearly negative for the other one. Table 3.1 depicts one sample RNSE message for the Royal Bank of Scotland, a company listed on the LSE and also the one in the sample with the most negative messages.

The analysis in this chapter relies on the RNSE sentiment measure which is either 1 for positive, -1 for negative, and 0 for neutral news messages. Through the sentiment measure, I derive information about the average daily general tone of public information that arrives at trading desks. Since I am interested how the stock specific sentiment of public information influences the price discovery process, per firm public information dummies are constructed which can be used in a regression on a daily basis. To construct the public information variables for one specific trading day and firm, I aggregate all news from the end of trading of the last trading day to the end of trading of the current trading day for which the variable is constructed. In the case of weekends, the variable contains news from a hypothetical end of trading on Sundays to the end of trading on Mondays. If, during an aggregation period, no news messages arrive for a specific firm and day, a neutral sentiment is assigned to this firm/day combination. If the aggregated sentiment is above zero, this day is considered a day with positive public information for the specific firm, if it is below zero it is considered to be a negative day, and if it is zero a neutral daily sentiment is assigned to the respective firm and trading day.

3.4.3 Sample Selection

The sample is based on FTSE 100 constituents which continuously trade in the index over the year 2009. The FTSE 100 is the most important British stock market also including the British blue chips. The FTSE 100 represents 85.67% of UK market capitalization as of 31 March 2010[15] which results in a net market cap of 1,460,100 mGBP. All constituents are traded on the LSE as well as on Chi-X and represent a broad cross-section of industries. Stocks in the index are free-float weighted to represent the publicly tradable investment opportunities. For this analysis, all stocks that are not continuously in the FTSE 100 index during 2009 and stocks which have less than ten trades on one day during 2009 on either the LSE or Chi-X are removed. Only two stocks are affected by the 'ten trade rule'. Additionally, I exclude 24 December 2009 and 31 December 2009 from the data since very little trading on those days results in extreme values for some measures. The final sample consists of 88 liquid stocks and 251 trading days in 2009. A complete list of sample firms including average market capitalization in 2009 can be found in Appendix A.

[15] FTSE 100 Index Factsheet,
http://www.ftse.com/Indices/UK_Indices/Downloads/FTSE_100_Index_Factsheet.pdf/.

3.5 Measures

3.5.1 Spreads and Trading Activity

Spread measures are calculated on tick-by-tick data to assess liquidity and also calculate measures for trading activity. Those measures are then aggregated to a daily frequency per firm for the regression analysis to capture the intraday market microstructure dynamics of each variable but to facilitate a comparison of different trading venues. Again, the standard Lee and Ready (1991) algorithm is used to sign trades with contemporaneous quotes as proposed by Bessembinder (2003a).

Quote based, ex-ante observable, liquidity is measured with the relative quoted half spread based on Bessembinder and Kaufman (1997) as described in Chapter 2 Section 2.5. This measure is based on a quote-to-quote process which is then aggregated to daily per firm and market averages for estimation purposes. Quoted spreads are also calculated as quoted spreads at trades for which I need the trade process. Those quoted spreads capture liquidity represented through the best bid and ask at the time of trades. Quoted spreads also influence how traders use market or limit orders. When spreads are narrow traders tend to use market orders while wide spreads incentivize the use of limit orders (Biais et al., 1995). The effective spread, the spread paid when an incoming market order trades against a limit order in the order book, is also calculated equivalently to Chapter 2 Section 2.5. The effective spread additionally captures institutional features of a market such as hidden liquidity through e.g. iceberg orders or real hidden orders and market depth. Hidden liquidity is available on the LSE from 14 December 2009 and on Chi-X over the entire observation period. Effective spreads are usually equal to or smaller than quoted spreads at trade time. If, however, markets feature hidden liquidity inside the spread, effective spreads might actually be smaller than quoted spreads at trades. For aggregate measures the relation between quoted spreads at trades and effective spreads fundamentally relies on the amount of visible and hidden liquidity as well as on other potential institutional details that might provide price improvement.

In addition to the liquidity measures quoted and effective spread which only include contemporaneous measures, I compute realized spreads and simple price impacts. The realized spread measures liquidity suppliers' revenues independent of the adverse selection costs imposed on the uninformed by the informed (Bessembinder and Kaufman, 1997). Let p_t be the execution price, D_t the trade direction, b_t the best bid, a_t the best ask then the realized spread is calculated with the midpoint five minutes after a trade ($z = 5$)[16] and the midpoint fifteen minutes after a trade ($z = 15$) as follows:

$$rs_t^z = D_t \times \frac{p_t - (a_{t+z} + b_{t+z})/2}{(a_t + b_t)/2} \times 10{,}000$$

Price impact is an approximate measure of the adverse selection component of the spread. The price impact is the effective spread minus the realized spread and tries to measure the information content of a trade. It approximates the permanent impact of a trade under the assumption that information impacts are permanent and realized at the 5-minute or 15-minute mark whereas other effects such as inventory costs are transitory. Following a trade, liquidity suppliers adjust their beliefs about the fundamental value of an asset depending on the information content of a trade (cf. Glosten and Milgrom, 1985). Using the same variable definitions as for the measures above, the simple price impact of a trade, pi_t^z, is calculated as follows:

$$pi_t^z = D_t \times \frac{(a_{t+z} + b_{t+z})/2 - (a_t + b_t)/2}{(a_t + b_t)/2} \times 10{,}000$$

The price impact provides an indication of the information content of a trade. I apply more robust information measures, not dependent on the spread decomposition, in the following (cf. Section 3.5.3). Spreads are calculated on both the LSE's and Chi-X's individual orderbooks and the consolidated orderbook. I also derive the trade based spread measures, effective spread, realized spread, and price impact, separated by different trade size categories. It is differentiated between five trade size categories measured by the number of shares traded[17]: 0-499 shares, 500-1,999, 2,000-4,999, 5,000-9,999 shares, and trades with 10,000 shares traded or more.

To assess trading activity, I calculate for the LSE and for Chi-X the number of trades per firm and day (#Trades), the number of shares traded per firm and day (Quantity), and the traded volume per firm and day in GPB (Volume). Comparable to spread measures on different trade size categories, also the number of trades per category is obtained. Based on daily per firm volumes the LSE and Chi-X market shares (MktShare) are computed relative to each other.

[16]The SEC uses the five minute mark in its definition of realized spreads (Regulation NMS, Rule 605).
[17]Trade size categories are based on SEC trade size categories (Regulation NMS, Rule 600).

Order Book 1

Price	Size
51.00	100
50.00	500
48.50	300
48.00	200

Order Book 2

Price	Size
50.00	200
49.50	300
48.50	100
47.50	200

Consolidated Order Book

Price	Size
51.00	100 = 100 + 0
50.00	700 = 500 + 200
49.50	300 = 0 + 300
48.50	400 = 300 + 100
48.00	200 = 200 + 0
47.50	200 = 0 + 200

Figure 3.1: **Consolidated Order Book.** Figure 3.1 shows an example of how individual order books are merged into one consolidated order book.

Spread measures are calculated for the individual order books of the LSE and Chi-X as well as for the consolidated order book. The individual order books consist of the quotes and trades of one trading venue, the LSE or Chi-X. The consolidated order book combines quotes and trades from both trading venues. The best bid or ask is taken from whatever order book provides the best prices. It might be that the best spread is only provided by one trading venue or that the bid is provided by one while the ask is provided by the other trading venue. Figure 3.1 graphically explains how two individual order books are combined to one consolidated order book. Trade based measures can either be calculated in the consolidated book for all trades not considering the specific trading venue or individually for both trading venues but with the consolidated order book as their reference. All spread measures are winsorized at 1% and 99% to account for potential extreme values through technical data recording errors.

3.5.2 Information Shares

To measure which market leads in quote based price discovery and in particular how this characteristic changes on days with high levels of firm specific public information, I compute Hasbrouck (1995) information shares (InfoShares) for each firm and day. The information shares measure assumes the existence of a common efficient price and provides information on the allocation of price discovery across markets. Joel Hasbrouck specifically intents this measure for fragemented market environments since "fragmentation, the dispersal of trading in a security in multiple sites, has emerged as a dominant institutional trend" (Hasbrouck, 1995). The assumption of a common efficient price across markets implies that stock prices are linked by arbitrage relationships (Hasbrouck, 1995). The information shares measure is based on the concept of cointegration of prices in multiple markets for one security. "Cointegration refers to the feature that while two price series [...] may be nonstationary, they do not diverge without bound from each other" (Hasbrouck, 1995). In principal, the econometric model for information shares attemps to determine which trading venue 'moves first'.

Econometrically, the price difference between a security trading in two markets is covariance stationary as a result of arbitrage relationships. The information share attributable to a trading venue is defined as "the proportion of the efficient price innovation variance that can be attributed to a market" (Hasbrouck, 1995). I use prevailing midpoints m_t of the consolidated order book, based on Thomson Reuters DataScope Tick History data, assumed to follow a random walk

$$m_t = m_{t-1} + u_t$$

to characterize the implicit efficient price. Then u_t follows a white noise process satisfying the following criteria: $E(u_t) = 0$, $E(u_t^2) = \sigma^2$, and $E(u_t u_s) = 0$ for $t \neq s$. The prices on the LSE and on Chi-X where p_t^j refers to the same security can be written as a vector defined as follows:

$$p_t = \begin{pmatrix} p_t^{LSE} \\ p_t^{Chi\text{-}X} \end{pmatrix}$$

Using above definitions, p_t can be written as

$$p_t = \begin{pmatrix} m_t & + & \epsilon_t^{LSE} \\ m_t & + & \epsilon_t^{Chi\text{-}X} \end{pmatrix} .$$

The vector of price changes Δp_t is covariance stationary and may thus be written in a vector moving average (VMA) representation

$$\Delta p_t = \epsilon_t + \psi_1 \epsilon_{t-1} + \psi_2 \epsilon_{t-2} + ... = \psi(L)\epsilon_t \tag{3.1}$$

where $\psi(L)$ is a polynomial in the lag operater and

$$\epsilon_t = \begin{pmatrix} \epsilon_t^{LSE} \\ \epsilon_t^{Chi\text{-}X} \end{pmatrix}$$

is a vector innovation process with $E(\epsilon_t) = 0$ and its covariance matrix $Var(\epsilon_t) = \Omega$. The components of ϵ_t reflect the new information that is incorporated on either the LSE (ϵ_t^{LSE}) or Chi-X ($\epsilon_t^{Chi\text{-}X}$). According to Huang (2002), Equation 3.1 can be rewritten as

$$\Delta p_t = \psi(1)\epsilon_t + (1-L)\sum_{i=1}^{\infty}\left(-\sum_{j=i+1}^{\infty}\psi_j\right)L^i\epsilon_t \tag{3.2}$$

where L are lag operators, $\psi(1) = (I_n + \sum_{i=1}^{\infty}\psi_i)$, and I_n is the identity matrix. $\psi(1)$ "constitutes the long-run impact of a disturbance on each of the prices" (Hasbrouck, 1995) since it comprises of the sum of all moving average coefficients (Huang, 2002). Based on Hasbrouck (1995) and Stock and Watson (1988) Equation 3.2 can be represented as follows:

$$p_t = p_0 + \psi(1)\sum_{i=1}^{t}\epsilon_i + \psi*(L)\epsilon_t$$

where $\psi*(L)$ is a matrix polynomial in the lag operator. "If price innovations are due to new information, the term $\psi(1)\sum_{i=1}^{t}\epsilon_i$ [greek symbols adjusted] captures the permanent impact of new information on prices" (Huang, 2002).

Observed midpoint prices are decomposed into a random walk common to all prices and a covariance stationary error. Based on above definitions, the variance of the random walk component, the representation of total price discovery, is

$$\sigma_u^2 = \psi\Omega\psi'$$

where ψ is an arbitrary row from $\psi(1)$. In my specific case the variance of the random walk reflects price discovery contributions from both trading venues, the LSE and Chi-X:

$$\sigma_u^2 = \left(\psi^{LSE}, \psi^{Chi\text{-}X}\right) \begin{pmatrix} \sigma_{LSE}^2 & \sigma_{LSE,Chi\text{-}X} \\ \sigma_{Chi\text{-}X,LSE} & \sigma_{Chi\text{-}X}^2 \end{pmatrix} \begin{pmatrix} \psi^{LSE} \\ \psi^{Chi\text{-}X} \end{pmatrix}$$

A diagonal covariance matrix Ω (i.e. $\sigma_i^2 = 0$) identifies the contribution of each individual trading venue without ambiguity. The fraction of the variance of a trading venue in relation to the entire variance of the random walk component then provides a measure of a market's contribution to price discovery. Formally, this fraction called information shares is defined by Hasbrouck (1995) as follows:

$$\text{IS}^j = \frac{\psi_j^2 \Omega_{jj}}{\psi \Omega \psi'}$$

where in this chapter $j \in \{LSE,\ Chi\text{-}X\}$. In a real market setting it might happen that contemporaneous midpoints of different trading venues are equal. As a result, midpoint prices may be correlated and Ω is not diagonal. Following Hasbrouck (1995), I determine upper and lower bounds for each trading venue through maximizing and minimizing the contribution of each to price discovery. Then the mean contribution of price discovery is calculated for both, the LSE and Chi-X:

$$\text{IS}^{j,mean} = \frac{\text{IS}^{j,upper} + \text{IS}^{j,lower}}{2}$$

Hasbrouck (1995) also proposes to "shorten the interval of observation". However, my data is already on a millisecond level and I need to resort to computing upper and lower bounds. In this chapter, information shares are calculated on a daily per firm basis. Also, information shares sum up to one by construction.

3.5.3 Trade and Quote Correlated Information

Changes in the efficient price are separated into trade and quote correlated components differentiating between trades executed on the LSE and Chi-X, $j \in \{LSE,\ Chi\text{-}X\}$, as in Hasbrouck (1991a,b). This results in a three-way vector autoregressive (VAR) model. Let x_t^j be the trade direction (-1 for a sell, 1 for a buy) for trades on the LSE or Chi-X, respectively, and 0 if the trade is not executed on the specific trading venue. r_t denotes the quote midpoint changes in the consolidated order book then the full model is defined as follows:

$$r_t = \sum_{i=1}^{10} \alpha_{t-i}^{r} r_{t-i} + \sum_{i=0}^{10} \alpha_i^{LSE} x_{t-i}^{LSE} + \sum_{i=0}^{10} \alpha_i^{Chi\text{-}X} x_{t-i}^{Chi\text{-}X} + u_{1,t}$$

$$x_t^{LSE} = \sum_{i=1}^{10} \beta_i^{r} r_{t-i} + \sum_{i=1}^{10} \beta_i^{LSE} x_{t-i}^{LSE} + \sum_{i=1}^{10} \beta_i^{Chi\text{-}X} x_{t-i}^{Chi\text{-}X} + u_{2,t}$$

$$x_t^{Chi\text{-}X} = \sum_{i=1}^{10} \gamma_i^{r} r_{t-i} + \sum_{i=1}^{10} \gamma_i^{LSE} x_{t-i}^{LSE} + \sum_{i=1}^{10} \gamma_i^{Chi\text{-}X} x_{t-i}^{Chi\text{-}X} + u_{3,t}$$

Then, the VAR model in its vector moving average (VMA) representation is as follows where L are lag polynomial operators:

$$\begin{pmatrix} r_t \\ x_t^{LSE} \\ x_t^{Chi\text{-}X} \end{pmatrix} = \begin{pmatrix} a^r(L) & a^{LSE}(L) & a^{Chi\text{-}X}(L) \\ b^r(L) & b^{LSE}(L) & b^{Chi\text{-}X}(L) \\ c^r(L) & c^{LSE}(L) & c^{Chi\text{-}X}(L) \end{pmatrix} \begin{pmatrix} u_{1,t} \\ u_{2,t} \\ u_{3,t} \end{pmatrix}$$

According to Hasbrouck (1991b) the sums of $\sum_{t=0}^{\infty} a^{LSE}$ and $\sum_{t=0}^{\infty} a^{Chi\text{-}X}$ are used to derive the cumulative impulse response functions (CIRF) for each trading venue. The CIRF is the permanent price impact of a trade and it is generally interpreted as the private information content of a trade. This measure provides for a more precise analysis of information than the simple price impact of Section 3.5.1. It represents the unexpected part of a trade, the trade innovation. Trades may contain information at lower frequencies than measured. However, this measure is used in other studies with the same interpretation (Barclay and Hendershott, 2003; Madhavan, 2000; Hendershott and Riordan, 2009).

Using the VMA representation from above, information can be decomposed into a trade correlated part for each trading venue and quote correlated portions (Hasbrouck, 1991b). The variance decomposition is as follows:

$$\sigma_v^2 = \left(\sum_{i=0}^{\infty} a_i^{r}\right)^2 \sigma_r^2 + \left(\sum_{i=0}^{\infty} a_i^{LSE}\right)^2 \sigma_{x^{LSE}}^2 + \left(\sum_{i=0}^{\infty} a_i^{Chi\text{-}X}\right)^2 \sigma_{x^{Chi\text{-}X}}^2$$

The information content of quotes (ICQuote) is the first term, the trade correlated portions for LSE the second (ICTrade^{LSE}), and the trade correlated part for Chi-X

($ICTrade^{Chi\text{-}X}$) the third. All lags are summed up to get the total trade correlated contribution of each market to price discovery. The results are reported in basis points for the CIRF and in percent for the information content of trades and quotes. The estimation is restarted for each trading day and firm in the sample.

To approximate the total contribution to price discovery $TPD^j_{i,d}$ of the LSE and Chi-X, I compute a combination of information shares and the variance decomposition. Information shares give the percentage that each market contributes to quote based price discovery whereas the variance decomposition provides the fraction of quote based contribution to price discovery and trade based contribution for each market separately. Then the following formula for the total contribution of market j for one stock on one day to price discovery emerges:

$$TPD^j = ICQuote \times IS^j + ICTrade^j.$$

3.6 Results and Interpretation

3.6.1 Descriptive Statistics

Before I analyze the influence of public information on trading, descriptive statistics on both markets and the current status of market fragmentation in FTSE 100 trading are presented. Market measures to assess market quality comprise of liquidity measures, trading activity measures, and information measures on a daily per instrument basis. Additionally, the trading venues' market shares are presented. I compute liquidity for both the individual order books of the LSE and Chi-X and for the consolidated order book. Table 3.2 reports liquidity measure descriptives. The difference between LSE and Chi-X measures is tested using clustered standard errors (cf. Petersen, 2009; Thompson, 2011). The most basic liquidity measure, the quoted spread, is 6.08 bps for the incumbent LSE and with 6.80 bps slightly higher for the MTF Chi-X. Not suprisingly, the consolidated order book provides a better average spread than the individual order books. The difference between the LSE and Chi-X is highly significant with a t-value of -8.86. I also compute the quoted spread on a trade-by-trade basis. Both markets have lower quoted spreads at trades than during periods without trades. This provides evidence in comparison to the overall quoted spreads that traders monitor the order books of both markets and trade when it is comparatively cheap to trade. The savings from monitoring the spreads seem to offset monitoring costs.

The difference for quoted spreads at trades between the LSE and Chi-X is small with -0.21 bps but still significant at the 1% level. The same pattern as for quoted spreads emerges for effective spreads which are slightly smaller by also 0.21 bps on the LSE than on Chi-X. In the consolidated order book, effective spreads are not significantly different between both markets, however this changes when effective spreads are splitted by trade size categories. When differences are statistically significant, it is always the LSE which has smaller effective spreads. Effective spreads are only marginally larger than quoted spreads at trades. The small difference is an indication that the majority of volume is executed at the best bid or ask which in turn shows that both markets are highly liquid in FTSE 100 trading. Summarized, the LSE quotes tighter spreads than Chi-X and provides more liquidity measured by ex-ante and ex-post liquidity measures. Realized spreads are negative on both the LSE and Chi-X which could be a result of the maker-taker pricing schemes, at least on Chi-X. I find positive price impacts at the five and fifteen minute marks. However, price impact measures for both markets are not statistically significantly different. Price impacts calculated on the consolidated order book are significantly higher for the LSE. Since price impact is a noisy information measure, I use more robust measures in the following paragraphs to analyze the price discovery process.

Panel B of Table 3.2 and Table 3.3 provide information on trade based spread measures for different trade sizes. Even for large trade sizes, effective spreads are quite small which indicates again a highly liquid market. For large trade sizes, the computed difference might be different to the difference of aggregated individual values. Since large trades do not exist for all firms and days, the difference can only be calculated when daily values for both markets exist. Realized spreads at both, the fifteen and the five minute marks, increase with larger trades sizes both on the LSE and on Chi-X. For the largest trade size, realized spreads at the 5-minute mark, liquidity suppliers' revenue, are close to zero at the LSE.

During the observation period the LSE has a relative market share of 73.70% measured both in volume traded and the number of shares traded. Chi-X attracts on average 26.30% of the order flow. The relative market share is the market share calculated against the consolidated volume or number of shares traded on the LSE and Chi-X, excluding other MTFs and OTC trading. The LSE and Chi-X have a combined market share of approximately 85% during 2009 in non-OTC trading. Market shares and other trading activity measures are reported in Table 3.4. The higher market share of the LSE is attended by more executed trades, higher volume and a higher number of shares traded on the LSE than on Chi-X per day and firm. It is interesting that the average trade size is much smaller on Chi-X than on the LSE with a high statistical significance at the 1% level. The average trade size in GBP is 10,276 on the LSE as compared to 6,160 GBP on Chi-X. One potential explanation could be that algorithmic traders are more likely to trade on Chi-X since it caters their need for low latency trading and small round trip times. Algorithmic traders often split orders extensively and use limit order strategies which could result in much smaller trade sizes (cf. Hendershott and Riordan, 2009; Hendershott et al., 2011). However, the data set in this chapter does not allow for a verification of this approach. Panel B of Table 3.4 reports the number of shares traded by trade size categories.

Existing evidence on the influence of market fragmentation on the price discovery process is mixed. Pagano (1989) finds that fragmentation has a negative effect on price discovery whereas Foucault and Menkveld (2008) argue that increased competition through fragmentation might lead to a deeper consolidated book and thus enhance the price discovery process. Table 3.5 provides descriptives on the price discovery process with measures calculated on the consolidated order book as presented in Section 3.5.2 and 3.5.3. My analysis focuses on the LSE and Chi-X. Since Riordan et al. (2010a) report that most of the price discovery in FTSE 100 stocks can be attributed to the LSE and Chi-X, this should not distort the results. The overall fraction of quote based price discovery is 45.18% with the remaining information being impounded through trades on the LSE and on Chi-X. 36.54% of total price discovery can be attributed to trades on the LSE and 18.28% to trades on Chi-X. Chowdhry and Nanda (1991) find that informed trading gravitates to the most liquid market, which is the LSE over the observaton period in this sample. This is a natural explanation given that informed traders try to reduce their impact on prices to a minimum and informed traders are also more likely to use market or marketable limit orders. However, information shares in Panel B of Table 3.5 show that Chi-X leads in quote based price discovery. 58.19% of quote based price discovery is attributable to Chi-X and only 41.81% to the LSE. The permanent impact of trade innovation is a proxy for private information impounded into markets through trades. The trade innovation results in Panel A of Table 3.5 illustrate that much more information, measured in basis points, is impounded through order flow on the LSE than on Chi-X. Since the LSE is more liquid than Chi-X, this cannot be a result of low liquidity. Panel C of Table 3.5 reports my measure of total contribution to price discovery computed through a combination of information shares and the variance decomposition. The LSE contributes 55.56% to total price discovery and Chi-X 44.44%.

The results show that price formation takes place on both the LSE and Chi-X and Chi-X also contributes significant liquidity to trading in FTSE 100 stocks. The further analyses focus on the impact of firm specific public information on characteristics in the individual markets and on characteristics of fragmentation.

3.6.2 The Effect of Public Information

News Descriptives

Figure 3.2 shows the number of news messages per month for the year 2009. The number of news per month is comparably steady with a peak in October and its minimum in December. Since December is a month with more holidays than the other months of the year, this result is not suprising. Figure 3.3 depicts the number of news messages per associated day of the week. Consistent with Berry and Howe (1994), a bit more news messages arrive Tuesday through Thursday than on Monday and Friday. The graph shows that neutral news messages amount for the least number of messages and negative messages for the most news messages. However, differences in the number of news messages for negative, positive, and neutral news are not dramatic.

Table 3.6 reports descriptive statistics on raw news messages and on the computed per day and firm public information sentiment. The average sentiment of news during 2009 is negatively skewed with the strongest negative average sentiment in January 2009 and an almost neutral average sentiment for the third quarter of 2009. 3.56 news messages arrive for an average firm per day, 1.23 positive messages, 1.60 negative, and 0.73 neutral items. Overall, the analysis in this chapter comprises 81,507 news messages with an average sentiment of -0.10. Panel B in Table 3.6 provides information about the calculated per firm and day public information variables. On average a firm has 45.49 positive, 57.50 negative, and 148.01 neutral days out of 251 trading days in 2009. The firm with the most positive days, 125, is Vodafone and the Royal Bank of Scotland features 179 days with on average negative public information which makes it the firm with the most negative days in 2009 probably as a result of the financial crisis.

Regression Model

To analyze the impact of the tone of public information on trading, I resort to a regression model. Let $m^j_{i,d}$ denote all calculated measures on liquidity, trading, and information for stock i, day d, and market j if applicable. $\text{PosN}_{i,d}$ and $\text{NegN}_{i,d}$ are dummy variables

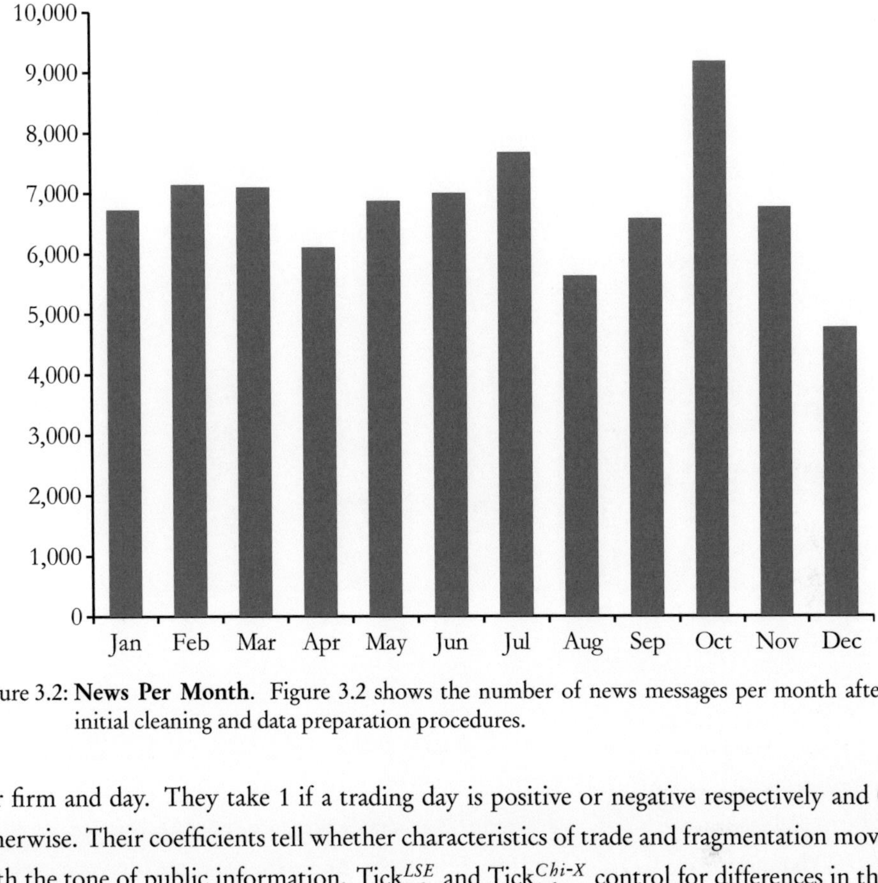

Figure 3.2: **News Per Month.** Figure 3.2 shows the number of news messages per month after initial cleaning and data preparation procedures.

per firm and day. They take 1 if a trading day is positive or negative respectively and 0 otherwise. Their coefficients tell whether characteristics of trade and fragmentation move with the tone of public information. $\text{Tick}_{i,d}^{LSE}$ and $\text{Tick}_{i,d}^{Chi\text{-}X}$ control for differences in the tick size between the LSE and Chi-X. $\text{Tick}_{i,d}^{LSE}$ takes one if the tick size for a specific stock and day is larger at the LSE than on Chi-X and $\text{Tick}_{i,d}^{Chi\text{-}X}$ takes 1 in case the tick size is larger on Chi-X. If tick sizes are equal between both markets both variables take 0. I include monthly dummy variables to control for time trends and to additionally capture changes in the maker-taker pricing scheme of the LSE as of 1 September 2009. Then the following regression model emerges:

$$m_{i,d}^{j} = a_i + p_1 \text{PosN}_{i,d} + p_2 \text{NegN}_{i,d} + c_1 \text{Tick}_{i,d}^{LSE} + c_2 \text{Tick}_{i,d}^{Chi\text{-}X} + \sum_{m=1}^{11} k_m \text{Month}_m + e_{i,t}^{j} \quad (3.3)$$

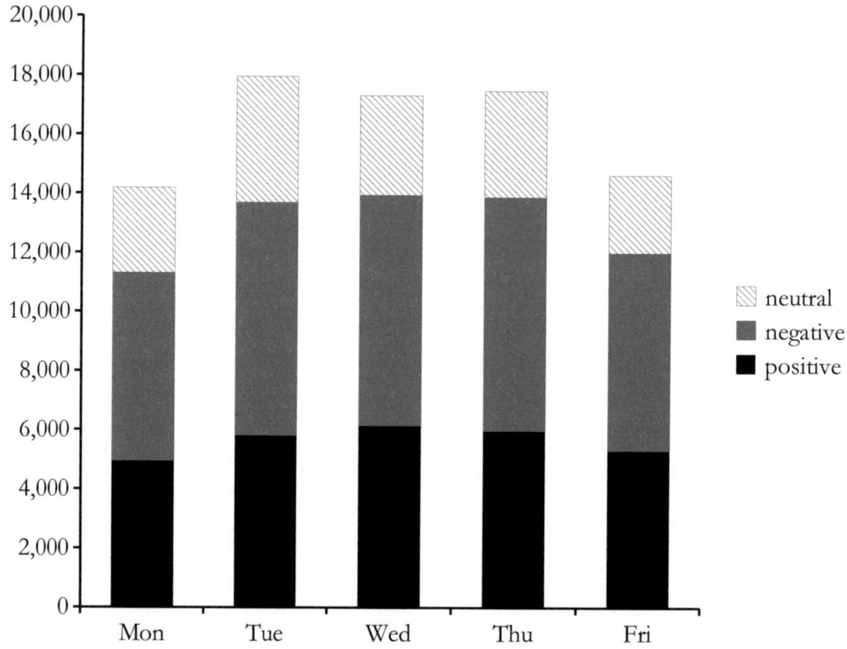

Figure 3.3: **News Per Associated Trading Day of the Week.** Figure 3.3 shows the number of news messages per associated trading day of the week after initial cleaning and data preparation procedures.

The model is estimated with firm-fixed effects and clustered standard errors (cf. Petersen, 2009; Thompson, 2011). I also test day of the week dummies, those are however insignificant and left out in the final model.

Liquidity and Trading Intensity

One of the most important aspects of financial markets is liquidity. Liquidity allows market participants to trade large sizes at any time at low implicit trading costs. As seen above, both, the LSE and Chi-X, are highly liquid in trading of FTSE 100 stocks. However, it remains unclear whether and how liquidity changes on individual markets and between both markets at times of high levels of firm specific public information. Table 3.7 reports results on different spread measures for the individual order books and for differences between the LSE and Chi-X for both the positive and negative public information coefficients ($\text{PosN}_{i,d}$ and $\text{NegN}_{i,d}$) from Regression 3.3.

Table 3.1: **Sample News.** Table 3.1 shows one intraday RNSE news message for the firm 'Royal Bank of Scotland' (RBS.L).

Sample RNSE News Item	
timestamp	20 AUG 2009 16:12:22.554
bcast_ref	RBS.L
stock_ric	RBS.L
item_id	2009-08-20_16.12.22.nN20424640.T1.bb216780
relevance	0.154303
sentiment	-1
sent_pos	0.0558151
sent_neut	0.12554
sent_neg	0.818645
lnkd_cnt1	0
lnkd_cnt2	0
lnkd_cnt3	0
lnkd_cnt4	0
lnkd_cnt5	0
lnkd_id1	.
lnkd_id2	.
lnkd_id3	.
lnkd_id4	.
lnkd_id5	.
lnkd_idpv1	.
lnkd_idpv2	.
lnkd_idpv3	.
lnkd_idpv4	.
lnkd_idpv5	.
item_type	ARTICLE
item_genre	NOT DEFINED
bcast_text	Fitch cuts European bank hybrid debt ratings
dsply_name	2
pnac	nN20424640
story_type	S
cross_ref	.
proc_date	20-AUG-2009
take_time	16:12:22
story_date	20-AUG-2009
story_time	16:12:22
named_item	.
take_seqno	1
attribtn	RTRS
prod_code	E U NAW D T NAT M PSC RNP DNP PTD EMK
topic_code	EUB EUROPE AAA LOA HYD BNK FIN DFIN GB INS NL DBT CDM FINS WEU LEN RTRS
co_ids	LLOY.L RBS.L ING.AS SR.AS
lang_ind	EN

Table 3.2: **Descriptive Statistics Spreads.** Panel A of Table 3.2 provides descriptive statistics for spread measures. Spread measures comprise quoted spreads, quoted spreads at trades, effective spreads, realized spreads, and price impacts. Realized spreads are computed both as 5-minute and 15-minute measures. All measures are first aggregated on a daily basis per firm, then tested and aggregated to overall averages. Table 3.2 presents values for the individual order books of the LSE and Chi-X as well as the differences (Diff) between the LSE and Chi-X in individual order books ($measure_{LSE}$-$measure_{Chi\text{-}X}$). In addition, values for the consolidated order book are reported for the LSE (LSE Cons) and Chi-X (Chi-X Cons) individually, for their differences within the consolidated order book (Diff Cons), and for values for the overall consolidated book (Cons). Panel B of Table 3.2 reports descriptives on effective spreads by trade size measured in the number of shares traded. Spreads are measured in basis points (bps). Robust t-statistics for the significance of the differences between the LSE and Chi-X are also reported. Standard deviations over per day and firm measures are reported in parantheses. 'a' indicates significance at the 1% level and 'b' indicates significance at the 5% level.

Measure	Panel A: Spread Measures								
	LSE	Chi-X	Diff	t-stat	LSE Cons	Chi-X Cons	Diff Cons	t-stat	Cons
Quoted Spread	6.08	6.80	-0.72[a]	-8.86					4.66
	(3.19)	(4.82)							(2.56)
Quoted Spread at Trades	4.62	4.83	-0.21[a]	-4.79	3.66	3.81	-0.15[a]	-10.30	3.72
	(2.25)	(2.68)			(1.92)	(1.93)			(1.91)
Effective Spread	4.69	4.90	-0.21[a]	-4.81	3.99	4.02	-0.03	-1.76	4.00
	(2.29)	(2.74)			(2.04)	(2.06)			(2.03)
Realized Spread 5	-0.57	-0.33	-0.24[a]	-6.48	-0.57	-0.31	-0.26[a]	-7.02	-0.47
	(1.80)	(1.93)			(1.77)	(1.88)			(1.57)
Realized Spread 15	-0.20	-0.03	-0.16[a]	-3.96	-0.23	-0.05	-0.18[a]	-4.30	-0.15
	(2.72)	(2.97)			(2.66)	(2.88)			(2.28)
Price Impact 5	5.29	5.26	0.03	0.64	4.60	4.33	0.27[a]	8.55	4.49
	(2.86)	(3.28)			(2.65)	(2.63)			(2.51)
Price Impact 15	4.92	4.97	-0.05	-0.93	4.26	4.07	0.19[a]	4.96	4.18
	(3.44)	(3.98)			(3.23)	(3.41)			(2.94)

Trade Size Category	Panel B: Effective Spread By Trade Size								
	LSE	Chi-X	Diff	t-stat	LSE Cons	Chi-X Cons	Diff Cons	t-stat	Cons
< 500	4.52	4.73	-0.21[a]	-4.96	3.81	3.82	-0.01	-0.29	3.82
	(2.26)	(2.70)			(2.05)	(1.95)			(1.98)
500 – 1,999	4.67	4.97	-0.30[a]	-5.88	3.96	4.09	-0.13[a]	-4.81	4.00
	(2.28)	(2.79)			(2.04)	(2.08)			(2.02)
2,000 – 4,999	4.89	5.36	-0.52[a]	-8.23	4.20	4.47	-0.32[a]	-8.87	4.25
	(2.36)	(3.02)			(2.12)	(2.36)			(2.10)
5,000 – 9,999	5.19	5.62	-0.65[a]	-9.35	4.46	4.71	-0.45[a]	-10.39	4.51
	(2.71)	(3.38)			(2.43)	(2.74)			(2.41)
≥ 10,000	6.19	5.83	-0.42[a]	-5.74	5.34	4.88	-0.22[a]	-4.68	5.34
	(3.39)	(3.79)			(3.44)	(3.18)			(3.41)

Table 3.3: **Descriptive Statistics Spreads by Trade Size.** Table 3.3 provides descriptive statistics for realized spreads and price impacts both at the 5 and 15 minute marks by trade size. All measures are first aggregated to per firm and day values, then tested and aggregated to overall averages. Table 3.3 presents values for the individual order books of the LSE and Chi-X as well as the differences (Diff) between the LSE and Chi-X in individual order books ($measure_{LSE}$-$measure_{Chi-X}$). Also, values for the consolidated order book (Cons) are reported not clustered by markets. Panel A of Table 3.3 reports descriptives on realized spreads and Panel B on price impacts. Spreads are measured in basis points (bps). Robust t-statistics for the significance of the differences between the LSE and Chi-X are also reported. Standard deviations over per day and firm measures are reported in parantheses. 'a' indicates significance at the 1% level and 'b' indicates significance at the 5% level.

Panel A

Trade Size Category	Realized Spread 5					Realized Spread 15				
	LSE	Chi-X	Diff	t-stat	Cons	LSE	Chi-X	Diff	t-stat	Cons
< 500	-0.04	0.03	-0.08	-1.34	0.02	0.18	0.29	-0.10	-1.54	0.24
	(2.84)	(3.03)			(2.35)	(4.65)	(4.73)			(3.77)
500 – 1,999	-0.51	-0.50	-0.01	-0.27	-0.49	-0.16	-0.20	0.04	0.77	-0.17
	(2.42)	(3.12)			(2.06)	(4.85)	(3.70)			(3.03)
2,000 – 4,999	-1.37	-1.27	-0.02	-0.31	-1.33	-0.86	-0.81	0.06	0.61	-0.88
	(4.37)	(6.72)			(4.12)	(6.28)	(10.50)			(5.81)
5,000 – 9,999	-2.07	-1.81	0.01	0.08	-2.03	-1.34	-1.06	-0.09	-0.55	-1.37
	(7.92)	(12.09)			(7.62)	(11.90)	(18.75)			(11.47)
≥ 10,000	-0.08	-2.51	1.05[a]	4.95	-0.18	1.20	-1.69	1.11[a]	3.21	1.05
	(15.09)	(15.56)			(14.34)	(21.75)	(23.99)			(20.81)

Panel B

Trade Size Category	Price Impact 5					Price Impact 15				
	LSE	Chi-X	Diff	t-stat	Cons	LSE	Chi-X	Diff	t-stat	Cons
< 500	4.58	4.73	-0.14[a]	-2.22	3.82	4.36	4.48	-0.12	-1.52	3.60
	(3.28)	(3.83)			(2.77)	(4.92)	(5.24)			(4.02)
500 – 1,999	5.21	5.50	-0.30[a]	-5.00	4.50	4.86	5.21	-0.36[a]	-4.45	4.19
	(3.21)	(4.18)			(2.73)	(4.18)	(5.60)			(3.49)
2,000 – 4,999	6.30	6.67	-0.51[a]	-5.41	5.62	5.80	6.22	-0.59[a]	-4.74	5.81
	(5.02)	(7.57)			(4.72)	(6.74)	(11.07)			(6.25)
5,000 – 9,999	7.35	7.51	-0.70[a]	-5.93	6.76	6.66	6.78	-0.60[a]	-3.95	6.16
	(8.26)	(12.50)			(7.63)	(11.98)	(18.97)			(11.18)
≥ 10,000	6.81	8.45	-1.37[a]	-6.55	7.32	5.94	7.65	-1.33[a]	-4.24	6.72
	(14.13)	(16.07)			(11.71)	(20.10)	(24.35)			(17.55)

Table 3.4: **Descriptive Statistics Trading Activity.** Table 3.4 provides descriptive statistics for trading activity measures. All measures are first aggregated on a daily basis per firm, then tested and aggregated to overall averages. Table 3.4 presents values for the individual order books of the LSE and Chi-X as well as the differences (Diff) between the LSE and Chi-X (measure$_{LSE}$-measure$_{Chi-X}$). Panel A reports descriptives on the number of trades per day and firm (#Trades), the volume in kGBP, the quantity, the average trade size in volume, the average trade size by shares traded, and market shares by volume and quantity. Panel B reports descriptives on the number of trades per day and firm splitted by trade size categories measured in the number of shares traded. Robust t-statistics for the significance of the differences between the LSE and Chi-X are reported in the last column. Standard deviations are reported in parantheses. 'a' indicates significance at the 1% level and 'b' indicates significance at the 5% level.

Measures	Panel A: Trading Activity			
	LSE	Chi-X	Diff	t-stat
#Trades	2,318	1,346	972[a]	11.16
	(1,967)	(1,154)		
Volume (in kGBP) Per Day and Firm	28,852	10,196	18,656[a]	7.49
	(40,029)	(13,378)		
Quantity (in kShares) Per Day and Firm	7,799	2,547	5,253[a]	4.71
	(18,706)	(5,611)		
Trade Size (Volume)	10,276	6,160	4,117[a]	19.97
	(5,484)	(3,251)		
Trade Size (Quantity)	2,723	1,610	1,114[a]	7.09
	(3,829)	(2,292)		
Market Share (Volume)	73.70%	26.30%	47.40%[a]	44.26
	(9.08%)	(9.08%)		
Market Share (Quantity)	73.70%	26.30%	47.40%[a]	44.26
	(9.08%)	(9.08%)		

Trade Size Category	Panel B: Number of Trades Per Day and Firm			
	LSE	Chi-X	Diff	t-stat
< 500	725.77	547.13	178.65[a]	8.24
	(721.75)	(589.86)		
$500 - 1,999$	810.85	496.34	314.51[a]	8.87
	(709.35)	(459.38)		
$2,000 - 4,999$	433.57	194.57	239.01[a]	9.98
	(485.73)	(276.71)		
$5,000 - 9,999$	192.33	67.75	124.58[a]	6.85
	(329.08)	(156.14)		
$\geq 10,000$	155.74	40.51	115.23[a]	3.95
	(474.13)	(159.16)		

Table 3.5: **Descriptive Statistics Price Discovery.** Table 3.5 provides descriptive statistics for information measures based on Hasbrouck (1991a,b, 1995). All measures are first computed per firm and day, then aggregated to overall averages and tested. Statistics on the LSE, Chi-X, and the differences between the two markets (Diff) are presented. Panel A reports descriptives on trade based price discovery: the share of trade based price discovery in total price discovery (% Trade Based) and the permanent impact of trade innovation in basis points (Trade Innovation). Panel B reports descriptives on quote based price discovery: the overall share of quote based price discovery in total price discovery and the share of the LSE and Chi-X respectively in quote based price discovery. Panel C provides information about the total contribution to price discovery of the LSE and Chi-X. Robust t-statistics for the significance of the differences between the LSE and Chi-X are also reported. Standard deviations over per day and firm measures are reported in parantheses. 'a' indicates significance at the 1% level and 'b' indicates significance at the 5% level.

Panel A: Trade Based Price Discovery

	% Trade Based		Trade Innovation	
	Value	StdDev	Value	StdDev
LSE	36.54%	(8.84%)	2.31	(2.11)
Chi-X	18.28%	(12.35%)	1.45	(2.51)
Diff	18.25%[a]		0.86[a]	
t-stat	27.33		15.16	

Panel B: Quote Based Price Discovery

	% Quote Based		Information Shares	
	Value	StdDev	Value	StdDev
Overall	45.18%	(15.59%)		
LSE			41.81%	(18.63%)
Chi-X			58.19%	(18.63%)
Diff			-16.38%[a]	
t-stat			-9.36	

Panel C: Total Contribution to Price Discovery

	Fraction of PD	
	Value	StdDev
LSE	55.56%	(14.69%)
Chi-X	44.44%	(14.69%)
Diff	11.12%[a]	
t-stat	7.38	

Table 3.6: **Descriptive Statistics News.** The news data are based on the FTSE 100 stock sample of my analysis with 88 firms. Panel A presents overall statistics on raw messages with standard deviations in parantheses. Statistics are presented for per day and firm averages, the whole year of 2009, and individual months of 2009. 'Positive News', 'Negative News' and 'Neutral News' report the raw number of news messages with the respective sentiment. 'All News' presents statistics about news not clustered by sentiment. 'Avg.Sentiment' gives the overall average sentiment of RNSE raw messages. Panel B reports results on the computed firm specific public information sentiment which is a per day and firm average value. Statistics for the whole year of 2009, each month, and the most extreme firms are presented. The number of positive, negative, and neutral days as well as the overall number of trading days per firm are reported.

	Panel A: Raw News Messages				
	Positive News	Negative News	Neutral News	All News	Avg.Sentiment
News Per Day and Firm (Avg.)	1.23 (3.09)	1.60 (4.17)	0.73 (4.22)	3.56 (8.65)	-0.08 (0.64)
Year 2009	28,158	36,638	16,711	81,507	-0.10
January	1,681	3,819	1,224	6,724	-0.32
February	2,022	3,819	1,296	7,137	-0.25
March	2,107	3,721	1,269	7,097	-0.23
April	1,976	2,950	1,178	6,104	-0.16
May	2,400	3,158	1,312	6,870	-0.11
June	2,406	3,132	1,461	6,999	-0.10
July	2,484	3,498	1,684	7,666	-0.13
August	2,214	2,244	1,172	5,630	-0.01
September	3,015	2,339	1,220	6,574	0.10
October	3,329	3,384	2,459	9,172	-0.01
November	2,692	2,582	1,489	6,763	0.02
December	1,832	1,992	947	4,771	-0.03

	Panel B: Per Day and Firm Computed Public Information Sentiment			
	Positive Days	Negative Days	Neutral Days	All Trading Days
Year 2009	45.49	57.50	148.01	251
January	2.82	5.64	12.55	21
February	2.69	5.41	11.19	20
March	3.10	6.25	12.65	22
April	3.38	4.83	11.80	20
May	3.49	4.89	10.63	19
June	3.75	5.18	13.07	22
July	4.05	5.77	13.18	23
August	3.55	3.80	12.66	20
September	5.27	3.82	12.91	22
October	4.92	4.66	12.42	22
November	4.88	4.08	12.05	21
December	3.60	3.18	12.22	19
Firm with most positive days (Vodafone)	125	85	41	251
Firm with most negative days (RBS)	49	179	23	251

Table 3.7: **Spreads and Public Information.** Table 3.7 provides regression (cf. Equation 3.3) results for spread measures: quoted spreads, quoted spreads at trade time, effective spreads, realized spreads, and price impacts. Realized spreads and price impacts are computed both as 5-minute and 15-minute measures. All measures are first aggregated to daily values per firm, then included in the regression model. The relevant variables are dummy variables for positive and negative public information days. Table 3.7 presents results for the individual order books of the LSE and Chi-X as well as the differences (Diff) between the LSE and Chi-X in individual order books of the two markets. I also report coefficients for regressions with the consolidated order book for the LSE (LSE Cons), Chi-X (Chi-X Cons), the differences of the two markets in the consolidated order book (Diff Cons), and the consolidated order book without clustering by markets (Cons). The regression model controls for tick size differences between the LSE and Chi-X, includes month of the year dummy variables, and is estimated with firm-fixed effects. Spreads are measured in basis points (bps). Robust t-statistics for the significance of the differences between the LSE and Chi-X are reported in parantheses. 'a' indicates significance at the 1% level and 'b' indicates significance at the 5% level.

Measure	Spreads in the Individual Order Books						Spreads in the Consolidated Order Book							
	LSE		Chi-X		Diff		LSE Cons		Chi-X Cons		Diff Cons		Cons	
	pos	neg	pos	neg	pos	neg	pos	neg	pos	neg	pos	neg	pos	neg
Quoted Spread														
Coeff.	-0.02	0.14[a]	0.04	0.21[b]	-0.05	-0.07							-0.03	0.07
t-stat	(-0.47)	(2.62)	(0.68)	(2.51)	(-1.51)	(-1.39)							(-1.06)	(1.88)
Quoted Spread at Trades														
Coeff.	-0.01	0.11[a]	0.01	0.11[a]	-0.02	0.01	-0.02	0.07[a]	-0.00	0.06[b]	0.00	0.01	-0.02	0.07[a]
t-stat	(-0.60)	(3.43)	(0.21)	(2.94)	(-1.60)	(0.53)	(-0.85)	(2.91)	(-0.11)	(2.49)	(0.07)	(1.50)	(-0.95)	(2.83)
Effective Spread														
Coeff.	-0.00	0.12[a]	0.02	0.12[a]	-0.02	0.01	-0.01	0.09[a]	-0.00	0.08[a]	-0.01	0.01	-0.01	0.09[a]
t-stat	(-0.19)	(3.67)	(0.51)	(3.18)	(-1.52)	(0.40)	(-0.48)	(3.37)	(-0.11)	(3.11)	(-0.85)	(1.00)	(-0.40)	(3.34)

continued on next page ...

...continued from Table 3.7

Measure	Spreads in the Individual Order Books						Spreads in the Consolidated Order Book							
	LSE		Chi-X		Diff		LSE Cons		Chi-X Cons		Diff Cons		Cons	
	pos	neg	pos	neg	pos	neg	pos	neg	pos	neg	pos	neg	pos	neg
Realized Spread 5														
Coeff.	0.05	-0.01	0.02	-0.07	0.03	0.06	0.06	-0.00	0.03	-0.06	0.04	0.06	0.04	-0.02
t-stat	(1.54)	(-0.23)	(0.66)	(-1.65)	(0.83)	(1.44)	(1.59)	(-0.06)	(0.71	(-1.65)	(0.77)	(1.55)	(1.25)	(-0.68)
Realized Spread 15														
Coeff.	-0.01	-0.08	-0.03	-0.17[a]	0.02	0.09	0.00	-0.06	-0.02	-0.15[a]	0.02	0.09	-0.01	-0.09[b]
t-stat	(-0.18)	(-1.40)	(-0.44)	(-2.53)	(0.34)	(1.37)	(0.04)	(-1.20)	(-0.33)	(-2.59)	(0.40)	(1.39)	(-0.24)	(-1.97)
Price Impact 5														
Coeff.	-0.05	0.13[b]	-0.01	0.19[a]	-0.05	-0.05	-0.06	0.09	-0.03	0.14[a]	-0.03	-0.05	-0.05	0.11[b]
t-stat	(-1.34)	(2.42)	(-0.14)	(3.31)	(-1.35)	(-1.31)	(-1.68)	(1.89)	(-0.81)	(3.06)	(-0.97)	(-1.22)	(-1.36)	(2.42)
Price Impact 15														
Coeff.	0.01	0.21[a]	0.04	0.29[a]	-0.04	-0.08	-0.01	0.15[b]	0.01	0.23[a]	-0.03	0.01	0.01	0.18[a]
t-stat	(0.13)	(2.68)	(0.67)	(4.02)	(-0.72)	(-1.39)	(-0.25)	(2.24)	(0.24)	(3.56)	(-0.52)	(0.82)	(0.01)	(2.93)

Overall, coefficients for liquidity are statistically significant for negative public information days and insignificant for all measures on positive public information days. Quoted spreads, quoted spreads at trades, and the ex-post measured effective spreads all increase on both, the LSE and on Chi-X, when traders receive on average negative public information. On the LSE, quoted spreads increase at the 1% significance level by 0.14 bps, quoted spreads at trades by 0.11 bps, and effective spreads by 0.12 bps. Quoted spreads increase at the 5% level by 0.21 bps on Chi-X while quoted spreads at trades increase by 0.11 bps and effective spreads by 0.12 bps. Although the magnitude of the coefficients suggests that the reduction in visible liquidity is stronger on Chi-X then on the LSE, I do not find statistically significant differences between the individual order books.

There is practically no difference in the reduction of liquidity at trade times measured by the quoted spread at trades and the effective spread. For days with positive public information, I do not find significant coefficients, neither for the individual order books nor for the difference between the LSE and Chi-X. The signs of coefficients for quoted spreads, quoted spreads at trade, and effective spreads are consistently negative for the LSE and positive for Chi-X, meaning an increase in liquidity at the LSE with a concurrent decrease in liquidity at Chi-X, but the coefficients are not statistically significant. Spreads in the consolidated order book react comparably to the individual order books. Quoted spreads at trades, pooled over both markets, significantly increase by 0.07 bps on negative days and do not significantly change on positive days. Effective spreads also increase by 0.09 bps on negative public information days which translates into higher execution costs, also over all trade size categories (Table 3.8) except for trades larger than 10,000 shares in the consolidated book.

Although, the analysis in Chapter 2 is performed on intraday high-frequency data, my results are quite consistent with the findings in Chapter 2. I find a significant drop in liquidity around negative news and an improvement in liquidity around positive news in Chapter 2 which can be explained with competition for liquidity supply in the limit order book. Possibly, due to the necessary daily aggregation of data in this chapter which is on a lower frequency, I do not find significant results for positive news. Overall, in this chapter liquidity drops on both markets on negative days and does not change significantly on positive days. Liquidity providers might want to protect themselves against better informed traders or highly capable public information processers in a negative firm specific public information environment (cf. Kim and Verrecchia, 1994). This argument is supported by the realized spread results for Chi-X as reported in Table 3.7. Realized spreads, liquidity suppliers' revenue, fall at the fifteen minute mark significantly by 0.17 bps for negative news. In the consolidated book, realized spreads at the fiveteen minute mark fall by 0.09 bps. Price impacts increase statistically significantly for both markets at the five and fifteen minute marks for days with negative firm specific public information. I do not find a change in price impact for positive days. An increase in price impact hints at more private information impounded, which fits the realized spread results and a slight observed reduction in liquidity. Differences between the LSE and Chi-X for realized spreads and price impacts are generally not significant. In the consolidated orderbook, on negative days a slight decrease in realized spreads, liquidity suppliers revenue, and an increase in price impacts is found. Overall, regressions with spreads calculated on the consolidated order book show qualitatively the same results as spreads calculated on the individual order books.

Effective spreads, realized spreads, and price impacts by trade size categories, reported in Tables 3.9, 3.10, and 3.11, paint on average essentially the same picture as the overall measures. One interesting aspect though is that mid-sized trades between 500 and 1,999 shares which have been found in previous research to be more informed (Barclay and Warner, 1993) need to pay even higher effective spreads on Chi-X than on the LSE on positive public information days than normal (see Table 3.9). The difference is statistically significant at the 5% level. Over all trading days, the difference for mid-sized trades between the LSE and Chi-X is already 0.30 bps (1% level, see Table 3.2) with the LSE having an average effective spread of 4.67 bps and Chi-X one of 4.97 bps. This difference increases by 0.03 bps on days with positive public information. Overall, trade size category 500 to 1,999 has also the largest difference for the absolute number of trades per day of 314.51 trades (Panel B, Table 3.4). Summerized, the LSE provides lower execution costs for mid-sized trades and has the higher market share in such trades which potentially have also a high level of private information.

Table 3.8: **Spreads in the Consolidated Order Book and Public Information**. Table 3.8 provides regression results for spread measures by trade size measured in the number of shares traded. Spread measures comprise effective spreads, realized spreads, and price impacts. Realized spreads and price impacts are computed both as 5-minute and 15-minute measures. All measures are first aggregated to daily values per firm and then included in the regression model. The relevant variables are dummy variables for positive and negative public information days. Table 3.8 presents results for the consolidated order book. The regression model controls for tick size differences between the LSE and Chi-X, includes month of the year dummy variables, and is estimated with firm-fixed effects. Spreads are measured in basis points (bps). Robust t-statistics for the significance of the differences between the LSE and Chi-X are reported in parantheses. 'a' indicates significance at the 1% level and 'b' indicates significance at the 5% level.

Trade Size Category	Consolidated Order Book									
	ESpread		RSpread 5		RSpread 15		PImpact 5		PImpact 15	
	pos	neg	pos	neg	pos	neg	pos	neg	pos	neg
< 500										
Coeff.	-0.02	0.06[a]	0.01	0.07	0.03	0.01	-0.03	-0.01	-0.05	0.06
t-stat	(-0.90)	(2.59)	(0.24)	(1.47)	(0.34)	(0.09)	(-0.70)	(-0.19)	(-0.66)	(0.72)
$500 - 1,999$										
Coeff.	-0.01	0.09[a]	0.05	0.02	-0.04	-0.01	-0.06	0.07	0.04	0.10
t-stat	(-0.28)	(3.37)	(1.69)	(0.48)	(-1.04)	(-0.19)	(-1.73)	(1.50)	(0.78)	(1.50)
$2,000 - 4,999$										
Coeff.	0.01	0.11[a]	0.03	0.03	0.04	-0.07	-0.02	0.08	-0.03	0.17[c]
t-stat	(0.60)	(3.97)	(0.35)	(0.49)	(0.31)	(-0.75)	(-0.24)	(1.30)	(-0.24)	(1.89)
$5,000 - 9,999$										
Coeff.	-0.00	0.11[a]	0.01	-0.19	0.03	-0.23	-0.07	0.20	-0.08	0.19
t-stat	(-0.02)	(2.98)	(0.10)	(-1.48)	(0.14)	(-1.14)	(-0.55)	(1.57)	(-0.43)	(1.01)
$\geq 10,000$										
Coeff.	0.02	0.08	-0.08	-0.34	-0.00	-0.17	-0.11	0.12	-0.30	-0.22
t-stat	(0.40)	(1.62)	(-0.24)	(-1.11)	(-0.01)	(-0.43)	(-0.50)	(0.55)	(-0.99)	(-0.65)

Table 3.9: **Effective Spread by Trade Size and Public Information.** Table 3.9 provides regression results for effective spreads by trade size measured in the number of shares traded. All measures are first aggregated to daily values per firm and then included in the regression model. The relevant variables are dummy variables for positive and negative public information days. Table 3.9 presents results for the individual order books of the LSE and Chi-X as well as the differences (Diff) between the LSE and Chi-X in individual order books of the two markets. I also report coefficients for regressions with the consolidated order book for the LSE (LSE Cons), Chi-X (Chi-X Cons), the differences of the two markets in the consolidated order book (Diff Cons), and the consolidated order book without clustering by markets (Cons). The regression model controls for tick size differences between the LSE and Chi-X, includes month of the year dummy variables, and is estimated with firm-fixed effects. Spreads are measured in basis points (bps). Robust t-statistics for the significance of the differences between the LSE and Chi-X are reported in parantheses. 'a' indicates significance at the 1% level and 'b' indicates significance at the 5% level.

Effective Spread												
Trade Size Cat.	Individual Order Books						Consolidated Order Book					
	LSE		Chi-X		Diff		LSE		Chi-X		Diff	
	pos	neg	pos	neg	pos	neg	pos	neg	pos	neg	pos	neg
< 500												
Coeff.	-0.02	0.09^{a}	-0.00	0.09^{b}	-0.02	0.00	-0.02	0.07^{a}	-0.02	0.06^{b}	-0.01	0.01
t-stat	(-0.94)	(3.05)	(-0.09)	(2.56)	(-1.31)	(0.25)	(-1.06)	(2.66)	(-0.81)	(2.34)	(-0.44)	(0.82)
$500 - 1,999$												
Coeff.	-0.00	0.12^{a}	0.03	0.12^{a}	-0.03^{b}	0.00	-0.01	0.09^{a}	-0.00	0.09^{a}	-0.02	0.00
t-stat	(-0.14)	(3.63)	(0.88)	(3.21)	(-1.96)	(0.19)	(-0.57)	(3.25)	(-0.21)	(3.43)	(-1.49)	(0.10)
$2,000 - 4,999$												
Coeff.	0.02	0.14^{a}	0.04	0.17^{a}	-0.03	-0.04^{b}	0.02	0.11^{a}	0.01	0.12^{a}	-0.01	-0.02
t-stat	(0.64)	(4.16)	(1.14)	(4.59)	(-1.59)	(-2.05)	(0.66)	(3.95)	(0.49)	(4.11)	(-0.29)	(-1.67)
$5,000 - 9,999$												
Coeff.	-0.01	0.15^{a}	-0.02	0.08	0.01	0.05	-0.00	0.11^{a}	-0.04	0.03	0.03	0.06
t-stat	(-0.29)	(3.35)	(-0.42)	(1.65)	(0.31)	(0.89)	(-0.03)	(3.00)	(-1.06)	(0.58)	(0.84)	(1.37)
$\geq 10,000$												
Coeff.	-0.02	0.09	0.13	0.15^{b}	-0.12^{b}	-0.01	-0.00	0.08	0.09	0.10	-0.09	-0.01
t-stat	(-0.34)	(1.30)	(1.82)	(2.52)	(-2.01)	(-0.23)	(-0.00)	(1.48)	(1.54)	(1.70)	(-1.58)	(0.22)

Table 3.10: **Realized Spread by Trade Size and Public Information.** Table 3.10 provides regression results for realized spreads at the 5- and 15-minute marks by trade size measured in the number of shares traded. All measures are first aggregated daily values per firm and then included in the regression model. The relevant variables are dummy variables for positive and negative public information days. Table 3.10 presents results for the individual order books of the LSE and Chi-X as well as the differences (Diff) between the LSE and Chi-X in individual order books of the two markets. The regression model controls for tick size differences between the LSE and Chi-X, includes month of the year dummy variables, and is estimated with firm-fixed effects. Spreads are measured in basis points (bps). Robust t-statistics for the significance of the differences between the LSE and Chi-X are reported in parantheses. 'a' indicates significance at the 1% level and 'b' indicates significance at the 5% level.

	Individual Order Books											
Trade Size Cat.	Realized Spread 5						Realized Spread 15					
	LSE		Chi-X		Diff		LSE		Chi-X		Diff	
	pos	neg	pos	neg	pos	neg	pos	neg	pos	neg	pos	neg
< 500												
Coeff.	0.05	0.11^b	-0.04	-0.01	0.09	0.12^b	0.09	0.10	-0.08	-0.12	0.17	0.22
t-stat	(0.83)	(2.00)	(-0.77)	(-0.24)	(1.70)	(2.53)	(0.88)	(0.86)	(-0.97)	(-1.73)	(1.53)	(1.77)
$500 - 1,999$												
Coeff.	0.07^b	0.02	-0.00	-0.05	0.08	0.06	-0.03	-0.00	-0.07	-0.04	0.04	0.04
t-stat	(2.12)	(0.44)	(-0.08)	(-0.83)	(1.37)	(1.47)	(-0.74)	(-0.01)	(-1.03)	(-0.53)	(0.53)	(0.51)
$2,000 - 4,999$												
Coeff.	0.00	-0.01	0.08	0.03	-0.02	-0.00	0.02	-0.06	-0.08	-0.28	0.16	0.22
t-stat	(0.05)	(-0.13)	(0.51)	(0.19)	(-0.15)	(-0.02)	(0.13)	(-0.66)	(-0.44)	(-1.45)	(0.87)	(1.13)
$5,000 - 9,999$												
Coeff.	0.02	-0.22	-0.20	-0.34	0.19	0.22	0.02	-0.24	-0.06	-0.37	0.10	0.18
t-stat	(0.16)	(-1.65)	(-0.65)	(-1.34)	(0.61)	(0.79)	(0.09)	(-1.12)	(-0.11)	(-0.80)	(0.18)	(0.37)
$\geq 10,000$												
Coeff.	-0.22	-0.47	-0.50	-0.21	0.22	-0.02	-0.46	-0.25	-1.41^b	-0.85	0.98	0.54
t-stat	(-0.64)	(-1.37)	(-1.41)	(-0.51)	(0.68)	(-0.05)	(-0.36)	(-0.55)	(-2.13)	(-1.27)	(1.54)	(0.81)

Table 3.11: **Price Impact by Trade Size and Public Information.** Table 3.11 provides regression results for price impacts at the 5- and 15-minute marks by trade size measured in the number of shares traded. All measures are first aggregated to values per firm on a daily basis and then included in the regression model. The relevant variables are dummy variables for positive and negative public information days. Table 3.11 presents results for the individual order books of the LSE and Chi-X as well as the differences (Diff) between the LSE and Chi-X in individual order books of the two markets. The regression model controls for tick size differences between the LSE and Chi-X, includes month of the year dummy variables, and is estimated with firm-fixed effects. Price impacts are measured in basis points (bps). Robust t-statistics for the significance of the differences between the LSE and Chi-X are reported in parantheses. 'a' indicates significance at the 1% level and 'b' indicates significance at the 5% level.

Individual Order Books												
Trade Size Cat.	Price Impact 5						Price Impact 15					
	LSE		Chi-X		Diff		LSE		Chi-X		Diff	
	pos	neg	pos	neg	pos	neg	pos	neg	pos	neg	pos	neg
< 500												
Coeff.	-0.07	-0.01	0.04	0.11	-0.11^b	-0.13^a	-0.11	-0.00	0.08	0.22^a	-0.19	-0.22
t-stat	(-1.18)	(-0.24)	(0.78)	(1.66)	(-2.13)	(-2.64)	(-1.06)	(-0.01)	(1.06)	(2.60)	(-1.74)	(-1.84)
$500 - 1,999$												
Coeff.	-0.07	0.11	0.03	0.17^a	-0.10	-0.06	0.03	0.12	0.10	0.16^b	-0.06	-0.03
t-stat	(-1.75)	(1.92)	(0.55)	(2.59)	(-1.95)	(-1.36)	(0.64)	(1.56)	(1.34)	(2.12)	(-0.96)	(-0.45)
$2,000 - 4,999$												
Coeff.	0.02	0.15^b	-0.06	0.14	0.00	-0.03	0.00	0.21	0.11	0.45^b	-0.18	-0.26
t-stat	(0.17)	(2.18)	(-0.34)	(0.96)	(0.02)	(-0.21)	(0.01)	(1.94)	(0.60)	(2.26)	(-0.98)	(-1.30)
$5,000 - 9,999$												
Coeff.	-0.03	0.36^b	0.13	0.39	-0.13	-0.13	-0.04	0.34	0.02	0.44	-0.08	-0.13
t-stat	(-0.25)	(2.37)	(0.42)	(1.59)	(-0.43)	(-0.50)	(-0.18)	(1.52)	(0.04)	(0.97)	(-0.14)	(-0.27)
$\geq 10,000$												
Coeff.	0.05	0.51	0.63	0.33	-0.35	0.08	-0.15	0.16	1.53^b	0.99	-1.12	-0.50
t-stat	(0.19)	(1.60)	(1.79)	(0.82)	(-1.01)	(0.17)	(-0.41)	(0.38)	(2.39)	(1.52)	(-1.83)	(-0.76)

Table 3.12 reports regression results for measures of trading activity. I apply the regression model to both the absolute difference between markets and the relative difference calculated through ratios. Ratios[18] give an impression of the change in trading activity relative to trading activity on normal days and account for the difference in market shares between the LSE and Chi-X. Results show a highly significant increase in trading activity on positive as well as on negative public information days measured by the number of trades per day, the number of shares traded, and volume. I use the natural logarithm of daily trading volume and quantity for the regression model. The increase in trading volume demonstrates that investors have differential interpretations of both negative and positive public information (cf. Kim and Verrecchia, 1991). The increase in trading activity is relatively equal between positive and negative days. For instance, on average the LSE has 2,318 trades per day and firm, Chi-X has 1,346. Negative days show an increase of 257 trades on the LSE and 106 on Chi-X compared to neutral days. On positive days, I find an increase of 218 on the LSE and 117 on Chi-X. Looking at volume, quantity, and the number of trades per day, I find that both measured by differences in trading activity and ratios, trading activity increases relatively more on the LSE than on Chi-X. The increase in trading activity is consistent with existing empirical (Ryan and Taffler, 2007; Mitchell and Mulherin, 1994) and theoretical literature (Kim and Verrecchia, 1991, 1994).

Per trade volume increases strongly on both markets but again statistically significantly stronger on the LSE than on Chi-X relative to their per trade volume during normal times. The absolute difference between the LSE and Chi-X as well as the ratio are both statistically significant. One possible explanation could be that high levels of public information increase differential interpretation among traders which can be seen through an increase in trading activity. If traders are more differential in their interpretation of certain stocks, they might want to execute their trades faster than normal and resort to larger trade sizes despite slightly worse liquidity on negative days and no increase in liquidity on positive days. It is interesting that the trade size increases stronger on the LSE, the more liquid market and the market with the a priori significantly larger average trade size (10,276 GBP on the LSE vs. 6,160 GBP on Chi-X). The LSE market share increases significantly on both positive and negative days. However, the increase is much stronger with 0.87% on positive days than with 0.30% on negative days. Since Chi-X's market share concurrently decreases by 0.87% on positive days I find a shift of almost 2% in trading of FTSE 100

[18] $ratio = \frac{measure^{LSE}}{measure^{Chi\text{-}X}}$

stocks on days with public information.

Panel B of Table 3.12 reports regression results on the number of trades per day and firm for different trade size categories. For positive public information days, one sees a significant rise of trading in all but the largest trade size category. On negative days, trading activity in all trade size categories increases significantly. The largest difference in the increase can be found in the mid-size trade category (500 – 1,999). The difference between the LSE and Chi-X increases by 38.16 trades for positive days and 41.64 trades for negative days both statistically significant at the 1% level. Interestingly, this is also the same trade size category with a significant change in the difference in effective spreads between the LSE and Chi-X on positive days (cf. Table 3.9). I find the highest absolute increase in trading activity by trade size for both the LSE and Chi-X again in the mid-size trade category. The patterns that are found in mid-sized trades will be examined more closely in the next section with robust information measures.

Information

To shed light on the question how stock specific markets characteristics and characteristics of fragmentation vary with firm specific public information, I take a look at the triad of liquidity, trading activity, and information with the help of robust information measures (see Section 3.5). Descriptive statistics (see Table 3.5) show that Chi-X contributes more to quote based price discovery, the LSE more to trade based price discovery and altogether also more to total price discovery.

Table 3.13 reports results on the price discovery process and public information. During times with high levels of public information, I do not find significant changes in the fractions of trade based and the fraction of quote based price discovery. On positive public information days, I find a strong decrease in private information on Chi-X of 0.19 bps and a slight but statistically insignificant decrease on the LSE. Overall, there is less private information impounded into the markets on positive days. Interestingly, the private information that still is impounded shifts to the LSE away from Chi-X. Additionally, information that translates into prices through quotes also shifts significantly to the LSE with a difference between the LSE and Chi-X of 1.17%. Both, quote based price discovery and trade based price discovery combined to total price discovery, shift from Chi-X to the LSE by 1.47% and statistically significant at the 1% level. I find different effects on days with public information of an on average negative tone. Private information increases on the LSE significantly while there is no statistically significant change on Chi-X. In combination, comparable to positive days, private information shifts from Chi-X to the LSE. A general increase in private information as a result of negative news is consistent with Chapter 2. Neither information shares nor the total contribution to price discovery change statistically significant on negative days.

Overall, I find that a negative tone of public information decreases liquidity, increases trading activity especially in mid-sized trades on the LSE, and slightly increases private information while also shifting private information processing to the LSE. On days with a positive tone of public information, I find no significant change in liquidity, again a strong increase in trading activity, and overall less private information impounded into markets but a significant shift of the remaining private information from Chi-X to the LSE. Also the total contribution to price discovery shifts to the LSE by 1.47%. One key finding is that negative and positive public information have an asymmetric impact on trading. For instance, Tetlock (2007) only finds a significant relation between pessimistic public information and S&P 500 returns, also I find significant asymmetric reactions to good and bad news in Chapter 2. Generally, it is expected that informed trading gravitate to the most liquid market (Chowdhry and Nanda, 1991). Through the arrival of news, the information environment and information processing of market participants change. The increase in trading intensity hints at differential interpretation by market participants both on positive and negative days. Positive information might be difficult to process such that aggregate private information slightly falls while the impact of positive public information is not strong enough to reduce competition for liquidity supply catering the increased need for liquidity of liquidity demanders. I find that trades in the mid-size trade category (500 – 1,999 shares) have to pay a significantly higher effective spread, compared to the normal difference, on Chi-X than on the LSE on positive days. Traders that are informed and have the information processing capability for positive information then move to the LSE, the more liquid market consistent with Chowdhry and Nanda (1991) and consistent with the trade innovation results.

I find on both markets a reduction in liquidity on negative days. Competition for liquidity supply reduces, possibly as a result of liquidity suppliers safeguarding themselves against better informed traders who are able to process the negative public information correctly. Liquidity supply is not sufficient to cater the growth in liquidity demand. Also more private information than normal is impounded into the market with again a significant shift from Chi-X to the LSE which is consistent with informed traders drawn to the

LSE (Chowdhry and Nanda, 1991). Robust measures are confirmed through a significant increase in the simple price impact on the LSE. However, trading in FTSE 100 stocks is overall still highly liquid on days with high levels of public information.

3.7 Conclusion

In this chapter, I study the effect of positive and negative firm specific public information on trading in FTSE 100 constituents. The analysis comprises the LSE and Chi-X, the two markets that account for the major part of non-OTC trading in FTSE 100 stocks. Individual order books as well as characteristics of market fragmentation are examined in this chapter. I find an asymmetric reaction to public information. Liquidity only decreases for a negative tone of public information whereas trading activity increases strongly for any type of public information. Price discovery shifts to the LSE on positive days and more private information is impounded on the LSE on negative days. My findings are consistent with existing literature (Kim and Verrecchia, 1991, 1994) within the individual order books and also on the fragmentation characteristics (Chowdhry and Nanda, 1991). Informed trading gravitates to the LSE, the most liquid market for FTSE 100 trading.

Overall, results also show that markets for FTSE 100 constituents are highly liquid and stocks are actively traded based on relatively efficient price discovery processes. In practice, traders spend a considerable amount of money to subscribe to newswires of Thomson Reuters, Bloomberg, or Dow Jones. Such newswires represent much of the real-time public information traders receive. I find that it is worthwile to observe the tone of public information to be able to adjust trading and order routing decisions. The study in this chapter confirms the important role that public information has in finding the efficient price in equity markets and today's computerized and fragmented trading landscape.

The perspective of the next chapter becomes broader and is not focused on market microstructure but analyzes how information production influences the comovement of international equity markets. It studies markets' important information processing function on an international level.

Table 3.12: **Trading Activity and Public Information.** Table 3.12 provides regression results for trading activity measures. All measures are first aggregated on a daily basis per firm, then included in the regression model. Panel A reports regression results on the number of trades (#Trades), the natural logarithm of volume in kGBP (lnVolume), the natural logarithm of quantity in kShares (lnQuantity), the average trade size in volume, the average trade size by shares traded, and market shares by volume and quantity. Ratios for volume and quantity are calculated on raw values not the natural logarithm of numbers. Panel B reports results on the number of trades per day and firm splitted by trade size categories measured in the number of shares traded. The relevant variables are dummy variables for positive and negative public information days. Table 3.12 presents results for the LSE and Chi-X as well as the differences (Diff) and ratios (Ratio) between the LSE and Chi-X. The regression model controls for tick size differences between the LSE and Chi-X, includes month of the year dummy variables, and is estimated with firm-fixed effects. Spreads are measured in basis points (bps). Robust t-statistics for the significance of the differences between the LSE and Chi-X are reported in parantheses. 'a' indicates significance at the 1% level and 'b' indicates significance at the 5% level.

Measure	Panel A: Trading Intensity and Trade Measures							
	LSE		Chi-X		Diff		Ratio	
	pos	neg	pos	neg	pos	neg	pos	neg
#Trades								
Coeff.	217.56[a]	256.54[a]	117.22[a]	105.62[a]	100.34[a]	150.92[a]	0.04[a]	0.01
t-stat	(8.29)	(7.14)	(7.36)	(4.55)	(5.47)	(6.23)	(2.93)	(0.42)
lnVolume								
Coeff.	0.17[a]	0.13[a]	0.13[a]	0.11[a]	0.21[a]	0.15[a]	0.12[a]	0.06[b]
t-stat	(10.82)	(9.54)	(9.43)	(8.11)	(10.63)	(9.05)	(4.04)	(2.11)
lnQuantity								
Coeff.	0.15[a]	0.15[a]	0.11[a]	0.13[a]	0.19[a]	0.16[a]	0.12[a]	0.06[b]
t-stat	(10.25)	(10.70)	(8.60)	(9.11)	(10.09)	(10.27)	(4.06)	(2.13)
Trade Size (Volume)								
Coeff.	582.79[a]	301.37[a]	193.34[b]	118.04[a]	389.46[a]	183.33[a]	0.03[a]	0.02[b]
t-stat	(2.99)	(3.46)	(2.45)	(2.85)	(3.13)	(2.88)	(3.51)	(2.42)
Trade Size (Quantity)								
Coeff.	47.63	142.15[a]	13.38	56.05[a]	34.25	86.10[a]	0.03[a]	0.02[b]
t-stat	(1.53)	(5.31)	(1.07)	(4.09)	(1.66)	(4.28)	(3.52)	(2.46)
Market Share (Volume)								
Coeff.	0.87%[a]	0.30%[b]	-0.87%[a]	-0.30%[b]	1.73%[a]	0.60%[b]		
t-stat	(6.23)	(2.38)	(-6.23)	(-2.38)	(6.23)	(2.38)		
Market Share (Quantity)								
Coeff.	0.87%[a]	0.30%[b]	-0.87%[a]	-0.30%[b]	1.73%[a]	0.60%[b]		
t-stat	(6.24)	(2.39)	(-6.24)	(-2.39)	(6.24)	(2.39)		

continued on next page ...

. . . continued from Table 3.12

Trade Size Category	Panel B: Number of Trades							
	LSE		Chi-X		Diff		Ratio	
	pos	neg	pos	neg	pos	neg	pos	neg
< 500								
Coeff.	66.37[a]	45.12[a]	51.29[a]	16.48	15.08[b]	28.64[b]	0.01	-0.00
t-stat	(6.74)	(4.44)	(5.21)	(1.15)	(2.49)	(2.37)	(0.88)	(-0.09)
$500 - 1,999$								
Coeff.	79.53[a]	84.80[a]	41.37[a]	43.16[a]	38.16[a]	41.64[a]	-0.00	-0.06
t-stat	(9.28)	(8.07)	(7.85)	(6.84)	(5.48)	(5.97)	(-0.06)	(-1.13)
$2,000 - 4,999$								
Coeff.	43.04[a]	58.96[a]	15.63[a]	24.31[a]	27.42[a]	34.65[a]	0.37[a]	0.11
t-stat	(7.55)	(6.92)	(4.95)	(5.05)	(6.28)	(6.34)	(2.71)	(1.07)
$5,000 - 9,999$								
Coeff.	19.59[a]	33.60[a]	6.44[b]	11.94[a]	13.14[a]	21.66[a]	1.08[a]	0.70[a]
t-stat	(3.93)	(4.53)	(2.55)	(3.37)	(3.64)	(4.15)	(4.09)	(3.43)
$\geq 10,000$								
Coeff.	9.03	34.06[a]	2.49	9.73[a]	6.54	24.33[a]	0.87[a]	0.46
t-stat	(1.46)	(3.09)	(1.74)	(2.95)	(1.26)	(2.75)	(3.00)	(1.61)

Table 3.13: **Price Discovery and Public Information.** Table 3.13 provides regression results (cf. Equation 3.3) for information measures based on Hasbrouck (1991a,b, 1995). All measures are computed on a daily basis per firm and then included in the regression model. Results on the LSE, Chi-X, and the differences between the two markets (Diff) are presented. Panel A reports results on trade based price discovery: the share of trade based price discovery in total price discovery (% Trade Based) and the permanent impact of trade innovation in basis points (Trade Innovation). Panel B reports descriptives on quote based price discovery: the overall share of quote based price discovery in total price discovery and the share of the LSE and Chi-X respectively in quote based price discovery. Panel C provides information about the total contribution to price discovery of the LSE and Chi-X. Robust t-statistics for the significance of the differences between the LSE and Chi-X are reported in parantheses. 'a' indicates significance at the 1% level and 'b' indicates significance at the 5% level.

Panel A: Trade Based Price Discovery				
	% Trade Based		Trade Innovation	
	Positive	Negative	Positive	Negative
LSE	0.05%	0.02%	-0.06	0.06[b]
t-stat	(0.20)	(0.12)	(-1.92)	(2.47)
Chi-X	0.02%	0.10%	-0.19[a]	-0.04
t-stat	(0.11)	(0.78)	(-2.74)	(-1.09)
Diff	0.03%	-0.09%	0.13[b]	0.10[a]
t-stat	(0.13)	(-0.36)	(2.48)	(2.61)

Panel B: Quote Based Price Discovery				
	% Quote Based		Information Shares	
	Positive	Negative	Positive	Negative
Overall	-0.07%	-0.16%		
t-stat	(-0.20)	(-0.48)		
LSE			0.85%[a]	0.44%
t-stat			(2.59)	(1.18)
Chi-X			-0.85%[a]	-0.44%
t-stat			(-2.59)	(-1.18)
Diff			1.17%[a]	0.89%
t-stat			(2.59)	(1.18)

Panel C: Total Contribution to Price Discovery		
	Fraction of PD	
	Positive	Negative
LSE	0.73%[a]	0.25%
t-stat	(3.09)	(0.97)
Chi-X	-0.73%[a]	-0.25%
t-stat	(-3.09)	(-0.97)
Diff	1.47%[a]	0.52%
t-stat	(3.09)	(0.97)

Chapter 4

Comovement in International Equity Markets and Public Information

4.1 Introduction

Over the last decades financial markets have become more globalized than ever. Financial instruments are traded 24/7 around the globe on market places based in small emerging economies as well as large developed countries. And still, we lack knowledge about price formation and how information influences financial markets specifically in different countries. Particularly in a globalized world with linked financial markets, it is essential to understand how markets process information in order to foster efficient and stable financial markets for the future. One aspect of interest is how firm specific stock returns vary in relation to market and industry returns. Literature suggests that a higher portion of firm specific stock price variability in the overall stock price variability is associated with more efficient stock markets (Roll, 1988; Durnev et al., 2003).

A firm's variability in stock prices can be either idiosyncratic, industry specific, or market driven. Idiosyncratic variability is often also called firm specific variability or firm specific volatility. The market driven component is also called stock market or systematic variability or volatility. The different components of stock price variability relate to eacher other. Market synchronicity, stock return comovement, or only comovement, is a measure that can be calculated in different ways but fundamentally expresses the degree to which stocks of individual firms in one market move together. It is the fraction of stock price changes that are explained by market and industry changes. Some studies also investigate how entire countries' stock markets move together. However, I base this chapter on the former definition of comovement. A change in comovement is a change in the relation of firm specific volatility to industry and market wide volatility. It is still not entirely clear what some underlying drivers of comovement are. Recent research suggests that information production and a country's information environment, e.g. transparency and other institutional settings, significantly influence stock return comovement (Brockman et al., 2010).

In this chapter, I am first interested whether changes in the overall firm specific public information flow are reflected in the synchronous movement of entire markets. Second, I study how country specific financial development and transparency characteristics influence the association of the firm specific information flow and stock return comovement. In contrast to existing research, the variability of firm specific information production is directly measured. Generally, one major source for firm specific public information flow is the Thomson Reuters newswire service. As in the previous chapters, it is again a suitable source for firm specific public information since "market participants use this news service on a regular basis, along with Dow Jones News Service and perhaps a few other newswires, as a prime news source for economic decision making" (Berry and Howe, 1994).

Generally, I find that the overall firm specific information flow has a significant influence on stock return comovement. An increase in relative firm specific public information reduces stock return comovement, thus increases idiosyncratic stock price variability. In addition, the strength of this association significantly depends on a country's institutional setting. The quality of a firm's information environment and legal protection of outside investors significantly determine how strong the association between firm specific information flow and stock return comovement is. Transparency and effective investor protection reduce the relation between the firm specific public information flow and stock market synchronicity.

The remainder of the chapter is organized as follows. Section 4.2 introduces related work. Section 4.3 provides a detailed description of the newswire data set, stock market data, additional cross sectional per firm and country data, and the sample selection process. Section 4.4 presents stock return comovement and news comovement measures while Section 4.5 introduces the regression framework and provides results. Section 4.6 finally concludes the chapter.

4.2 Related Work

One central paper for this chapter is the work by Campbell et al. (2001) who develop the comovement measure which is used in this chapter. In their paper, they show that firm specific volatility has increased over the last decades in the US market. Their data ranges from 1962 to 1997, a long time series to analyze trends. When firm specific volatility is high, stock market comovement is low and vice versa. Intuitively, high average firm specific volatility corresponds to high average firm specific risks which is how some papers, that base on the Campbell et al. (2001) measure, interpret firm specific volatility. With respect to the research question, many papers that use the Campbell et al. (2001) comovement measure focus on either the time series or cross sectional characteristics of comovement.

The source of time trends in stock return comovement has been of interest to numerous research papers. Cao et al. (2008) compute one measure of idiosyncratic firm volatility, comparable to the comovement measure used in this chapter, with high idiosyncratic firm volatility being equivalent to low comovement. In contrast to my analysis, they base their calculation on the market and firm volatility leaving out the industry component. The past decades have shown a time trend increase in idiosyncratic firm volatility in the US stock market which they explain with an increase in growth options or growth opportunities of firms. In their regression framework, time trends become insignificant once proxies for growth opportunities are included in the models. In an analysis of the G7 countries – Canada, France, Germany, Italy, Japan, the United Kingdom, and the United States – Guo and Savickas (2008) make essentially the same argument, that idiosyncratic firm volatility is related to changes in investment opportunities which are driven by growth opportunities. They also find a high correlation of average per market measured idiosyncratic volatility among the G7 countries which the other way around also means a high correlation of stock market comovement. In another study of the US market, Fink et al. (2006) find that idiosyncratic risk computed with the Campbell et al. (2001) comovement measure is driven by firm age at initial public offerings (IPO) plus the increase in the number of IPOs over time. During the last decades, the average age of firms at IPOs has decreased dramatically. Since younger firms tend to be riskier, this effect in combination with a higher number of IPOs has driven the time trend in comovement.

Consistently, Brown and Kapadia (2007) study the time trend of comovement in the United States based on a very long time series from 1963 to 2004. They use the relation of firm specific risk to market wide risk as a type of comovement measure. The authors interpret low stock return comovement as the presence of higher firm specific risk in relation to the market wide risk. One driver of time trends is, according to their analysis, the change in characteristics of publicly traded firms. Over time smaller companies and riskier industries have been listed on the public stock market increasing firm specific risk and thus reducing the overall stock market synchronicity. They do not use the Campbell et al. (2001) measure of comovement but directly compare their results to the results of Campbell et al. (2001) which are consistent. Irvine and Pontiff (2009) explain the increase in firm specific volatility over the last decades specifically in the US market with an increase in economy wide competition. In the light of the Brown and Kapadia (2007) results, Irvine and Pontiff (2009) conclude that "financial innovation allows small, risky firms to raise capital, thus inducing greater economy-wide competition". Irvine and Pontiff (2009) extend their analysis to international markets and find the same effect. In non-US markets, economy-wide competition also increases firm specific volatility thus reduces stock market comovement.

In another study of the US stock market, Chun et al. (2004) propose that an increase in firm specific volatility, thus a reduction in comovement, is related to the dramatic development of information technology and its increased use in firms. They argue that, like electricity a hundred years ago, information technology has become a general purpose technology. Information technology improves production processes and puts more importance to intangible outputs. Firm specific, or idiosyncratic, volatility increases since possibilities for improvement based on information technology are used differently by firms and result in higher heterogeneity of firm performance. Chun et al. (2004) also find that industries which rely stronger on information technology exhibit higher firm specific volatility than other industries.

Hamao et al. (2003) study firm specific and market wide risk in the Japanese stock market, one of the few analyses that does not include the US market. They also use the Campbell et al. (2001) measure. In contrast to the United States, the Japanese stock market shows a strong decrease in firm specific volatility after its crash in 1990. Hamao et al. (2003) attribute this decrease in firm specific volatility, or increase in comovement, to homogeneity in the performance of Japanese firms and the protection from bankruptcies which resulted in a "lack of creative destruction [...] and added to the difficulty of sorting out healthy firms in the capital allocation process" (Hamao et al., 2003). Thus, Hamao et al. (2003) show that the time trend properties of comovement do not need to necessarily be the same in different countries.

One stream of literature links stock return comovement with firm specific information using information related proxies. In the interpretation of this literature, the focus often lies on the firm level, i.e. specific firm attributes and not the average firm. Durnev et al. (2003) analyze the US market over the the years 1983 to 1995. They study whether price informativeness, proxied through accounting measures such as future earnings, relates to firm specific stock price variation which in their analysis is the complement to comovement. Their definition of firm specific stock price variation is close to mine of "firm-specific price variation as the portion of a firm's stock return variation unexplained by market and industry returns" (Durnev et al., 2003). One major result is that higher firm specific variation, lower comovement, indicates more informative stock market prices. "Firm-specific variation in U.S. stock returns most likely reflects the capitalization of firm-specific information into stock prices" (Durnev et al., 2003). Durnev et al. (2004) analyze the relation of the efficiency of corporate investment[1], or broadly speaking efficient capital allocation, with firm specific return variation in the US market from 1993 to 1997. Higher economic efficiency of corporate investment positively correlates with firm specific stock return variation. According to Piotroski and Roulstone (2004), an interpretation of the Durnev et al. (2004) results is that "a stronger flow of firm-specific information should allow for greater monitoring and reduced information asymmetry between insiders and outsiders, the observed relations between low synchronicity and efficient capital allocation decisions indirectly support the interpretation that synchronicity reflects the flow of firm-specific information".

Piotroski and Roulstone (2004) present another analysis of the US market. The focus on one country ensures that the results are not driven by country differences. Their study reveals that analyst forcast activity increases comovement. Analysts are by design outsiders with relatively little firm specific information in contrast to insiders. They increase industry level information which reduces firm specific volatility. Insider trading, insiders having presumably firm specific information, on the other hand reduces stock return comovement. Their results suggest that firm specific information reduces comovement while comovement is increased by market wide or industry wide information. Hameed et al. (2010) present an analysis of the US market from 1984 to 2007. If one stock is heavily covered by analysts, other less covered stocks within the same industry follow. They "document that the stock returns of firms followed by many analysts contribute to the syn-

[1]Their measure for the efficiency of corporate investiment is Tobin's marginal q ratio.

chronicity of stock returns" (Hameed et al., 2010), not necessarily for the whole market but for firms whose fundamentals are close. Interestingly, this behavior is more pronounced if the base level of analyst coverage is low. However, Hameed et al. (2010) restrict their finding to the US market and speculate that market behavior could be different in other markets, especially in emerging economies. Their study is consistent with Piotroski and Roulstone (2004) who postulate that analysts disseminate mainly industry information.

Hutton et al. (2009) provide evidence that opaqueness is linked to stock return comovement using US market data from 1991 to 2005. "When less firm specific information is publicly available, fewer observable reasons exist for individual stock returns to depart from broad market indexes and market synchronicity increases" (Hutton et al., 2009). In contrast to other papers they study opaqueness and comovement directly at the firm level using earnings management as a firm specific opaqueness measure. "Firms with opaque financial reports have stock returns that are more synchronous with the market" (Hutton et al., 2009).

All studies above mostly study the differences of firms within the US market, including the linkage between information and comovement, or the time trend proporties of comovement. I focus on a determinant of comovement that is neither a time trend nor purely country specific but driven by the time-varying characteristics of information production, in particular of firm specific information. The association of time-varying variables might differ as a result of cross sectional country characteristics, e.g. institutional settings. Consequently, the area of literature that studies different characteristics among countries, their relation to comovement, and the association with a firm's information environment is also important for this chapter.

Jin and Myers (2006) provide a study of 40 countries around the world analyzing the years 1990 - 2001. They find that opaqueness in a country increases comovement, called R^2 in their paper. Weaker control rights and lower availability of firm specific information shift some firm specific risk from investors to managers. If firms are less transparent, insiders, for instance managers, can more easily divert cash flows to themselves. However, in doing so they also carry more firm specific risk since they can divert more if inside firm specific information is positive and less when it is negative. Insiders carrying more firm specific risk then increases the synchronicity of stock returns. In short, Jin and Myers (2006) provide evidence that the information environment and a firm's intrinsic transparency level to outside investors can have a significant influence on the comovement of a country's stock market. One conclusion which can be drawn from their findings is that a high amount of firm specific information might result in a reduction of stock return comovement.

Morck et al. (2000) study the impact of institutional development on the degree of comovement. Their sample includes poor emerging countries and rich developed economies. A particular institutional feature of interest in their work is the strength of property rights. The lack of strong property rights of outside investors in poor countries explains high stock market comovement. Morck et al. (2000) conjecture that those effects can be attributed to less informed trading on proprietary firm specific information. If the political class has more influence on stock prices through direct influence on firms, the uncertainty of future returns increases. In addition, informed outside traders might not even be able to keep their profits based on a lack of property rights. Both factors discourage informed trading. Their study shows that a country's institutional setting might affect how much private firm specific information is capitalized into stock prices, also among developed countries. Li et al. (2004) study the relation between comovement and financial market openness for different emerging markets. They find that lower comovement is associated with higher financial market openness. Using emerging markets provides the opportunity for an acadamic analysis to still find markets that are not financially open in contrast to developing countries. One of their proxies for financial market openness is "good government" which subsumes the rule of law, efficiency of the legal system, and freedom from corruption. Karolyi et al. (2009) study stock markets of 40 countries around the world from 1995 to 2004 including both developed and emerging economies. Consistent with existing literature, they find that comovement is larger in countries with weak investor protection and opaque information environments. They not only investigate stock return comovement but also liquidity comovement and find a strong positive correlation between both.

Bushman et al. (2004) analyze the determinants of corporate transparency which they define as "the availability of firm-specific information to those outside publicly traded firms". They find two main factors that characterize a countries firm specific information environment, financial transparency and governance transparency. The financial transparency factor, for instance, captures information dissemination by media outlets. The governance factor is strongly related to a country's legal system with higher governance transparency in common law countries. High financial transparency is driven by low state ownership of firms and low risk of state expropriation. One additional finding is "that financial transparency is significantly higher where firms are larger" (Bushman et al., 2004).

Their paper shows that political and legal characteristics of a country substantially influence a firms information environment.

Wurgler (2000) studies characteristics of efficient capital allocation across 65 countries based on approximately 30 years of return observations for each individual country. He finds a negative correlation between efficient capital allocation and stock return comovement which is interpreted as a measure of how much firm specific information is incorporated into stock prices. In addition, one result is that efficient capital allocation correlates positively with the legal protection of minority investors, a financial development indicator. Bris et al. (2007) provide additional evidence that institutional characteristics of countries influence the firm specific variation of stock returns, thus also comovement, and as such the informativeness of stock prices. Their analysis comprises of 46 stock markets from all over the world over the years 1990 to 2001. Bris et al. (2007) find that less negative firm specific information measured by lower idiosyncratic stock return variability is incorporated into stock prices when short selling is restricted.

In the paper that is probably the closest to this chapter, Brockman et al. (2010) hypothesize that the comovement in stock returns is driven by time-varying information production. Based on recent research (Veldkamp, 2005) which connects information production and aggregate economic activity, Brockman et al. (2010) connect stock return comovement with measures of aggregate economic activity, for instance with gross domestic product (GDP) growth. Veldkamp (2005) presents a theoretical model which predicts that information production is high during times of economic expansion and that information production is low during times of economic decline. Since demand is lower for information during times of economic decline, costs for information rise as the fixed costs of information have to be apportioned to a lower number of information demanders. As a result "with less firm-specific information available comovement increases" (Brockman et al., 2010). Brockman et al. (2010) find in their analysis a negative relation of economic growth and stock return comovement. Using economic growth as a proxy for information production, its time-varying characteristics have an influence on stock return comovement. A low amount of firm specific news drives an increase in stock return comovement. To measure comovement driven by aggregate economic activity as a proxy for information production, Brockman et al. (2010) "study the relation between economic activity and comovement while jointly controlling for country and time effects using panel data".

A theoretical model that also motivates the analysis in this chapter is presented by Veldkamp (2006) who analyzes the market for information and its relation to comovement.

Her model predicts that comovement increases when many investors only demand a subset of information as a result of costly information. However, when the number of information signals increases and information is additionally available for more stocks then comovement decreases. Less investors infer information about an asset from another asset's information. High levels of information production should associate with low levels of comovement which is important when countries exhibit different information environments, e.g. influenced through institutional settings. Also, a relatively low amount of firm specific information should increase stock return comovement.

Based on previous research, especially Brockman et al. (2010), I first hypothesize that an increase in the directly measured relative per firm information production in a market, as one factor, reduces stock return comovement after controlling for country effects and time trends. Second, this relation should vary with financial development and transparency characteristics of individual countries. I remove time and country specific effects comparable to Brockman et al. (2010) through time trend and per country controls in the regression models and, in contrast to existing research, I apply a direct proxy for firm specific information based on Thomson Reuters newswire messages.

4.3 Data and Sample Selection

The data in this chapter bases on manifold sources. The major data source is firm specific stock market and news data which are both cross-sectional as well as time-series data. In addition, pure cross-sectional per country data as well as cross-sectional per firm data are included in the analyses.

4.3.1 Market Data

I retrieve daily per firm prices and volumes as well as foreign exchange data for the years 2005 to 2009 from the Thomson Reuters DataScope Tick History archive through SIRCA as in the previous chapters. Sample stock market data can be found in Appendix B. Per firm data includes stock split information and dividend payments. All prices are reported in local currencies in the raw data. Daily returns are simple returns and calculated stock split and dividend adjusted. Trading volume is derived from local currency trading volume in combination with the daily US dollar foreign exchange rate and reported in US dollars. Daily excess returns for firms, industries, and countries are calculated in excess of daily one-month US Treasury Bill returns derived from Kenneth French's data library[2]. To control for extreme returns or data recording errors, excess returns are winsorized at 99% and 1% comparable to Brockman et al. (2010).

4.3.2 News Data

This chapter's analysis is based on RNSE news data as presented in Chapter 2 Section 2.4, the data which are used throughout this thesis. The entire news data for firms traded worldwide are used as a basis for this chapter. It is again important to recall that one news item is scored separately for different firms. A more detailed description of RNSE data fields is available in Appendix C. This chapter bases on the sentiment and relevance scores of RNSE data. Again, sentiment reflects the stock specific tone of one news item and is either positive (1), negative (-1), or neutral (0). Relevance is a stock specific score between 0 and 1 (including 1 and not 0) for a single message. The closer relevance is to one, the more relevant a news message is for a particular firm.

News data are aggregated to daily per firm measures for further analyses in a two step approach. First, I weight sentiment with the relevance of a news message. I compute for each single message the product of sentiment and relevance. Second, I calculate the average daily value of this product ('sentrel') for a specific firm. If no news message arrives for a firm on a specific day, 0 is assigned as a value to this specific firm and day combination. Daily aggregate measures range between -1 and 1. To check for robustness of the analyses, daily aggregated values are also calculated without weighting sentiment measures by relevance. If news variables are zero, news volatility is low, if news variables indicate firm specific news, news volatility is driven up. If no news arrives, news variability is by definition zero, in line with intuition. The analysis is based on 4,442,097 raw news messages items in the final sample of firms and countries over the years 2005 to 2009 (cf. Section 4.3.4).

4.3.3 Cross-Sectional Data

The study in this chapter also uses country and firm specific cross-sectional data based on literature presented in Section 4.2. Country specific variables consist of the Corruption Perceptions Index (CPI), the ICT Development Index, stock market size, per capita gross domestic product (GDP), an index of antidirector rights, an index of accounting quality, and finally whether a country is a civil law country or not.

[2]http://mba.tuck.dartmouth.edu/pages/faculty/ken.french/data_library.html.

For the CPI, the 2007 ranking is used since year to year changes in the CPI are not comparable. In addition, 2007 lies in the middle of the sample period. The CPI measures perceived corruption on a scale from 0 to 10 and is retrieved from Transparency International[3], a non-governmental organisation fighting against and reporting on corruption globally. A value of 10 would characterize a country without any corruption. The ICT development index is compiled by the International Telecommunication Union (ITU), a United Nations agency. The index measures the advancement of information and communication technology in a country. I derive the 2007 numbers which are the most current data in the 2009 'Measuring the Information Society' report (International Telecommunication Union, 2009). Stock market size is retrieved from the World Federation of Exchanges (WFE)[4] and measured by the average entire domestic market capitalization in US dollars over the years 2005 to 2009 for each country in the sample.

The data for antidirector rights and accounting quality are derived from Andrei Shleifer's data sets.[5] "Antidirector rights measure how strongly the legal system favors minority shareholders against managers or dominant shareholders in the corporate decision-making process, including the voting process" (La Porta et al., 1998). Antidirector rights consist of six rights, if each is granted to investors in a country, the index variable is six, if investors have not a single of the six rights, the variable takes zero, and otherwise the number of given rights is counted. Thus, the antidirector rights index ranges from zero to six with higher values being better. The first right is the right for absent voting, for instance via mail, for an investor to be able to execute voting rights. The second area is whether shareholders need to deposit shares around shareholders' meetings in order to execute voting righs, if they do, minority shareholders are discouraged to come to shareholders' meetings and vote. The third is the right for cumulative voting or proportional board representation which protects minority shareholders. The fourth is whether legal mechanisms against directors exist for minority shareholders. The fifth is whether shareholders' have a preemption of new issues. And the final antidirector right is the necessary percentage of share capital to call an extraordinary shareholders' meeting. Since a percentage cannot be directly expressed in terms of whether a right is given or not, La Porta et al. (1998) introduce a barrier of 10%. Below and at it is counted as one for the total calculation of the antidirector measure and above it is calculated as zero.

[3]http://www.transparency.org/.
[4]http://www.world-exchanges.org/statistics/.
[5]http://www.economics.harvard.edu/faculty/shleifer/dataset/.

The accounting quality index is constructed by La Porta et al. (1998) and described as "an index created by examining and rating companies' 1990 annual reports on their inclusion or omission of 90 items falling in the categories of general information, income statements, balance sheets, funds flow statement, accounting standards, stock data, and special items" (La Porta et al., 2000). If the numerical value of the accounting quality index is higher, the respective country has a higher accounting quality. Per capita GDP is derived in US dollars from the Worldbank database.[6] Whether a country is a civil or common law country is compiled from own research.[7]

In addition to cross-sectional country data, I retrieve the Thomson Reuters Business Classification[8] (TRBC), a market oriented schema to globally classify firms. TRBC includes four hierarchies: 10 economic sectors, 25 business sectors, 52 industry groups, and 124 industries. For the purpose of this analysis, I rely on the TRBC business sector hierarchy level to differentiate firms by their industry affiliation. A descriptive summary of the classification for this chapters's sample (see Section 4.3.4) can be found in Table 4.1. Most stocks are traded in the 'Banking and Investment Services' business sector with an average yearly trading volume of almost four trillion US dollars. In the 'Energy' sector 322 stocks are traded, 200 less than in 'Banking and Investment Services'. However, the average yearly trading volume is only 500 billion US dollars lower than in the 'Banking and Investment Services' category which increases the average per firm trading volume considerably. The highest average yearly per firm trading volume can be found in the 'Telecommunication Services' sector with a little more than 12 billion US dollars. The by far smallest average yearly per firm turnover is found in 'Investment Trusts' with 0.7 billion US dollar which consequently has the effect that those firms have barely an influence on the comovement measures. The next smallest turnover measure is observed for 'Industrial Services' averaging 2.53 billion US dollars per year and firm.

[6]http://databank.worldbank.org/.

[7]Information about a country's legal system can be, for instance, found in the CIA World Factbook database, https://www.cia.gov/library/publications/the-world-factbook/index.html.

[8]http://thomsonreuters.com/products_services/financial/thomson_reuters_indices/trbc/.

Table 4.1: **Descriptive Statistics Thomson Reuters Business Classification**. This table presents the Thomson Reuters Business Classification Scheme used to define industries for the comovement calculation. 'Number of Stocks' reports the overall number of stocks in the entire sample that belong to one business sector. The average yearly trading volume is reported in billion US dollars.

Economic Sector	Business Sector	Number of Stocks	Avg. Trading Volume (bnUSD)
Energy	Energy	322	3,572.64
Basic Materials	Chemicals	102	651.72
	Mineral Resources	212	1,759.84
	Applied Resources	57	163.26
Industrials	Industrial Goods	283	1,205.56
	Industrial Services	236	597.97
	Industrial Conglomerates	25	290.75
	Transportation	130	546.31
Cyclical Consumer Goods and Services	Automobiles and Auto Parts	64	518.41
	Cyclical Consumer Products	184	728.21
	Cyclical Consumer Services	268	1,042.28
	Retailers	163	1,046.78
Non-Cyclical Consumer Goods and Services	Food and Beverages	139	1,016.39
	Personal and Household Products and Services	69	313.11
	Food and Drug Retailing	39	391.30
Financials	Banking and Investment Services	522	3,994.36
	Insurance	159	1,464.81
	Real Estate	174	583.96
	Investment Trusts	28	19.71
Healthcare	Healthcare Services	231	631.44
	Pharmaceuticals and Medical Research	239	1,495.20
Technology	Technology Equipment	279	2,139.67
	Software and IT Services	231	1,568.37
Telecommunication Services	Telecommunication Services	104	1,276.24
Utilities	Utilities	148	993.54

4.3.4 Sample Selection

The selection of securities in this study is based on available Thomson Reuters newswire messages, only stocks and countries that are covered by RNSE data from 2005 to 2009 are taken into consideration for this analysis. Stocks in the final sample have to have at least one news message per year such that I know that a firm is still covered by RNSE archive data. A country requires at least 10 traded firms to stay in the sample while existence of stock split information and dividend data is another necessary condition. After considering all conditions, the sample consists of 4,408 securities traded in 23 countries over the years 2005 to 2009 with 4,442,097 raw news messages. Decriptive market statistics for the sample are provided in Table 4.2 and statistics for the Thomson Reuters Business Classification of the sample can be found in Table 4.1 which shows that the sample also covers a broad section of industries. The sample comprises with Argentina, India, and Indonesia three developing countries based on the Worldbank classification as of August 2010.[9]

Market summary statistics in Table 4.2 show that the firm sample is by far the largest in the United States comprising of approximately three quarters of all sample stocks. This phenomenon is also evidence for the fact that most firm specific public information flow, here proxied through Thomson Reuters news messages, is disseminated for US listed firms in contrast to the rest of the world. The average yearly per firm trading volume is with a bit less than five billion US dollars quite small for the United States compared to the rest of financially developed countries. It seems as if a huge number of stocks, that are relatively small in comparison to the average firm size in the market, is followed by Thomson Reuters news in the United States which does not appear to be the case in other countries. The smallest per firm yearly trading volume is found in the Argentinian sample with only 211 million US dollars. Argentina is also one of the three countries in the sample that are classified as a developing country by Worldbank standards. The global overall volume in share trading on regulated exchanges is, according to the World Federation of Exchanges (WFE), on average 83.3 trillion US dollars per year from 2005 to 2009. All firms in my sample have a combined average yearly trading volume of 28.1 trillion US dollars which is almost 34% of global equity trading based on 23 countries with 4,408 traded firms that are the basis for my analysis.

Domestic market capitalization of the entire market is not based on sample firms but reports values for a country's entire regulated stock market as reported by the World Fed-

[9]http://data.worldbank.org/about/country-classifications/.

eration of Exchanges. The average domestic market capitalization of all countries in the sample is approximately 35.6 trillion US dollars. The overall market capitalization of exchanges that report to the World Federation of Exchanges is on average 46.6 trillion US dollars over the years 2005 to 2009. The 23 sample countries constitute almost 80% of the world's entire market capitalization and as such those countries should be representative for global investor behavior.

The yearly average annual returns, dividend and stock split adjusted, compare well to Brockman et al. (2010) considering that the sample periods are different. The only strongly negative average annual return is recorded for Ireland at a value of -7.70%. The major driver for that development is the financial crisis which had a dramatic negative effect on returns in 2008 and 2009. The annual returns for 2008 and 2009 on average decrease the average annual returns for most countries in the analysis. The highest average annual return rate is observed for India at 57.44%, closely followed by Indonesia at 51.85%. Both countries are developing countries as defined by the Worldbank and their stock markets should include additional risks for outside investors in comparison to developed financial markets. The equal weighted average over all countries is 10.50%, a reasonable number for the time period from 2005 to 2009 without risk adjustments.

Table 4.2: **Market Summary Statistics.** This table presents market statistics for the sample for the observation period from 2005 to 2009. The domestic market capitalization is based on World Federation of Exchanges' data for the entire domestic equity market. All other measures are based on the firms in the sample over the years 2005 to 2009. Average annual returns are simple dividend adjusted returns for a country compiled from trading volume weighted firm returns for the country return computation. Averages in the 'Overall' line are equal weighted over all countries. All monetary measures are reported in US dollars.

Country	Number of Stocks	Number of Observations	Average Yearly Per Firm Trading Volume (Mio. USD)	Yearly Trading Volume (Mio. USD)	Domestic Market Cap Entire Market (Mio. USD)	Average Annual Returns (%)
Argentina	15	17,594	211	3,172	48,299	31.16
Australia	163	202,761	4,654	748,625	1,028,794	15.23
Austria	18	22,077	3,521	63,374	150,449	7.94
Canada	134	167,311	5,902	790,932	1,615,941	16.99
Denmark	13	15,988	4,748	61,725	161,063	19.86
France	124	156,014	13,388	1,660,066	1,726,260	3.40
Germany	38	47,801	24,228	920,663	1,473,370	10.73
Greece	45	55,650	1,726	77,650	164,234	8.49
Hongkong (China)	41	49,646	16,712	685,199	1,811,656	27.19
India	73	89,581	1,402	102,352	1,984,010	57.44
Indonesia	25	30,001	1,417	35,429	149,142	51.85
Ireland	20	23,998	2,955	59,101	106,408	-7.70
Italy	80	100,693	13,584	1,086,688	815,010	2.24
Netherlands	25	31,671	25,899	647,483	978,219	5.30
New Zealand	37	45,342	453	16,754	38,522	-0.38
Norway	18	22,493	13,490	242,823	239,471	21.68
Portugal	12	15,008	4,388	52,660	81,299	7.35
Singapore	27	33,578	4,661	125,857	385,405	21.19
Spain	35	44,247	26,000	910,012	1,289,370	9.33
Sweden	19	23,141	16,301	309,727	465,941	16.31
Switzerland	34	42,238	31,522	1,071,744	1,072,765	3.92
United Kingdom	278	346,682	12,849	3,572,035	3,073,759	8.37
United States	3,134	3,765,037	4,735	14,838,089	16,719,301	11.08
Overall	4,408	5,348,552	6,373	28,092,161	35,578,688	10.50

4.4 Measures

4.4.1 Stock Market Comovement

To calculate stock market comovement, I resort to the definition of Brockman et al. (2010) which is based on a decomposition into firm specific, industry specific , and market wide volatility (Campbell et al., 2001) without the use of firm specific betas. Numerous other research articles also use this volatility decomposition.[10] Comovement measures are calculated separately for each country and each month. Since GDP growth data is only available by quarters for most countries, Brockman et al. (2010) compute their comovement measure on a quarterly basis. I do not have such data restrictions and perform the decomposition analogous to Campbell et al. (2001) on a monthly level.

The first step of the Campbell et al. (2001) volatility decomposition is to calculate daily weighted market excess returns and daily weighted industry excess returns. Excess returns are calculated against the risk free rate represented by daily returns of one-month US Treasury Bills. Let c denote a market (country), i an industry, and j an individual firm. Days are identified by the variable s. Let $w_{i,c,s}$ be the weight of an industry i in country c on day s. The weight of firm j in industry i in a country c on day s is $w_{j,i,c,s}$. Let $R_{j,i,c,s}$ denote an individual firm's excess return. Then, industry excess returns are defined as

$$R_{i,c,s} = \sum_{j \in i} w_{j,i,c,s} R_{j,i,c,s}. \tag{4.1}$$

Market, and as such country, excess returns are defined as

$$R_{c,s} = \sum_{i \in c} w_{i,c,s} R_{i,c,s}. \tag{4.2}$$

In this study, returns are weighted by daily trading volume. The originally proposed volatility decomposition is based on market value weights but the decomposition is valid for any weighting scheme (Campbell et al., 2001). In addition, there should be not much difference between weighting by trading volume and market value. Based on above returns, the three volatility components – market wide, industry specific, and firm specific – are estimated monthly for each country. Let μ_c be the mean weighted market excess

[10] Cao et al. (2008), Fink et al. (2006), and Irvine and Pontiff (2009) study die US market Hamao et al. (2003) analyze the Japanese market and Guo and Savickas (2008) present a study on the G7 countries, Canada, Germany, France, Italy, Japan, the UK, and the US.

return for country c over the entire sample period and days are denoted by s then $\text{MKT}_{c,t}$, the market wide volatility of country c in month t, is computed as

$$\text{MKT}_{c,t} = \sum_{s \in t} \left(R_{c,s} - \mu_c\right)^2. \tag{4.3}$$

Industry volatility $\text{IND}_{c,t}$ of country c in month t is the weighted average industry volatility in month t and country c and defined as

$$\text{IND}_{c,t} = \sum_{i \in c} \left(w_{i,c,s} \sum_{s \in t} \left(R_{i,c,s} - R_{c,s}\right)^2 \right). \tag{4.4}$$

Firm volatility $\text{FIRM}_{c,t}$ of country c in month t is the weighted average firm volatility in month t and country c and defined as

$$\text{FIRM}_{c,t} = \sum_{i \in c} \left(w_{i,c,s} \sum_{j \in i} \left(w_{j,i,c,s} \sum_{s \in t} \left(R_{j,i,c,s} - R_{i,c,s}\right)^2 \right) \right). \tag{4.5}$$

Using above equations, comovement in the spirit of Brockman et al. (2010) for a country c in month t is calculated as

$$\text{COMV}_{c,t} = 1 - \frac{\text{FIRM}_{c,t}}{\text{MKT}_{c,t} + \text{IND}_{c,t} + \text{FIRM}_{c,t}}. \tag{4.6}$$

The comovement measure is in principal 1 minus relative firm specific volatility which then measures the fraction of volatility explained through market and industry stock return variation. Complete comovement, the absence of idiosyncratic volatility, is illustrated through a $\text{COMV}_{c,t}$ measure of 1. The complete absence of comovement is illustrated through a $\text{COMV}_{c,t}$ measure of 0. Since stock return comovement will be the dependent variable in a subsequent regression model, it could potentially introduce autocorrelation. To avoid potential autocorrelation in the residuals, a measure derived from $\text{COMV}_{c,t}$ is calculated. Based on each country's c individual time series of 60 $\text{COMV}_{c,t}$ values, the measure is obtained from the following regression, an AR(1) process, with $\text{COMV}_{c,t}$ as the raw stock return comovement and months denoted by t:

$$\text{COMV}_{c,t} = \alpha_c + \beta_c \times \text{COMV}_{c,t-1} + \epsilon_{c,t} \tag{4.7}$$

The residual $\epsilon_{c,t}$ then is the derived stock market comovement measure $\text{CMRes}_{c,t}$ which can be used as the dependent variable in the next steps. Durbin-Watson tests are used in the following regressions to assess whether significant autocorrelation is still existent in the residuals after transformation.

4.4.2 News Comovement

News comovement measures the comovement of daily news, equivalent to the definition of stock market comovement. It is comparably based on a decomposition of news volatility into market wide news volatility, industry specific news volatility, and firm specific news volatility. If higher firm specific volatility is recorded, a higher amount of public information that is not specific to an industry or entire market should be disseminated. Instead of using excess returns, the decomposition uses the daily news variable as specified in Section 4.3.2: the daily 'sentrel' measure (daily relevance weighted average sentiment of the news messages of a particular firm) and daily 'sentiment' measure. With a high measure of comovement the public information flow consists of relatively little firm specific information relative to the overall public information flow while low news comovement implies a high public information flow for specific firms relative to the overall flow of information.

First, daily weighted market news variables and daily weighted industry news variables have to be computed. Weights $\text{w}_{i,c,s}$ and $\text{w}_{j,i,c,s}$ are the same as in the previous section. Let $N_{j,i,c,s}$ denote an individual firm's j daily s news variable ('sentrel' and 'sentiment') in country c and industry i then industry news variables are defined as

$$N_{i,c,s} = \sum_{j \in i} w_{j,i,c,s} N_{j,i,c,s}. \tag{4.8}$$

Market news, and as such also country news, variables are defined as

$$N_{c,s} = \sum_{i \in c} w_{i,c,s} N_{i,c,s}. \tag{4.9}$$

Based on the definition of daily market wide, industry specific, and firm specific news variables, three news volatility components are estimated on a monthly basis for each country. Let $\text{N}_{c,\mu}$ be the mean of the weighted market news variable for country c over the entire sample period, then $\text{MNV}_{c,t}$, the markt wide news volatility of country c in month t, is computed as

$$\mathrm{MNV}_{c,t} = \sum_{s \in t} \left(N_{c,s} - N_{c\mu} \right)^2 . \tag{4.10}$$

Industry specific news volatility $\mathrm{INV}_{c,t}$ of country c in month t is defined as

$$\mathrm{INV}_{c,t} = \sum_{i \in c} \left(w_{i,c,s} \sum_{s \in t} \left(N_{i,c,s} - N_{c,s} \right)^2 \right) . \tag{4.11}$$

Firm specific news volatility $\mathrm{FNV}_{c,t}$ of country c in month t is defined as

$$\mathrm{FNV}_{c,t} = \sum_{i \in c} \left(w_{i,c,s} \sum_{j \in i} \left(w_{j,i,c,s} \sum_{s \in t} \left(N_{j,i,c,s} - N_{i,c,s} \right)^2 \right) \right) . \tag{4.12}$$

Using above equations, news comovement for a country c in month t is computed as

$$\mathrm{NCMV}_{c,t} = 1 - \frac{\mathrm{FNV}_{c,t}}{\mathrm{MNV}_{c,t} + \mathrm{INV}_{c,t} + \mathrm{FNV}_{c,t}} . \tag{4.13}$$

$\mathrm{NCMV}_{c,t}$ is the fraction of news variability that cannot be explained by market or industry wide news. If news exhibits high variability it should also contain some new information, if it exhibits high firm specific variability it should contain some new firm specific information.

4.5 Results and Interpretation

4.5.1 Descriptive Statistics

For each country, 60 monthly stock market comovement COMV values and 60 news comovement values NCMV are observed in the observation period from 2005 to 2009 which provides overall 1,380 observation for the entire panel. For CMRes, only 59 observations per country are available since the measure is constructed with a lagged variable, January 2005 is missing. An overview of all stock return comovement and news comovement measures is presented in Table 4.3. I find, consistent with existing literature (e.g. Morck et al., 2000; Brockman et al., 2010), the lowest stock return comovement of 0.460 in the United States followed by the United Kingdom. A comovement of 0.460 implies that 46% of return fluctuation is common to stocks in the US sample. The United States stock market is probably the most developed financial market in the world which should lead to low comovement. The overall equal weighted mean of stock return comovement is 0.778. The highest stock market comovement is observed in Denmark, followed by Portugal. Portugal is also the country with the least number of firms among all countries. Interestingly, all stock return comovements below 0.7 are found in common law countries (see also Table 4.7). The overall median is quite close to the overall mean with 0.801. By design, the mean of CMRes should be 0 which is also the case. However, the absolute level of stock market comovement is not important to the analysis of the time-variation of comovement in this chapter.

The lowest mean for news comovement can again be found in the United States with 0.572. The highest mean for news comovement is computed from Argentinian public information flow. This can be driven by two slightly distinct factors. First, only a little amount of public information arrives at the market which also implies that little firm specific public information arrives. Or second, if public information arrives it is not firm specific but industry or market wide information. Still, the absolute level of comovement tells nothing about how stock market comovement interacts with a variation of news comovement over time. The overall mean of news comovement is, like stock return comovement, 0.778 with a median of 0.800 which is again close to the mean.

Table 4.4 presents regression results of country specific comovement COMV on world comovement WCMV for each country individually with robust Newey and West (1987) standard errors. World comovement is calculated in three different ways. First, as the equal weighted average of country comovements, second, as the trading volume weighted average of country comovements, and third, as the WFE domestic market capitalization weighted average of country comovements. For all countries but Portugal[11] – whose coefficient is insignificant – a positive, and mostly significant, coefficient for the variation with world comovement can be observed. Country comovements fluctuate more than the equal weighted world comovement and mostly more than the volume and market capitalization weighted world comovement. Consistent with existing literature (Guo and Savickas, 2008), a common global comovement correlation seems to exist. Time fixed effects in subsequent regressions remove such global trends since the analysis in this chapter focuses on the time-varying relation of stock return comovement and news comovement.

[11] Excluding Portugal from the analyses in this chapter does not change any results.

Table 4.3: **Descriptive Statistics Monthly Comovement.** This table reports descriptive statistics on the monthly stock market comovement $COMV_{c,t}$ and $NCMV_{c,t}$ for each country in the sample . Stock market comovements (COMV) and news comovements (NCMV) are computed for each month over the years 2005 to 2009. Additionally, stock market comovement measures which are the residuals from the per country regression $COMV_{c,t} = \alpha_c + \beta_C \times COMV_{c,t-1} + \epsilon_{c,t}$ are reported ($CMRes_{c,t}$). Measures over all countries are equal weighted.

		COMV			CMRes			NCMV ('sentrel')		
Country	#Obs	Mean	Median	Std.Dev.	Mean	Median	Std.Dev.	Mean	Median	Std.Dev.
Argentina	60	0.904	0.908	0.052	0.000	0.011	0.046	0.919	0.943	0.077
Australia	60	0.603	0.595	0.072	0.000	-0.002	0.069	0.686	0.689	0.084
Austria	60	0.874	0.875	0.044	0.000	0.004	0.044	0.811	0.828	0.088
Canada	60	0.651	0.645	0.079	0.000	-0.004	0.068	0.643	0.647	0.121
Denmark	60	0.922	0.934	0.044	0.000	0.009	0.043	0.902	0.927	0.070
France	60	0.749	0.755	0.066	0.000	0.009	0.051	0.783	0.785	0.057
Germany	60	0.827	0.833	0.051	0.000	0.006	0.048	0.864	0.869	0.041
Greece	60	0.760	0.754	0.076	0.000	0.004	0.067	0.732	0.729	0.120
Hongkong (China)	60	0.776	0.773	0.058	0.000	-0.007	0.049	0.724	0.736	0.096
India	60	0.695	0.705	0.077	0.000	0.007	0.075	0.758	0.767	0.077
Indonesia	60	0.775	0.778	0.066	0.000	0.003	0.063	0.608	0.608	0.144
Ireland	60	0.847	0.863	0.068	0.000	0.002	0.057	0.828	0.843	0.112
Italy	60	0.841	0.860	0.066	0.000	0.005	0.052	0.892	0.900	0.040
Netherlands	60	0.886	0.891	0.045	0.000	0.009	0.044	0.879	0.880	0.043
New Zealand	60	0.776	0.775	0.065	0.000	0.011	0.058	0.915	0.921	0.049
Norway	60	0.813	0.844	0.084	0.000	0.020	0.078	0.790	0.786	0.065
Portugal	60	0.908	0.919	0.056	0.000	0.015	0.054	0.913	0.921	0.064
Singapore	60	0.723	0.733	0.067	0.000	0.011	0.064	0.733	0.746	0.090
Spain	60	0.835	0.838	0.063	0.000	0.003	0.054	0.789	0.796	0.063
Sweden	60	0.859	0.863	0.043	0.000	0.003	0.042	0.747	0.766	0.110
Switzerland	60	0.818	0.817	0.062	0.000	-0.001	0.052	0.803	0.805	0.062
United Kingdom	60	0.601	0.615	0.064	0.000	-0.001	0.056	0.601	0.604	0.066
United States	60	0.460	0.443	0.103	0.000	-0.007	0.069	0.572	0.569	0.089
Overall	1,380	0.778	0.801	0.129	0.000	0.006	0.057	0.778	0.800	0.133

Table 4.4: **Regression of Country Comovement on World Comovement.** This table reports the relation between individual country stock market comovements (COMV) and average world comovement (WCMV). World comovement is computed in three different ways. First, world comovement is calculated as the simple mean of all country comovements. Second, it is calculated as the US dollar trading volume weighted average of country comovements and third, it is calculated as the entire domestic market capitalization weighted average of individual countries. The table reports coefficients and t-statistics from the following regression per country c: $COMV_{c,t} = \alpha_c + \eta_c \times WCMV_{c,t} + \epsilon_{c,t}$. Standard errors are heteroskedasticity and autocorrelation consistent Newey and West (1987) standard errors and t-statistics are reported in parantheses. Significance at the 1% level is indicated through an 'a'. 5% and 10% levels are indicated through a 'b' and 'c'.

	Not Weighted		Volume Weighted		MCap Weighted	
Country	Coeff.	t-stat	Coeff.	t-stat	Coeff.	t-stat
Argentina	2.377[a]	(3.71)	1.548[b]	(2.24)	1.528[b]	(2.53)
Australia	2.960[a]	(6.11)	2.013[a]	(3.20)	1.778[a]	(4.15)
Austria	2.845[a]	(3.56)	2.133[c]	(1.98)	1.848[a]	(2.75)
Canada	2.499[a]	(10.83)	1.256[a]	(8.00)	1.297[a]	(8.38)
Denmark	2.652[b]	(2.60)	1.770[c]	(1.78)	1.618[b]	(2.22)
France	2.005[a]	(9.87)	1.093[a]	(6.20)	1.100[a]	(6.69)
Germany	4.376[c]	(1.80)	2.685	(1.28)	2.911	(1.35)
Greece	3.267[a]	(3.94)	1.844[a]	(3.23)	1.951[a]	(3.46)
Hongkong (China)	1.898[a]	(8.49)	1.003[a]	(6.01)	1.065[a]	(6.64)
India	2.713[a]	(5.76)	1.617[a]	(3.78)	1.639[a]	(4.17)
Indonesia	3.383[a]	(3.96)	1.701[a]	(4.12)	1.910[a]	(4.02)
Ireland	3.097[a]	(6.55)	1.288[a]	(5.65)	1.527[a]	(5.74)
Italy	2.302[a]	(7.28)	1.032[a]	(8.08)	1.148[a]	(7.26)
Netherlands	2.022[a]	(4.34)	1.174[a]	(3.17)	1.373[a]	(2.91)
New Zealand	9.426	(1.31)	6.354	(0.92)	11.916	(0.61)
Norway	3.203[a]	(4.71)	1.472[a]	(6.06)	1.612[a]	(5.31)
Portugal	-97.610	(-0.10)	-5.654	(-0.83)	-5.587	(-0.90)
Singapore	2.386[a]	(6.49)	1.421[a]	(4.29)	1.344[a]	(5.04)
Spain	2.090[a]	(7.23)	1.088[a]	(5.42)	1.144[a]	(5.32)
Sweden	2.433[a]	(4.21)	1.591[b]	(2.03)	1.785[b]	(2.18)
Switzerland	2.147[a]	(6.67)	1.210[a]	(4.73)	1.197[a]	(5.66)
United Kingdom	1.957[a]	(9.10)	0.939[a]	(9.63)	0.984[a]	(10.49)
United States	2.990[a]	(13.64)	1.360[a]	(12.43)	1.396[a]	(23.97)
Mean	-1.417	(5.74)	1.389	(4.50)	1.673	(5.22)
Median	2.499	(5.76)	1.421	(4.12)	1.527	(4.17)

4.5.2 Influence of News Comovement on Stock Market Comovement

To generally assess the influence of news comovement on stock market comovement and to find their time-varying relation (research question 1), a two-way fixed effects model with month fixed effects and country fixed effects is applied removing the country specific components and common time trends. Let $M_{c,t}$ be either the raw stock market comovement COMV or CMRes from the first step regression and c, t denotes a country month combination then the following two-way fixed effects model emerges:

$$M_{c,t} = \alpha_{c,t} + \delta \times \text{NCMV}_{c,t} + \epsilon_{c,t} \tag{4.14}$$

The standard errors for the two-way fixed effects model are clustered standard errors (cf. Petersen, 2009; Thompson, 2011). I also compute the influence of news comovement on stock market comovement with three news comovement lags, to check whether there are also lagged dependencies in addition to the contemporaneous relation, using CMRes as the dependent variable $M_{c,t}$:

$$M_{c,t} = \alpha_{c,t} + \sum_{k=0}^{3} \left(\delta_{-k} \times \text{NCMV}_{c,t-k} \right) + \epsilon_{c,t} \tag{4.15}$$

Brockman et al. (2010) also present pooled regressions with additional control variables like the industry Herfindahl index, firm Herfindahl index, and the number of stocks. However, most of those variables are insignificant in the two-way fixed effects setting and the number of stocks does not vary in my data set.

The models are estimated using both the 'sentrel' and the simple 'sentiment' measures (cf. Section 4.3.2 of this chapter for details on the variable construction). However, I will focus on the 'sentrel' results, 'sentiment' results are reported for robustness only and yield qualitatively the same results. Table 4.5 reports the main results while Table 4.6 reports only the 'sentiment' results; these results are not used in the further discussion.

Table 4.5 reports three models. Model A is based on the normal comovement measure COMV, Model B uses the derived CMRes measure, and Model C introduces three lags. The most basic regression, Model A, exhibits a highly significant coefficient of 0.133 with a t-value of 4.804 which indicates that there is a significant time-varying association between how firm specific news is disseminated and how stocks in equity markets comove. The F-test for fixed effects significantly rejects the null hypothesis of no-fixed effects justifying the usage of a two-way fixed effects model. The Hausman test as well as the Breusch-Pagan Lagrange Multiplier test for random effects significantly reject the null hypothesis of random effects which in combination with the F-test again justifies the fixed effects model. R^2 is very high at 84.71%, probably strongly driven through the fixed effects. Durbin-Watson statistics indicate strong positive autocorrelation in the residuals which is why I resort to the CMRes measure that has the first order autocorrelation of COMV removed. Durbin-Watson statistics are calculated for each country over the time-series and mean as well as median values are presented in Table 4.5.

Model B presents the contemporaneous association of news comovement with CMRes. However, I lose all January 2005 observations for the panel since the derivation of CMRes requires a lagged variable. The coefficient for NCMV is still highly significant with a value of 0.094 for the estimate. Tests for no-fixed effects and random effects still significantly reject the null hypotheses. The two-way fixed effects model is also suitable for the model based on CMRes. Adjusted R^2 is significantly reduced in comparison to using COMV as the dependent variable. However, one must not be tempted to compare the R^2 measures. Deriving CMRes from COMV greatly reduces fixed effects which drives a reduction in adjusted R^2 and it is by far no sign of Model B being worse than Model A. Durbin-Watson statistics for Model B show that there is no significant autocorrelation left in the residuals.

In addition to the purly contemporaneous regressions, I also introduce Model C with three lags. By design, this again reduces the number of available months per country. The contemporaneous coefficient is still significant, positive, and almost the same as for Model B. Lags one through three are all not significant and the effect of the contemporaneous term is not mitigated. Since lags do not add explanatory value to the model, further regressions focus on the contemporaneous association between stock return comovement and news comovement.

Economically, a significant positive coefficient confirms my hypothesis that a part of stock return comovement is driven by time-varying information production proxied through RNSE firm specific newswire messages. These results confirm Brockman et al. (2010) who also find that information production has a significant impact on stock return comovement. Their analysis is based on a lower frequency than mine which suggests that there are influences of information production on stock return comovement on different frequencies. Brockman et al. (2010) ultimately relate their stock return comovement measures to business cycles which are measured on a three months frequency. The novelty of my results, in contrast to existing literature, is that I am able to directly relate a major source of information production with stock return comovement. The results in Table 4.5 show that a relatively high flow in public firm specific information reduces comovement. The coefficient is positive in the regression since high news comovement implies relatively little firm specific information. Two cases for high news comovement can generally be distinguished, it might be the case that no public information arrives or that only market and industry wide information is disseminated.

I show in Chapter 2 that market participants obtain private information from public information sources, potentially through analysis and interpretation. Market participants have limited cognition and limited research resources, a fact that can drive informed trading even if information is public. Some market participants are better than others in processing firm specific public information while others again are just slow to observe that firm specific information has even arrived. The reduction in comovement due to a higher relative amount of firm specific news is then potentially a result of derived private information that is capitalized into stock returns. The capitalization of private information increases idiosyncratic variability of stock prices which in turn reduces stock return comovement (Durnev et al., 2003).

In addition, a relatively high firm specific public information flow might incentivize market participants to obtain additional private information. This, in turn, enhances the comovement reducing effect of firm specific public information and increases idiosyncratic stock volatility. A higher firm specific information flow enhances the firm specific information environment making a firm more transparent to the market. A trader has limited time and intellectual capacity to observe stocks and profitable trading opportunities. Additional firm specific public information might lead a certain fraction of traders to the conclusion that it could be interesting to trade in a certain stock. If they generate additional private information through research, analysis, and purchasing information this private information is eventually priced into the stock price once they trade on their information. This trading then increases a firm's idiosyncratic volatility and reduces stock market comovement.

My results are also consistent with the theoretical model of Veldkamp (2006) which predicts that a relatively little flow of firm specific information increases comovement and higher information production decreases stock return comovement. In general, prices should be more efficient when more information is capitalized into individual stocks (Durnev et al., 2004). Results from Table 4.5 provide evidence for the link between a time variation of stock market comovement and the flow of firm specific information.

However, this analysis focuses on the overall panel of countries and not subsamples based on country characteristics. The next section investigates whether there are cross-sectional characteristics that influence the association between news comovement and stock return comovement (research question 2).

4.5.3 Cross-Country Analysis

Existing research shows that stock return comovement varies substantially between countries (cf. Jin and Myers, 2006; Morck et al., 2000; Karolyi et al., 2009). Since country characteristics influence stock return comovement, it is reasonable to assume that the association of news comovement and stock returns might also be influenced by country characteristics, e.g. transparency or corruption.

Table 4.7 provides a descriptive overview on additional country specific information such as information about a country's legal system, corruption, ICT development, per capita GDP, antidirector rights, accounting quality, and whether a country is a developing country or not. The detailed description of those variables is available in Section 4.3.3 of this chapter. The sample of 23 countries comprises of 9 common law countries and 14 civil law countries which describes countries with either a French, German, or Scandinavian legal tradition. The Corruption Perceptions Index (CPI) is by far the lowest for the three developing countries in my sample, Argentina, Indonesia, and India. The countries with the lowest perceived corruption (highest index values) are Denmark, New Zealand, Singapore, and Sweden. On average, the index is on the level of the United States or Germany which shows that considering the cross-section of countries that exist in the world, the sample comprises relatively few overly corrupt countries. The ICT development index shows two clear outliers with Indonesia and India both having on average underdeveloped information and communication systems. This might seem strange for India since it is one of the major countries to which the US outsources call centers, software development, or even administrative medical work. However, one must keep in mind that India still has a huge rural population without access to communication or information systems. Again, per capita GDP is by far the lowest for the three developing countries in the sample. Norway has the highest per capita GDP with an average of 78,705 US dollars over the years 2005 to 2009, largely driven by their immense oil and gas resources.

Table 4.5: **Influence of News Comovement on Stock Market Comovement.** This table presents regression results for the influence of news comovement on stock market comovement. Three regression models are provided. Model A is the naive approach, regressing the raw stock market comovement COMV on news comovement NCMV. In model B the residuals of the country specific regressions $\mathrm{COMV}_{c,t} = \alpha_c + \beta_c \times \mathrm{COMV}_{c,t-1} + \epsilon_{c,t}$ (CMRes) are regressed on contemporaneous news comovement. Model C adds three lags to model B. Regressions are two-way fixed effects models over all countries and all month; models with lags naturally lose observations. Adjusted R^2 and additional statistics to assess the two-way fixed effects model are provided. The F-test tests for no-fixed effects while the Hausman and Breusch-Pagan Lagrange Multiplier tests test for random effects. Mean and median values of the Durbin-Watson statistics for per country regressions without fixed effects are also provided. Robust t-statistics are reported in parantheses. Significance at the 1% level ist denoted by an 'a'.

	Model A (COMV)	Model B (CMRes)	Model C (CMRes)
NCMV			
Coeff.	0.133[a]	0.094[a]	0.091[a]
t-stat	(4.804)	(3.804)	(3.357)
NCMV_{lag1}			
Coeff.			-0.010
t-stat			(-0.333)
NCMV_{lag2}			
Coeff.			0.023
t-stat			(1.446)
NCMV_{lag3}			
Coeff.			0.005
t-stat			(0.210)
Number of Observations	1,380	1,357	1,311
Adj. R^2	84.71%	29.64%	30.25%
F-Test (No FE)			
F-stat	49.60	6.52	6.58
p-value	< 0.0001	< 0.0001	< 0.0001
Hausman Test (RE)			
m-stat	27.86	18.38	12.44
p-value	< 0.0001	< 0.0001	0.0060
Breusch-Pagan LM Test (RE)			
m-stat	9,188	915	938
p-value	< 0.0001	< 0.0001	< 0.0001
DW Statistics			
Mean	1.310	2.111	2.118
Median	1.297	2.101	2.099
DW p-value (Pr < DW)			
Mean	0.058	0.636	0.632
Median	0.002	0.649	0.636
DW p-value (Pr > DW)			
Mean	0.942	0.365	0.368
Median	0.998	0.351	0.364

Table 4.6: **Influence of News Comovement on Stock Market Comovement – 'Sentiment' Only.** This table presents regression results for the influence of news comovement on stock market comovement. To check robustness, news comovement in this table is based on the sentiment measure only. Three regression models are provided. Model A is the naive approach, regressing the raw stock market comovement COMV on news comovement NCMV. In model B the residuals of regressions $COMV_{c,t} = \alpha_c + \beta_c \times COMV_{c,t-1} + \epsilon_{c,t}$ (CMRes) are regressed on contemporaneous news comovement. Model C adds three lags to model B. Regressions are two-way fixed effects models over all countries and all month; models with lags naturally lose observations. Adjusted R^2 and additional statistics to assess the two-way fixed effects model are provided. The F-test tests for no-fixed effects while the Hausman and Breusch-Pagan Lagrange Multiplier tests test for random effects. Mean and median values of the Durbin-Watson statistics for per country regressions without fixed effects are also provided. Robust t-statistics are reported in parantheses. Significance at the 1% level ist denoted by an 'a'.

	Model A (COMV)	Model B (CMRes)	Model C (CMRes)
NCMV			
Coeff.	0.159[a]	0.101[a]	0.093[a]
t-stat	(3.829)	(3.001)	(2.746)
$NCMV_{lag1}$			
Coeff.			-0.027
t-stat			(-1.443)
$NCMV_{lag2}$			
Coeff.			0.042
t-stat			(1.426)
$NCMV_{lag3}$			
Coeff.			0.025
t-stat			(0.780)
Number of Observations	1,380	1,357	1,311
Adj. R^2	84.60%	29.11%	29.84%
F-Test (No FE)			
F-stat	44.21	6.42	6.54
p-value	< 0.0001	< 0.0001	< 0.0001
Hausman Test (RE)			
m-stat	35.58	13.65	10.58
p-value	< 0.0001	0.0002	0.0142
Breusch-Pagan LM Test (RE)			
m-stat	8,091	911	935
p-value	< 0.0001	< 0.0001	< 0.0001
DW Statistics			
Mean	1.334	2.123	2.112
Median	1.312	2.114	2.097
DW p-value (Pr $<$ DW)			
Mean	0.050	0.635	0.618
Median	0.003	0.655	0.629
DW p-value (Pr $>$ DW)			
Mean	0.950	0.365	0.382
Median	0.997	0.345	0.371

Table 4.7: **Descriptive Statistics Countries.** This table presents descriptive statistics for each country. Legal System indicates whether a country is a common law or civil law country. The Corruption Perceptions Index is based on the year 2007; a higher number indicates lower perceived corruption in a country. The United Nations ICT Development Index represents a higher standard in information and communication technology the higher the number. Per capita GDP is based on the average over the years 2005 to 2009 and reported in US dollars. Antidirector rights and accounting quality are derived from Andrei Shleifer's data set. The potential range for antidirector rights is 1 to 6 while a higher number indicates stronger antidirector rights. The accounting quality index represents a higher accounting quality with higher index numbers. The classification into a developing country is taken from the Worldbank classification.

Country	Legal System	Corruption Perceptions Index	ICT Development Index	Per Capita GDP (US Dollars)	Antidirector Rights	Accounting Quality	Developing Country
Argentina	Civil Law	2.9	4.12	6,550	4	45	Yes
Australia	Common Law	8.6	6.58	40,354	4	75	
Austria	Civil Law	8.1	6.32	43,157	2	54	
Canada	Common Law	8.7	6.34	40,407	5	74	
Denmark	Civil Law	9.4	7.22	54,592	2	62	
France	Civil Law	7.3	6.16	39,248	1	69	
Germany	Civil Law	7.8	6.61	39,003	2	62	
Greece	Civil Law	4.6	5.25	26,733	4	55	
Hongkong (China)	Common Law	8.3	6.70	28,638	3	69	
India	Common Law	3.5	1.59	983	5	57	Yes
Indonesia	Civil Law	2.3	2.13	1,893	2	n/a	Yes
Ireland	Common Law	7.5	6.37	54,269	5	n/a	
Italy	Civil Law	5.2	6.18	34,211	2	62	
Netherlands	Civil Law	9.0	7.14	45,817	5	64	
New Zealand	Common Law	9.4	6.44	28,056	4	70	
Norway	Civil Law	8.7	7.09	78,705	1	74	
Portugal	Civil Law	6.5	5.47	20,282	2	36	
Singapore	Common Law	9.3	6.57	35,474	4	78	
Spain	Civil Law	6.7	5.91	30,582	4	64	
Sweden	Civil Law	9.3	7.50	46,422	3	83	
Switzerland	Civil Law	9.0	6.94	56,315	4	68	
United Kingdom	Common Law	8.4	6.78	40,507	3	78	
United States	Common Law	7.2	6.44	45,460	5	71	
Mean		7.29	5.99	36,420	3.30	65.24	
Median		8.10	6.44	39,248	4.00	68.00	

Both variables for antidirector rights and accounting quality are based on Andrei Shleifer's data sets. The least antidirector rights are granted to investors in France and Norway, both civil law countries. Most rights are given to investors in the United States, Canada, India, Ireland, and the Netherlands, all but the Netherlands common law countries. The theoretical highest value of 6 is reached by non of the countries in my sample. The highest accounting quality can be found in Sweden and the lowest in Portugal. Accounting quality data for Ireland and Indonesia are missing.

To assess whether country characteristics influence the association between stock return comovement and news comovement, different subsamples based on country and market (stock market price and volume data based) specific criteria are compiled. Regression models are estimated for a subset of data exactly comparable to Equation 4.14. Only Model B is estimated for country subsamples which implies that the dependent variable is always CMRes. Depending on country characteristics, the flow of firm specific information might have different magnitudes of influence on stock return comovement and thus also on the idiosyncratic variability of stock prices. Tables 4.8 and 4.9 present the results for different subsamples. Table 4.8 presents subsample estimations based on the entire domestic market capitalization, the per firm trading volume in US dollars in the sample, whether a country is a civil law country or not, and perceived corruption in a country. Market capitalization and per firm value are both based on market criteria while civil law country and corruption concern the entire institutional setting of one country. Table 4.9 presents results for measures that focus more on economic indicators and institutional settings: the per capita GDP, the strength of antidirector rights, and accounting quality. Specifically, the legal tradition and corruption as well as investors' rights against management and a firm's transparency measured through its accounting quality potentially have a significant direct impact on the overall information environment of firms. Tables 4.8 and 4.9 additionally provide information on the number of observations, adjusted R^2, and tests for no-fixed effects and random effects.

The division into subsamples by domestic market capitalization and per firm trading volume yields very similar results. Those countries with smaller domestic market capitalization and a lower per firm trading volume have a highly significant association of contemporaneous news comovement NCMV with stock return comovement having coefficients of 0.143 and 0.136 respectively. The t-values of both regressions are highly significant at 4.706 and 4.616. Coefficients are not statistically significant for both market capitalization and per firm trading volume in countries with high domestic market capitalization and high per firm trading volume. Although not significant, both coefficients still have the expected sign. This is consistent with the fact that larger firms are more transparent to outside investors (Bushman et al., 2004). If large firms are more transparent it might be that additional firm specific information does not add much to existing firm specific information which is already at a high level. Also, such information is more likely to be already capitalized into individual stock prices. But if additional firm specific information does not add much to existing firm specific information, the relation between the flow of public firm specific information and stock return comovement or idiosyncratic variability of stock prices should be low. This is exactly what I find in the subsamples with high domestic market capitalization and high per firm trading volume. If transparency is lower on the other hand, firm specific public information might add much more to the firm specific information set and also incentivizes other traders to obtain private information. Such behavior and information characteristics can then lead to a stronger association of news comovement with stock return comovement as observed for countries with small domestic market capitalization and small per firm trading volume.

The legal tradition of a country, common law or civil law, is an important characteristic for the economic environment of both firms and external investors. Dividing the sample of 23 countries into civil law countries and common law countries, unfortunately results in two samples which are of different size. The subsamples contain 826 observations for civil law countries and only 531 for common law countries. Civil law countries have a positive and significant coefficient of 0.128 for the relation of stock return comovement with news comovement. The coefficient for common law countries is only 0.048 and not statistically significant. However, I cannot asses whether the statistical insignificance for common law countries is not partially driven by the smaller sample size. Bushman et al. (2004) find higher corporate governance transparency in common law countries in comparison to civil law countries. In addition, previous research finds on average lower stock return comovement in common law countries (Khandaker and Heaney, 2009) which the comovement descriptive statistics in this chapter confirm (cf. Table 4.3). Thus, the difference in the association of stock return comovement and the comovement of firm specific news might be driven by two factors in the civil law and common law subsamples, transparency and the prevailing average level of stock return comovement. As in the previous paragraph, higher transparency might have a decreasing effect on the association of firm specific information flow with stock return comovement. If the prevailing level of idiosyncratic volatility is already high, as in common law countries, prices might already comprise more firm specific information which gives less leeway for the idiosyncratic variability of stock prices to increase. This results in a lower average association of news comovement with stock market comovement in common law countries.

One measure that is related to transparency and also defines a firm's general information environment is corruption, an important institutional feature of a country. I find that in countries with more corruption the association between stock return comovement and news comovement is highly significant with a coefficient of 0.130 and a t-value of 5.610. It is not significant for the less corrupt half of countries in my sample. However, in comparison to the differentiation by market capitalization and per firm trading volume the coefficient is very close to being significant. Karolyi et al. (2009) and Li et al. (2004) include corruption in their good government measures. In combination, the rule of law and freedom from corruption have a decreasing effect on stock return comovement in their studies. Again, the same explanation as for the paragraphs above applies. Lower corruption potentially increases transparency to investors and enhances the general information environment in a country. Lower transparency increases the effect that additional firm specific information has on the association between stock return comovement and news comovement. The same effect is found for subsamples constructed on the per capita GDP in US dollars (cf. Table 4.9) consistent with existing literature which also adresses transparency as a determinant of stock return comovement in less developed countries (Karolyi et al., 2009). The coefficient of the half of the sample with lower per capita GDP, which still are mostly developed countries, is 0.139 and highly statistically significant. Although positive, the coefficient is only 0.056 and not significant for the countries in the sample with higher per capita GDP.

The separation of subsamples in Table 4.9, by antidirector rights and accounting quality, focuses on certain specific aspects that influence a firm's information environment and the disposition of investors to acquire firm specific information. In contrast to all previous subsample pairs, both, the subsamples for antidirector rights as well as for accounting quality, do not exhibit such clear cut differences. The coefficient for countries with less antidirector rights is 0.103 and highly significant at the 1% level while the coefficient for countries with more antidirector rights is only 0.074 while being still significant at the 10% level. Existing literature confirms that lower porperty rights disincentivize investors to obtain private firm specific information (Morck et al., 2000). In turn, this might lead to a higher impact of firm specific news on idiosyncratic stock price variability. Once firm specific information arrives, it still needs to be capitalized into stock prices since the information might not have been obtained as firm specific private information by investors before. The specific characteristic of accounting quality as a country specific institutional variable directly influences a firm's transparency and is linked to different legal systems. For the half of countries with the lower accounting quality, the coefficient for the association of news comovement with stock return comovement is 0.144 and highly significant. The coefficient for countries with higher accounting quality is much lower at 0.069 but still significant at the 10% level. Again, an explanation for this behavior is the influence of transparency.

Summarizing the subsample results, it becomes clear that different institutional settings, characterized through a variety of country parameters, considerably influence the association between stock return comovement and news comovement. The results are driven by two comprehensive factors: a firm's information environment and the legal protection of investors which indirectly also influences firm specific information in stock prices. In more opaque stock markets, stock markets where firms are less transparent to outside investors, additional firm specific information can have a stronger influence on firm specific stock price volatility. Since less information is capitalized into stock prices on a base level, new firm specific information potentially has a stronger effect on idiosyncratic volatility. Also, in opaque markets it is more likely that firm specific news still contains information that has not yet been found by outside investors. Direct effects of a disadvantageous information environment are potentially amplified through lower investor protection that disincentivizes private information gathering. News specifically seems to enhance the efficieny of stock prices in an environment where it is legally as well as economically more difficult for outside investors to obtain firm specific information.

Table 4.8: **Influence of News Comovement on Stock Market Comovement – Subsamples 1**. This table presents regression results for the influence of news comovement on stock market comovement for subsamples of the 23 countries. Subsamples are constructed based on the fact whether countries have a civil law legal system or not, whether countries belong to the lower half or upper half of the entire domestic market capitalization, based on the average per firm trading volume, and on whether countries belong to the more or less corrupt half in the sample. Stock market size is the entire domestic market capitalization averaged over the years 2005 to 2009 in US dollars based on data from the World Federation of Exchanges. Average per firm trading volume is average yearly per firm trading volume in US dollars over the years 2005 to 2009. Corruption is based on the the Corruptions Perceptions Index from the year 2007. In all subsample regressions the residuals of the country specific regressions $COMV_{c,t} = \alpha_c + \beta_c \times COMV_{c,t-1} + \epsilon_{c,t}$ (CMRes) are regressed on contemporaneous news comovement (NCMV). Regressions are two-way fixed effects models over all countries and all months; the first observation of each country's time series is lost as a result of the specification of the dependent variable. Adjusted R^2 and additional statistics to assess the two-way fixed effects model are provided. The F-test tests for no-fixed effects while the Hausman and Breusch-Pagan Lagrange Multiplier tests test for random effects. Robust t-statistics are reported in parantheses. Significance at the 1% level ist denoted by an 'a'.

	Domestic MCap		Per Firm Volume		Civil Law Country		Corruption (CPI)	
	Lower Half	Upper Half	Lower Half	Upper Half	Yes	No	More Corrupt	Less Corrupt
NCMV								
Coeff.	0.143[a]	0.024	0.136[a]	0.025	0.128[a]	0.048	0.130[a]	0.059
t-stat	(4.706)	(0.711)	(4.616)	(0.768)	(4.910)	(1.209)	(5.610)	(1.537)
Number of Observations	708	649	708	649	826	531	708	649
Adj. R^2	25.75%	43.46%	28.29%	40.18%	29.51%	42.18%	28.98%	37.39%
F-Test (No FE)								
F-stat	2.84	6.54	3.41	5.71	4.11	5.09	3.52	5.06
p-value	< 0.0001	< 0.0001	< 0.0001	< 0.0001	< 0.0001	< 0.0001	< 0.0001	< 0.0001
Hausman Test (RE)								
m-stat	12.40	0.52	14.34	0.53	13.87	1.79	12.73	3.59
p-value	0.0004	0.4730	0.0002	0.4686	0.0002	0.1814	0.0004	0.0581
Breusch-Pagan LM Test (RE)								
m-stat	72.84	467.46	122.08	381.44	223.63	257.54	136.90	308.04
p-value	< 0.0001	< 0.0001	< 0.0001	< 0.0001	< 0.0001	< 0.0001	< 0.0001	< 0.0001

Table 4.9: **Influence of News Comovement on Stock Market Comovement – Subsamples 2.** This table presents regression results for the influence of news comovement on stock market comovement for subsamples of the 23 countries. Subsamples are constructed on the per capita GDP in US dollars, the antidirector rights index, and the accounting quality index. Lower half in this tables indicates, the half of the countries with the lower per capita GDP, less antidirector rights, and less transparent accounting standards. No accounting quality measures exist for Indonesia and Ireland such that for the accounting quality regression only 21 countries are taken into account. In all subsample regressions the residuals of the country specific regressions $\text{COMV}_{c,t} = \alpha_c + \beta_c \times \text{COMV}_{c,t-1} + \epsilon_{c,t}$ (CMRes) are regressed on contemporaneous news comovement (NCMV). Regressions are two-way fixed effects models over all countries and all months; the first observation of each country's time series is lost as a result of the specification of the dependent variable. Adjusted R^2 and additional statistics to assess the two-way fixed effects model are provided. The F-test tests for no-fixed effects while the Hausman and Breusch-Pagan Lagrange Multiplier tests test for random effects. Robust t-statistics are reported in parantheses. Significance at the 1% level ist denoted by an 'a', 'b' at the 5% level, and 'c' at the 10% level.

	Per Capita GDP		Antidirector Rights		Accounting Quality	
	Lower Half	Upper Half	Lower Half	Upper Half	Lower Half	Upper Half
NCMV						
Coeff.	0.139[a]	0.056	0.103[a]	0.074[c]	0.144[a]	0.069[c]
t-stat	(4.481)	(1.590)	(3.244)	(1.836)	(4.430)	(1.762)
Number of Observations	708	649	649	708	649	590
Adj. R^2	29.56%	36.78%	28.87%	34.55%	30.38%	42.69%
F-Test (No FE)						
F-stat	3.62	4.92	3.38	4.72	3.36	5.77
p-value	< 0.0001	< 0.0001	< 0.0001	< 0.0001	< 0.0001	< 0.0001
Hausman Test (RE)						
m-stat	13.21	3.26	10.85	4.52	8.24	4.30
p-value	0.0003	0.0708	0.0010	0.0335	0.0041	0.0381
Breusch-Pagan LM Test (RE)						
m-stat	145.63	293.88	129.26	286.42	120.80	342.37
p-value	< 0.0001	< 0.0001	< 0.0001	< 0.0001	< 0.0001	< 0.0001

In addition to constructing subsamples, I provide correlations of news comovement, the association of news comovement with CMRes, and institutional variables for individual countries. One has to keep in mind that the sample for the correlation coefficient is quite small with only 23 observations and only 21 for accounting quality. Correlation coefficients are Spearman's rank correlation coefficients (cf. Brockman et al., 2010). To calculate country specific associations, I compute for each country c and month t

$$\text{CMRes}_{c,t} = \alpha_c + \gamma_c \times \text{NCMV}_{c,t} + \epsilon_{c,t} \tag{4.16}$$

resulting in 23 individual γ_cs. However, one caveat in comparison to the panel regressions remains, I cannot incorporate monthly time dummies. Results of the correlation analysis are presented in Table 4.10. Variables that correlate significantly with the average per country news comovement are the civil law variable, domestic stock market size, and accounting quality. A civil law country is more likely to have high news comovement while a large stock market and higher accounting quality relate to lower news comovement. Those observations are consistent with the descriptive statistics presented earlier in this chapter. The country specific association of news comovement with stock market comovement is significantly negatively related to stock market size and accounting quality, consistent with subsample results. ICT development is highly negatively correlated with corruption and has a high positive correlation with per capita GDP. A negative and significant correlation coefficient shows that civil law countries have on average less antidirector rights than common law countries. Interestingly, accounting quality is significantly correlated with all variables but antidirector rights. All correlation coefficients for accounting quality exhibit the expected direction. Accounting quality is higher in more developed countries with large stock markets, it is higher in countries with a common law legal tradition, with high ICT developement, and low corruption. Countries with high accounting quality have a significantly lower association of news comovement with stock return comovement. Interestingly, per capita GDP has a correlation with a country's legal tradition that is close to zero.

In general, the significant correlation results are consistent with the subsample analyses. The insignificant correlation of accounting quality and antidirector rights shows that not all characteristics which are used to build subsamples are necessarily highly correlated but nonetheless have explanatory power. Different characteristics of a country's institutional setting can influence the association of news comovement and stock return comovement.

Table 4.10: **Cross-Sectional Correlations**. This table reports correlations between cross-sectional characteristics of countries. News Comovement is the average news comovement in a country. The association of news comovement with CMRes is the coefficient of the country c specific regressions $\text{CMRes}_{c,t} = \alpha_c + \gamma_c \times \text{NCMV}_{c,t} + \epsilon_{c,t}$. The Corruptions Perceptions Index is based on the year 2007; a higher number indicates lower perceived corruption in this country. The United Nations ICT Development Index represents a higher standard in information and communication technology the higher the number. 'Civil Law Country' indicates whether a country is a civil law country or not. 'Stock Market Size' is the entire domestic market capitalization averaged over the years 2005 to 2009 in US dollars based on data from the World Federation of Exchanges. Per capita GDP is based on the average over the years 2005 to 2009 and reported in US dollars. Antidirector rights and accounting quality are derived from Andrei Shleifer's data set. The potential range for anti-director rights is 1 to 6 while a higher number indicates stronger antidirector rights. The accounting quality index represents a higher accounting quality with higher index numbers. Correlation coefficients are Spearman's rank correlation coefficients and p-values are reported in parantheses. Significance at the 1% level ist indicated through an 'a'. 5% and 10% levels are indicated through 'b' and 'c'.

N = 23 (Accounting, N = 21)	Corruption Perceptions Index	ICT Development Index	Civil Law Country	Stock Market Size (Domestic MCap)	Per Capita GDP (US Dollars)	Antidirector Rights	Accounting Quality
News Comovement (Country Mean)	0.080 (0.716)	-0.006 (0.977)	0.457^b (0.029)	-0.612^a (0.002)	-0.018 (0.936)	-0.193 (0.378)	-0.617^b (0.003)
Association of NCMV with CMRes ($\text{CMRes}_{c,t} = \alpha_c + \gamma_c \times \text{NCMV}_{c,t} + \epsilon_{c,t}$)	-0.202 (0.356)	-0.279 (0.198)	0.269 (0.215)	-0.522^b (0.011)	-0.194 (0.376)	-0.060 (0.787)	-0.476^b (0.030)
Corruption Perceptions Index (0 - 10, 10 = no corruption)		0.843^a (< 0.001)	-0.195 (0.373)	-0.012 (0.957)	0.642^a (0.001)	0.037 (0.868)	0.617^a (0.003)
ICT Development Index (higher = more developed)			-0.040 (0.855)	0.176 (0.422)	0.783^a (< 0.001)	-0.084 0.703	0.578^a 0.006
Civil Law Country (1 = yes, 0 = no)				-0.336 (0.117)	0.067 (0.761)	-0.567^a (0.005)	-0.520^b (0.016)
Stock Market Size (Domestic MCap)					0.130 (0.553)	0.187 (0.392)	0.370^c (0.098)
Per Capita GDP (US Dollars)						-0.029 0.897	0.475^b 0.030
Antidirector Rights (1-6, 6 = strongest rights)							0.126 (0.588)

Table 4.11: **Influence of News Comovement on Stock Market Comovement – USA Only**. This table presents regression results for influence of news comovement on stock market comovement for the United States only. The complete US sample of 3134 stocks is splitted into 20 quantiles by average per firm trading volume. Comovement and news comovement are calculated for each quantile separately. Subsamples for quantiles 1-5, 5-10, 11-15, and 16-20 are also reported. In the overall sample as well as subsamples the residuals of the country specific regressions $\text{COMV}_{c,t} = \alpha_c + \beta_c \times \text{COMV}_{c,t-1} + \epsilon_{c,t}$ (CMRes) are regressed on contemporaneous news comovement (NCMV). Regressions are two-way fixed effects models. The first observation of each quantiles's time series is lost as a result of the specification of the dependent variable. Adjusted R^2 and additional statistics to assess the two-way fixed effects model are provided. The F-test tests for no-fixed effects while the Hausman and Breusch-Pagan Lagrange Multiplier tests test for random effects. Robust t-statistics are reported in parantheses. Significance at the 1% level ist denoted by an 'a'.

	Overall	Quantiles 1-5	Quantiles 6-10	Quantiles 11-15	Quantiles 16-20
Number of Stocks	3134	782	785	785	782
NCMV					
Coeff.	0.013	0.022^b	0.009	0.017	0.002
t-stat	(0.938)	(2.265)	(0.647)	(1.295)	(0.044)
Number of Observations	1,180	295	295	295	295
Adj. R^2	26.69%	77.85%	64.78%	45.65%	28.61%
F-Test (No FE)					
F-stat	5.12	13.04	6.83	3.07	1.47
p-value	< 0.0001	< 0.0001	< 0.0001	< 0.0001	0.0231
Hausman Test (RE)					
m-stat	0.03	0.19	0.00	0.30	2.15
p-value	0.8605	0.6601	0.9638	0.5824	0.1427
Breusch-Pagan LM Test (RE)					
m-stat	572.38	309.80	186.73	60.38	8.31
p-value	< 0.0001	< 0.0001	< 0.0001	< 0.0001	0.0039

4.5.4 US Specific Analysis

The analysis for only the United States is based on the same methodology as the international analysis in Section 4.5.2 of this chapter. In contrast to the international subsample analysis, all stocks are traded within the same institutional setting in the United States such that all country specific variables used in the previous section do not vary. Consequently, firm specific and not external characteristics drive potential differences. Considering all countries in the main sample, the United States have a highly developed stock market with transparent firms and strong investor protection. All 3134 stocks in the US sample are separated into 20 quantiles based on the average per firm trading volume which enables the usage of the panel regression methodology. Quantile 1 includes the firms with the largest trading volume and quantile 20 those with the smallest trading volume. In addition, panel regressions are also computed on subsamples: quantiles 1-5, quantiles 6-10, quantiles 11-15, and quantiles 16-20. Table 4.11 presents results for the overall and subsample regressions including the F-test, Hausman test, and Breusch-Pagan Lagrange Multiplier test statistics. The coefficient of the overall regression is slightly positive but insignificant. The only coefficient that is found to be significant is for quantiles one to five which includes the 782 stocks with the largest average per firm trading volume. The significant coefficient of quantiles one to five is also very small in comparison to the international analysis. Although not significant, all coefficients are positive.

Within the US (same institutional setting), Irvine and Pontiff (2009) show that smaller firms are riskier and thus have a higher idiosyncratic volatility. Larger US firms also enjoy higher analyst coverage which can increase stock return comovement (Piotroski and Roulstone, 2004). If idiosyncratic volatility is already high it might be the case that additional firm specific information does not significantly further increase firm specific volatility. Such characteristics could explain why I only find a significant association of news comovement and stock return comovement for the 782 largest stocks in the US sample. At first the results may seem a bit contradictory to results from previous sections. However, it is important to keep in mind that in this analysis, institutional settings along the cross section do not vary, only firm characteristics vary. In addition, multiple factors influence the association of stock market comovement and news comovement. Such a design implies that institutional settings cannot drive differences among quantiles. The important finding is that also for the US stock market alone, all regression coefficients show at least the expected sign, consistent with results from previous sections.

4.6 Conclusion

In this chapter, I study the effect of the flow of firm specific public information on stock return comovement, thus also firm specific stock price variability, over 23 countries. In contrast to existing literature, a direct measure of firm specific information based on Thomson Reuters newswire messages is applied. The modelling of stock return comovement is based on Campbell et al. (2001) and Brockman et al. (2010) while I construct a news comovement measure similar to stock return comovement. Specifically, I am interested in the time-varying influence of firm specific information on stock return comovement, overall and in addition separated by country characteristics. The regression framework uses monthly measures from 2005 to 2009.

Results provide evidence that stock return comovement is linked to the relative amount of firm specific public information that arrives at a stock market. The relative amount is defined through the construction of the news comovement measure. If news comovement decreases, more firm specific information is disseminated relative to market or industry information. More relative firm specific information reduces stock return comovement consistent with existing empirical literature that uses proxies for information production (Brockman et al., 2010) and consistent with theoretical models (Veldkamp, 2006). The firm specific flow of public information seems to contain information that is not yet capitalized into stock returns which in turn increases idiosyncratic volatility of stock prices. In addition, a relative increase of firm specific information might incentivize investors to obtain further private firm specific information amplifying the stock return comovement reducing effect. Country specific institutional characteristics significantly affect the strenght of the association of news comovement with stock return comovement. The information environment of firms and investor protection are the major drivers of differences between countries. More developed financial markets with transparent firms and strong outside investor protection generally show a lower magnitude of association between the firm specific flow of public information and stock return comovement.

The main contribution of this chapter is that I show that information production, in contrast to existing literature directly measured through firm specific public information, significantly influences stock return comovement and thus the efficiency of financial markets. In addition, I find that despite global integrated financial markets, strong differences in the information processing capabilities of international stock markets remain, also as a result of external characteristics.

Chapter 5

Conclusion

5.1 Summary

The central message of this thesis is that the firm specific flow of public information has a significant impact on financial markets. In addition, I find that today's equity markets show expeditious reactions to news and as a result speedy information processing. As an overall research matter, this thesis investigates the effect of firm specific news on equity markets from three different perspectives. Chapter 2 analyzes high-frequency intraday market dynamics around the arrival of firm specific news, Chapter 3 focuses on the impact that firm specific news has on trading in fragmented market and on fragmentation characteristics, while Chapter 4 takes a broader perspective and investigates the association of firm specific public information and stock return comovement in international equity markets. The overarching question that motivates this thesis is how information influences financial markets and how it is incorporated into prices. Understanding those mechanisms is central to our comprehension of modern financial markets.

Chapter 2 introduces two specific research questions. How do firm specific news messages, separated by their tone, influence intraday market dynamcis, i.e. price discovery, liquidity, and trading intensity? In addition, one central question is how those market measures interact around firm specific newswire messages. In contrast to existing literature, I am able to differentiate by the tone of a newswire message. The empirical results of Chapter 2 provide evidence for an asymmetric reaction of market participants to the arrival of newswire messages of different sentiments. I find higher adverse selection around negative news messages than around positive news messages. Liquidity increases around positive and neutral news messages while it has the tendency to decrease around negative news messages. Only trading intensity increases around all types of news. An explanation for the increase in adverse selection around news is that traders aquire costly firm specific information prior to a news message and that market participants have different capabilities to process new firm specific public information. Both types of behavior lead to higher information asymmetry among market participants. Liquidity is sustained around positive news as a result of competition for liquidity supply, new positive information is, in the view of market participants, not disruptive enough for a breakdown of liquidity supply. Ambiguity aversion of a proportion of traders at the TSX is a concept that potentially explains the asymmetricity of trader behavior with respect to positive and negative news.

The analysis in Chapter 3 is focused on firm specific public information and fragmented markets, specifically the London Stock Exchange and Chi-X which both offer trading in FTSE 100 stocks. In such a trading environment, information has multiple opportunities to translate into prices which yields two research questions. How does firm specific information influence price discovery, liquidity, and trading intensity on individual trading venues in fragmented markets and how does it influence characteristics of market fragmentation? Again, market participants' reactions to the daily general firm specific tone of public information, based on aggregated newswire messages, are asymmetric. For daily averages, liquidity only decreases on days with predominantely negative firm specific information while it remains stable on positive days. With respect to fragementation characteristics, one result is that overall price discovery shifts to the LSE on positive days in contrast to neutral days. Also, more trade based information is found to be impounded into the LSE than on Chi-X on negative days. Within individual order books, results can be explained with pre-news information gathering of a fraction of market participants in combination with different post-news information processing capabilities. Consistent with existing theory (Chowdhry and Nanda, 1991), informed trading, which is higher on positive and negative news day, gravitates to the LSE, the most liquid market. The empirical analysis also reveals that the market for FTSE 100 stocks is highly liquid and price discovery is based on relatively efficient processes even on positive and negative news days.

Finally, Chapter 4 takes a more general view on financial markets and considers the association between the firm specific public information flow and stock return comovement, thus also idiosyncratic volatility. International equity markets all show some amount of stock return synchronicity which cannot be explained by existing theoretical asset pricing models. Recent research suggests that information production has an influence on the time-varying properties of stock return comovement (Brockman et al., 2010). Also, comovement varies significantly between different countries. These observations, in combination with the ability to measure a direct proxy for firm specific information through Thomson Reuters newswire messages, lead to two research questions. How does the relative flow of firm specific information influence stock return comovement and how might such an association be influenced by country characteristics. Results show that an increase in the flow of firm specific public information relative to public industry and market information reduces stock return comovement. The firm specific flow of news still includes information that needs to be capitalized into stock prices and thus increases stocks' idiosyncratic variability. Additionally, firm specific news might incentivize investors to obtain more firm specific information. I also find that a country's institutional setting has an effect on the association between firm specific public information and stock return comovement. More transparent countries and countries with higher investor protection show a lower association between firm specific news and comovement. The attenuation of the association is an indication that in such countries the price already contains more of the firm specific information found in news.

Newswire messages, such as the Thomson Reuters data used in this thesis, represent much of the real-time information traders receive. I find that they are a significant source of information for financial markets. In general, this thesis confirms the important role that public information has in discovering the efficient price in equity markets and it contributes to the understanding how such public information facilitates efficient financial markets.

5.2 Outlook

Equity trading has undergone a process of automation and computerization during the last decades. Now, more than half of all equity trading in developed financial markets is based on algorithms and computers making buy or sell decisions and placing orders. It is reasonable to assume that with increasing computing power and available data this computerization will heavily expand into news and information analysis. Already today, traders, banks, and hedge funds use automatic news analysis to support trading decisions. Recent news products like the Thomson Reuters Sentiment Engine or News Analytics what it is called now, Dow Jones Elementized News Feed, and machine readable products from other information providers directly cater to algorithmic and to high-frequency traders. Research that would be interesting for regulators and the securities trading industry alike could study how an increase in machine driven analysis will change the incorporation of new information into prices. Whether this trend will increase price efficiency and provide a broader incorporation of information into prices or whether such a development is a cause for concern has not been answered yet. The question of what happens to financial markets if not only trading but also information based decision making is taken over by computers, is an interesting area for future research. Another question is whether an increased linkage of international financial markets through computers will alleviate differences among financial markets in terms of price discovery and capitalization of information.

This dissertation focuses on equity markets. However, behavior on other markets like futures, options, foreign exchange, or bond markets might be different and questions arising from this area provide for numerous potential research questions. Some potential explanations for observed trader behavior might also require additional experimental analyses in laboratory settings to control for external influences. For instance, one might gain more insight into ambiguity aversion in financial markets through controlled economic experiments but also through datasets that directly identfy individual traders.

This thesis answers some fundamental questions concerning the relation of firm specific public information and equity markets. But in an ever changing financial market environment, many potential research areas remain and provide for interesting and challenging research questions in the future.

Appendix A

Sample Firms LSE/Chi-X

Table A.1: **Chapter 3 Sample Firms.** Table A.1 reports the sample firms for the LSE/Chi-X analysis including the average daily market capitalization in Million GBP over 2009 and the LSE and Chi-X Reuters Instrument Codes (RIC).

Firm	LSE RIC	Chi-X RIC	MCap (Mio. GBP)
Anglo American	AAL.L	AALl.CHI	23,740.97
Associated British Foods	ABF.L	ABFl.CHI	5,974.56
Admiral Group	ADML.L	ADMLl.CHI	2,575.62
AMEC	AMEC.L	AMECl.CHI	2,251.58
Antofagasta	ANTO.L	ANTOl.CHI	6,543.08
AstraZeneca	AZN.L	AZNl.CHI	38,371.10
Autonomy Corp	AUTN.L	AUTNl.CHI	3,200.30
Aviva	AV.L	AVl.CHI	9,456.08
BAE Systems	BAES.L	BAESl.CHI	12,171.70
Barclays	BARC.L	BARCl.CHI	26,206.12
British American Tobacco	BATS.L	BATSl.CHI	36,064.97
British Airways	BAY.L	BAYl.CHI	1,935.43
BG Group	BG.L	BGl.CHI	35,568.91
British Land Company	BLND.L	BLNDl.CHI	3,462.31
BHP Billiton	BLT.L	BLTl.CHI	94,010.22
Bunzl	BNZL.L	BNZLl.CHI	1,866.82
BP	BP.L	BPl.CHI	96,823.48

continued on next page ...

...continued from Table A.1

British Sky Broadcasting	BSY.L	BSYl.CHI	8,714.49
BT Group	BT.L	BTl.CHI	8,852.04
Cadbury	CBRY.L	CBRYl.CHI	8,527.92
Carnival	CCL.L	CCLl.CHI	14,242.51
Centrica	CNA.L	CNAl.CHI	12,596.55
Cairn Energy	CNE.L	CNEl.CHI	3,306.94
Cobham	COB.L	COBl.CHI	2,287.52
Compass Group	CPG.L	CPGl.CHI	6,545.79
Capita Group	CPI.L	CPIl.CHI	4,385.28
Cable & Wireless	CW.L	CWl.CHI	3,647.77
Diageo	DGE.L	DGEl.CHI	22,802.81
Man Group	EMG.L	EMGl.CHI	4,534.63
Eurasion Natural Resources	ENRC.L	ENRCl.CHI	8,679.94
Experian	EXPN.L	EXPNl.CHI	5,023.78
G4S	GFS.L	GFSl.CHI	3,031.86
GlaxoSmithKline	GSK.L	GSKl.CHI	60,284.53
Hammerson	HMSO.L	HMSOl.CHI	2,204.38
Home Retail Group	HOME.L	HOMEl.CHI	2,330.51
HSBC Holdings	HSBA.L	HSBAl.CHI	95,189.54
ICAP	IAP.L	IAPl.CHI	2,473.58
InterContinental Hotels Group	IHG.L	IHGl.CHI	1,948.98
Imperial Tobacco	IMT.L	IMTl.CHI	17,423.58
International Power	IPR.L	IPRl.CHI	3,941.14
Inmarsat	ISA.L	ISAl.CHI	2,405.31
Invensys	ISYS.L	ISYSl.CHI	1,871.73
Johnson Matthey	JMAT.L	JMATl.CHI	2,708.75
Kazakhmys	KAZ.L	KAZl.CHI	4,047.00
Kingfisher	KGF.L	KGFl.CHI	4,442.22
Land Securities Group	LAND.L	LANDl.CHI	4,033.45
Legal & General Group	LGEN.L	LGENl.CHI	3,785.92
Liberty International	LII.L	LIIl.CHI	2,233.84
Lloyds Banking Group	LLOY.L	LLOYl.CHI	19,401.84
Marks and Spencer	MKS.L	MKSl.CHI	5,034.66
Morrison Supermarkets	MRW.L	MRWl.CHI	6,947.18
National Grid	NG.L	NGl.CHI	14,540.55

continued on next page ...

...continued from Table A.1

NEXT	NXT.L	NXTl.CHI	3,104.02
Old Mutual	OML.L	OMLl.CHI	4,245.73
Prudential	PRU.L	PRUl.CHI	11,536.79
Pearson	PSON.L	PSONl.CHI	5,794.91
Reckitt Benckiser Group	RB.L	RBl.CHI	20,231.46
Royal Bank of Scotland	RBS.L	RBSl.CHI	19,729.10
Royal Dutch Shell A	RDSa.L	RDSal.CHI	103,901.99
Royal Dutch Shell B	RDSb.L	RDSbl.CHI	103,901.99
Reed Elsevier	REL.L	RELl.CHI	5,574.24
Rexam	REX.L	REXl.CHI	2,081.97
Rio Tinto	RIO.L	RIOl.CHI	48,231.79
Rolls Royce	RR.L	RRl.CHI	7,173.48
Randgold Resources	RRS.L	RRSl.CHI	3,165.69
RSA Insurance Group	RSA.L	RSAl.CHI	4,261.03
SABMiller	SAB.L	SABl.CHI	20,762.99
Sainsbury	SBRY.L	SBRYl.CHI	5,815.61
Schroders	SDR.L	SDRl.CHI	2,625.49
Sage Group	SGE.L	SGEl.CHI	2,579.61
Shire	SHP.L	SHPl.CHI	5,448.85
Standard Life	SL.L	SLl.CHI	4,341.68
Smiths Group	SMIN.L	SMINl.CHI	3,192.63
Smith & Nephew	SN.L	SNl.CHI	4,460.47
Serco Group	SRP.L	SRPl.CHI	2,153.39
Scottish and Southern Energy	SSE.L	SSEl.CHI	10,370.69
Standard Chartered	STAN.L	STANl.CHI	23,873.95
Severn Trent	SVT.L	SVTl.CHI	2,465.39
Thomas Cook Group	TCG.L	TCGl.CHI	1,922.35
Tullow Oil	TLW.L	TLWl.CHI	7,775.12
Tesco	TSCO.L	TSCOl.CHI	29,228.68
TUI Travel	TT.L	TTl.CHI	2,721.68
Unilever	ULVR.L	ULVRl.CHI	47,908.85
United Utilities Group	UU.L	UUl.CHI	3,379.39
Vedanta Resources	VED.L	VEDl.CHI	4,082.57
Vodafone	VOD.L	VODl.CHI	67,698.88
WPP	WPP.L	WPPl.CHI	5,917.92
Xstrata	XTA.L	XTAl.CHI	20,061.58

Appendix B

Sample Data

The following tables report sample data for trade and quote data, depth data, and daily data as retrieved from the Thomson Reuters DataScope Tick History archive. Table B.1 depicts trade and quote data from the Toronto Stock Exchange. The firm is 'Research in Motion' indicated through the Reuters Instrument Code (RIC) RIM.TO. Bid and ask sizes are reported in hundreds. The Qualifiers column usually comprises of exchange specific information. In this sample, 'Low[USER]' indicates that this has been the lowest trading price on that trading day up to that specific point in time. Table B.2 reports depth data for 'Research in Motion' traded on the Toronto Stock Exchange. The sample data are from 2006. Still, the thirty data entries only show a snapshot of a little less than three seconds. Nowadays, the quote update frequency is even higher. A new line in the data appears as soon as either volume or price changes occur at any depth level reported by the data. Table B.3 reports Chi-X trade and quote data for 'Vodafone' which is listed on the LSE. Prices are reported in Pence not British Pounds. The raw data are different to the TSX data, only data fields that change are reported while TSX raw data also includes unchanged data fields. For instance, if the bid size is updated on Chi-X only the new bid size is reported while the TSX also features the non changed data fields for bid price, ask size, and ask price in the same line. Table B.4 reports daily data including traded volume and prices. In this sample the firm is 'General Electric' traded on the New York Stock Exchange. Daily data are very similar for different exchanges.

Table B.1: **Raw TAQ Data – TSX:** This table presents raw trade and quote data from the Toronto Stock Exchange. In this sample the firm is 'Research in Motion'.

#RIC	Date[G]	Time[G]	GMT Offset	Type	Price	Volume	Bid Price	Bid Size	Ask Price	Ask Size	Qualifiers
RIM.TO	01-AUG-2006	14:16:28.018	-4	Quote			71.79	12	71.8	2	
RIM.TO	01-AUG-2006	14:16:28.265	-4	Quote			71.77	6	71.8	2	
RIM.TO	01-AUG-2006	14:16:28.265	-4	Quote			71.77	4	71.8	2	
RIM.TO	01-AUG-2006	14:16:28.683	-4	Quote			71.77	1	71.8	2	
RIM.TO	01-AUG-2006	14:16:28.683	-4	Quote			71.76	1	71.8	2	
RIM.TO	01-AUG-2006	14:16:28.744	-4	Quote			71.78	6	71.8	2	
RIM.TO	01-AUG-2006	14:16:29.225	-4	Quote			71.77	10	71.8	2	
RIM.TO	01-AUG-2006	14:16:29.471	-4	Quote			71.78	5	71.8	2	
RIM.TO	01-AUG-2006	14:16:32.563	-4	Quote			71.77	10	71.8	2	
RIM.TO	01-AUG-2006	14:16:32.563	-4	Trade	71.77	200					Low[USER]
RIM.TO	01-AUG-2006	14:16:32.866	-4	Quote			71.77	8	71.8	2	
RIM.TO	01-AUG-2006	14:16:32.866	-4	Quote			71.78	5	71.8	2	
RIM.TO	01-AUG-2006	14:16:33.560	-4	Trade	71.78	500					
RIM.TO	01-AUG-2006	14:16:33.560	-4	Quote			71.75	12	71.78	5	
RIM.TO	01-AUG-2006	14:16:33.560	-4	Trade	71.75	200					Low[USER]
RIM.TO	01-AUG-2006	14:16:33.560	-4	Quote			71.75	10	71.77	5	
RIM.TO	01-AUG-2006	14:16:33.910	-4	Quote			71.75	8	71.77	5	
RIM.TO	01-AUG-2006	14:16:33.910	-4	Quote			71.75	6	71.77	5	
RIM.TO	01-AUG-2006	14:16:33.910	-4	Quote			71.75	5	71.77	5	
RIM.TO	01-AUG-2006	14:16:33.910	-4	Quote			71.75	4	71.77	5	
RIM.TO	01-AUG-2006	14:16:33.910	-4	Quote			71.75	5	71.77	5	
RIM.TO	01-AUG-2006	14:16:34.153	-4	Quote			71.75	6	71.77	5	
RIM.TO	01-AUG-2006	14:16:34.153	-4	Quote			71.75	7	71.77	5	
RIM.TO	01-AUG-2006	14:16:34.153	-4	Quote			71.75	8	71.77	5	
RIM.TO	01-AUG-2006	14:16:34.274	-4	Quote			71.75	10	71.77	5	
RIM.TO	01-AUG-2006	14:16:35.573	-4	Quote			71.75	8	71.77	5	
RIM.TO	01-AUG-2006	14:16:35.756	-4	Quote			71.75	7	71.77	5	
RIM.TO	01-AUG-2006	14:16:35.756	-4	Quote			71.75	6	71.77	5	
RIM.TO	01-AUG-2006	14:16:35.756	-4	Quote			71.75	5	71.77	5	
RIM.TO	01-AUG-2006	14:16:35.756	-4	Quote			71.75	4	71.77	5	

Table B.2: **Raw Depth Level 3 Data – TSX:** This table presents raw depth data at three levels into the order book from the Toronto Stock Exchange. Depth data is similar on most exchanges available in the Thomson Reuters DataScope Tick History archive. In this sample the firm is 'Research in Motion'.

#RIC	Date[G]	Time[G]	GMT Offset	Type	L1 Bid Price	L1 Bid Size	L1 Ask Price	L1 Ask Size	L2 Bid Price	L2 Bid Size	L2 Ask Price	L2 Ask Size	L3 Bid Price	L3 Bid Size	L3 Ask Price	L3 Ask Size
RIM.TO	01-AUG-2006	13:43:28.013	-4	Market Depth	73.26	300	73.31	900	73.25	1000	73.32	900	73.24	800	73.33	100
RIM.TO	01-AUG-2006	13:43:28.159	-4	Market Depth	73.26	300	73.31	1000	73.25	1000	73.32	900	73.24	800	73.33	100
RIM.TO	01-AUG-2006	13:43:28.160	-4	Market Depth	73.26	300	73.31	1000	73.25	1000	73.32	900	73.24	800	73.36	100
RIM.TO	01-AUG-2006	13:43:28.161	-4	Market Depth	73.26	300	73.31	1000	73.25	1000	73.32	900	73.24	800	73.34	100
RIM.TO	01-AUG-2006	13:43:28.226	-4	Market Depth	73.26	300	73.31	1100	73.25	1000	73.32	900	73.24	800	73.34	100
RIM.TO	01-AUG-2006	13:43:28.229	-4	Market Depth	73.26	300	73.31	1100	73.25	1000	73.32	300	73.24	800	73.34	100
RIM.TO	01-AUG-2006	13:43:28.229	-4	Market Depth	73.26	300	73.31	2200	73.25	1000	73.32	300	73.24	800	73.34	100
RIM.TO	01-AUG-2006	13:43:28.296	-4	Market Depth	73.26	300	73.31	2600	73.25	1000	73.32	300	73.24	800	73.34	100
RIM.TO	01-AUG-2006	13:43:28.361	-4	Market Depth	73.26	300	73.31	2600	73.25	1000	73.32	300	73.24	800	73.34	100
RIM.TO	01-AUG-2006	13:43:28.361	-4	Market Depth	73.26	300	73.31	2600	73.25	1000	73.32	300	73.24	800	73.34	100
RIM.TO	01-AUG-2006	13:43:28.361	-4	Market Depth	73.26	300	73.31	2600	73.25	1100	73.32	300	73.24	800	73.34	100
RIM.TO	01-AUG-2006	13:43:28.803	-4	Market Depth	73.26	300	73.31	2600	73.25	1100	73.32	300	73.24	800	73.34	100
RIM.TO	01-AUG-2006	13:43:28.912	-4	Market Depth	73.26	300	73.31	2600	73.25	1100	73.32	300	73.24	600	73.34	100
RIM.TO	01-AUG-2006	13:43:28.914	-4	Market Depth	73.26	300	73.31	2600	73.25	1100	73.32	300	73.24	400	73.34	100
RIM.TO	01-AUG-2006	13:43:28.984	-4	Market Depth	73.26	300	73.31	2600	73.25	1100	73.32	300	73.24	200	73.34	100
RIM.TO	01-AUG-2006	13:43:29.126	-4	Market Depth	73.26	300	73.31	2600	73.25	1100	73.32	300	73.24	200	73.34	100
RIM.TO	01-AUG-2006	13:43:29.131	-4	Market Depth	73.26	300	73.31	2600	73.25	1100	73.32	300	73.24	200	73.34	100
RIM.TO	01-AUG-2006	13:43:29.203	-4	Market Depth	73.26	300	73.31	2600	73.25	1000	73.32	300	73.24	200	73.34	100
RIM.TO	01-AUG-2006	13:43:29.355	-4	Market Depth	73.26	300	73.31	2600	73.25	1000	73.32	300	73.24	200	73.34	100
RIM.TO	01-AUG-2006	13:43:29.593	-4	Market Depth	73.26	300	73.31	2600	73.25	1000	73.32	300	73.24	200	73.34	100
RIM.TO	01-AUG-2006	13:43:30.177	-4	Market Depth	73.26	300	73.31	2600	73.25	1000	73.32	300	73.24	200	73.34	100
RIM.TO	01-AUG-2006	13:43:30.180	-4	Market Depth	73.26	300	73.31	2600	73.25	1000	73.32	300	73.24	400	73.34	100
RIM.TO	01-AUG-2006	13:43:30.389	-4	Market Depth	73.26	300	73.31	2600	73.25	1000	73.32	300	73.24	600	73.34	100
RIM.TO	01-AUG-2006	13:43:30.389	-4	Market Depth	73.26	300	73.31	2600	73.25	1000	73.32	300	73.24	600	73.34	100
RIM.TO	01-AUG-2006	13:43:30.606	-4	Market Depth	73.26	300	73.31	1500	73.25	1000	73.32	300	73.24	600	73.34	100
RIM.TO	01-AUG-2006	13:43:30.610	-4	Market Depth	73.26	300	73.31	1500	73.25	1000	73.32	300	73.24	600	73.34	100
RIM.TO	01-AUG-2006	13:43:30.897	-4	Market Depth	73.26	300	73.31	1500	73.25	1100	73.32	300	73.24	600	73.34	100
RIM.TO	01-AUG-2006	13:43:30.901	-4	Market Depth	73.26	300	73.31	1500	73.25	1100	73.32	300	73.24	600	73.34	100
RIM.TO	01-AUG-2006	13:43:30.901	-4	Market Depth	73.26	300	73.31	2600	73.25	1100	73.32	300	73.24	600	73.34	100
RIM.TO	01-AUG-2006	13:43:30.966	-4	Market Depth	73.26	300	73.31	2600	73.25	1100	73.32	300	73.24	600	73.34	100

Table B.3: **Raw TAQ Data – Chi-X:** This table presents raw trade and quote data from Chi-X. In this sample the firm is 'Vodafone' which is listed on the London Stock Exchange.

#RIC	Date[G]	Time[G]	GMT Offset	Type	Price	Volume	Bid Price	Bid Size	Ask Price	Ask Size	Qualifiers
VODl.CHI	01-SEP-2009	08:47:09.615	+1	Quote				1496			
VODl.CHI	01-SEP-2009	08:47:09.922	+1	Quote				4505		27148	
VODl.CHI	01-SEP-2009	08:47:13.255	+1	Quote				1496		30157	
VODl.CHI	01-SEP-2009	08:47:14.780	+1	Trade	132.9	104					
VODl.CHI	01-SEP-2009	08:47:14.780	+1	Quote				1392			
VODl.CHI	01-SEP-2009	08:47:14.780	+1	Trade	132.9	1392					
VODl.CHI	01-SEP-2009	08:47:14.780	+1	Quote			132.85	56793			
VODl.CHI	01-SEP-2009	08:47:16.306	+1	Quote				40593			
VODl.CHI	01-SEP-2009	08:47:16.445	+1	Quote				32519			
VODl.CHI	01-SEP-2009	08:47:16.445	+1	Quote				16419			
VODl.CHI	01-SEP-2009	08:47:16.445	+1	Quote				10419		38257	
VODl.CHI	01-SEP-2009	08:47:16.445	+1	Quote						46357	
VODl.CHI	01-SEP-2009	08:47:16.489	+1	Quote				16419			
VODl.CHI	01-SEP-2009	08:47:18.464	+1	Quote			132.9	14212			
VODl.CHI	01-SEP-2009	08:47:21.038	+1	Trade	132.9	14212					
VODl.CHI	01-SEP-2009	08:47:21.038	+1	Quote			132.85	38593			
VODl.CHI	01-SEP-2009	08:47:21.038	+1	Quote				24493			
VODl.CHI	01-SEP-2009	08:47:21.038	+1	Quote				16419			
VODl.CHI	01-SEP-2009	08:47:22.632	+1	Quote			132.9	1421			
VODl.CHI	01-SEP-2009	08:47:34.921	+1	Trade	132.9	8					
VODl.CHI	01-SEP-2009	08:47:34.921	+1	Quote				1413			
VODl.CHI	01-SEP-2009	08:47:34.938	+1	Quote						41357	
VODl.CHI	01-SEP-2009	08:47:36.143	+1	Quote						46357	
VODl.CHI	01-SEP-2009	08:47:37.294	+1	Quote				3413		30157	
VODl.CHI	01-SEP-2009	08:47:37.649	+1	Quote				5413			
VODl.CHI	01-SEP-2009	08:47:41.579	+1	Trade	132.9	1413					
VODl.CHI	01-SEP-2009	08:47:41.579	+1	Quote				4000			
VODl.CHI	01-SEP-2009	08:47:41.579	+1	Trade	132.9	2000					
VODl.CHI	01-SEP-2009	08:47:41.579	+1	Quote				2000			
VODl.CHI	01-SEP-2009	08:47:41.579	+1	Trade	132.9	2000					

Table B.4: **Raw Daily Data:** This table presents raw daily data. In this sample the firm is 'General Electric' traded on the New York Stock Exchange.

#RIC	Date[L]	Time[L]	Type	Qualifiers	Open	High	Low	Last	Volume
GE.N	01-AUG-2006		End Of Day		32.65	32.67	32.48	32.56	7580000
GE.N	02-AUG-2006		End Of Day		32.55	32.81	32.42	32.6	8597600
GE.N	03-AUG-2006		End Of Day		32.5	32.87	32.43	32.73	9784600
GE.N	04-AUG-2006		End Of Day		32.88	32.99	32.6	32.8	8594900
GE.N	05-AUG-2006		End Of Day	No Trades					
GE.N	06-AUG-2006		End Of Day	No Trades					
GE.N	07-AUG-2006		End Of Day		32.68	32.78	32.51	32.69	8162200
GE.N	08-AUG-2006		End Of Day		32.8	32.8	32.2	32.34	11718100
GE.N	09-AUG-2006		End Of Day		32.48	32.72	32.24	32.28	8877000
GE.N	10-AUG-2006		End Of Day		32.35	32.78	32.28	32.67	12836500
GE.N	11-AUG-2006		End Of Day		32.78	32.78	32.43	32.5	8555800
GE.N	12-AUG-2006		End Of Day	No Trades					
GE.N	13-AUG-2006		End Of Day	No Trades					
GE.N	14-AUG-2006		End Of Day		32.8	33.43	32.77	32.82	12432100
GE.N	15-AUG-2006		End Of Day		33.2	33.28	33.04	33.2	9318700
GE.N	16-AUG-2006		End Of Day		33.35	33.84	33.32	33.71	12016900
GE.N	17-AUG-2006		End Of Day		33.7	34	33.65	33.92	9120800
GE.N	18-AUG-2006		End Of Day		33.98	34	33.8	34	10654900
GE.N	19-AUG-2006		End Of Day	No Trades					
GE.N	20-AUG-2006		End Of Day	No Trades					
GE.N	21-AUG-2006		End Of Day		34	34.1	33.77	33.96	6276500
GE.N	22-AUG-2006		End Of Day		33.9	34.18	33.68	33.96	7653400
GE.N	23-AUG-2006		End Of Day		33.75	33.86	33.6	33.79	9313400
GE.N	24-AUG-2006		End Of Day		33.94	34.01	33.77	33.85	7243000
GE.N	25-AUG-2006		End Of Day		33.72	33.91	33.71	33.84	6236400
GE.N	26-AUG-2006		End Of Day	No Trades					
GE.N	27-AUG-2006		End Of Day	No Trades					
GE.N	28-AUG-2006		End Of Day		33.7	34	33.7	33.93	6890900
GE.N	29-AUG-2006		End Of Day		33.9	34.23	33.9	34.19	10029400
GE.N	30-AUG-2006		End Of Day		34.25	34.44	34.21	34.27	6691100

Appendix C

RNSE File Format

The following table provides a data description of RNSE data fields. The RNSE data format includes 41 fields overall, however only the relevant data fields used in this thesis are introduced here. The following information and description is copied with only minor changes directly from Thomson Reuters (2008b):

TIMESTAMP: The date and time of the news item as timestamped by the NewsScope Archive, presented in GMT, millisecond precision.
Format: DD MMM YYYY hh:mm:ss.sss
Length: 24

BCAST_REF: Reuters Instrument Code (RIC) of the company for which the scores apply. *Note: While company may trade on a foreign exchange under a different RIC, the scores are referenced to its Home RIC.*
Format: String: <CompanyID>.<Market>
Length: 10

RELEVANCE: A real valued number indicating the relevance of the news item to the company. It is calculated by comparing how relevant the article is about each of the companies mentioned in it. For stories with multiple companies mentioned, the company with the most mentions will have the highest relevance. A company with a lower amount of mentions will have a lower relevance score.
Format: Real: 0.0-1.0
Length: 10

SENTIMENT: This field indicates the predominant sentiment class for this news item with respect to this company. The indicated class is the one with the highest probability.
Format: Integer (1: Positive, 0: Neutral, -1: Negative)
Length: 15

LNKD_CNTn: These fields (n: 1-5) contain a list of the number of linguistically similar items found by the RNSE in each of five history periods: 12 hours, 24 hours, 3 days, 5 days and 7 days. The RNSE takes a "vocabulary fingerprint" of the current news item and compares it with the fingerprints of other stories from each of the history periods that mention the current company. The count of linked articles in a particular time period gives a measure of the novelty of the news being reported – the higher the linked count value, the less novel the story is. If the count is zero, then the currrent item can be considered novel as there are no similar items reporting the story within the history period.
Format: Unsigned Integer
Length: 15

PNAC: Primary News Access Code – a semi-unique story identifier. PNACS are often reused.
Format: String
Length: 14

References

Akhtar, S., R. Faff, B. Oliver, and A. Subrahmanyam (2011). The power of bad: The negativity bias in Australian consumer sentiment announcements on stock returns. *Journal of Banking and Finance 35*(5), 1239–1249.

Andersen, T. G., T. Bollerslev, F. X. Diebold, and C. Vega (2007). Real-time price discovery in global stock, bond and foreign exchange markets. *Journal of International Economics 73*(2), 251–277.

Antweiler, W. and M. Z. Frank (2004). Is all that talk just noise? the information content of internet stock message boards. *The Journal of Finance 59*(3), 1139–1167.

Bagehot (Pseud.), W. (1971). The only game in town. *Financial Analysts Journal 27*(2), 12–14.

Barber, B. M. and D. Loeffler (1993). The "dartboard" column: Second-hand information and price pressure. *The Journal of Financial and Quantitative Analysis 28*(2), 273–284.

Barber, B. M. and T. Odean (2008). All that glitters: The effect of attention and news on the buying behavior of individual and institutional investors. *The Review of Financial Studies 21*(2), 785–818.

Barclay, M. J. and T. Hendershott (2003). Price discovery and trading after hours. *The Review of Financial Studies 16*(4), 1041–1073.

Barclay, M. J., T. Hendershott, and D. McCormick (2003). Competition among trading venues: Information and trading on electronic communications networks. *The Journal of Finance 58*(6), 2637–2665.

Barclay, M. J. and J. B. Warner (1993). Stealth trading and volatility: Which trades move prices? *Journal of Financial Economics 34*(3), 281–305.

Bennett, P. and L. Wei (2006). Market structure, fragmentation, and market quality. *Journal of Financial Markets 9*(1), 49–78.

Berry, T. D. and K. M. Howe (1994). Public information arrival. *The Journal of Finance 49*(4), 1331–1346.

Bessembinder, H. (2003a). Issues in assessing trade execution costs. *Journal of Financial Markets 6*(3), 233–257.

Bessembinder, H. (2003b). Trade execution costs and market quality after decimalization. *Journal of Financial and Quantitative Analysis 38*(4), 747–777.

Bessembinder, H. and H. M. Kaufman (1997). A cross-exchange comparison of execution costs and information flow for NYSE-listed stocks. *Journal of Financial Economics 46*(3), 293–319.

Biais, B., P. Hillion, and C. Spatt (1995). An empirical analysis of the limit order book and the order flow in the paris bourse. *The Journal of Finance 50*(5), 1655–1689.

Blöhdorn, S. and A. Hotho (2009). Ontologies for machine learning. In S. Staab and R. Studer (Eds.), *Handbook on Ontologies*, International Handbooks on Information Systems, pp. 637–661. Springer Berlin / Heidelberg.

Boehmer, B. and E. Boehmer (2003). Trading your neighbor's ETFs: Competition or fragmentation? *Journal of Banking and Finance 27*(9), 1667–1703.

Bris, A., W. N. Goetzmann, and N. Zhu (2007). Efficiency and the bear: Short sales and markets around the world. *The Journal of Finance 62*(3), 1029–1079.

Brockman, P., I. Liebenberg, and M. Schutte (2010). Comovement, information production, and the business cycle. *Journal of Financial Economics 97*(1), 107–129.

Brown, G. and N. Kapadia (2007). Firm-specific risk and equity market development. *Journal of Financial Economics 84*(2), 358–388.

Bushman, R. M., J. D. Piotroski, and A. J. Smith (2004). What determines corporate transparency? *Journal of Accounting Research 42*(2), 207–252.

Cai, C. X., R. Hudson, and K. Keasey (2004). Intra day bid-ask spreads, trading volume and volatility: Recent empirical evidence from the london stock exchange. *Journal of Business Finance and Accounting 31*(5–6), 647–676.

Campbell, J. Y., M. Lettau, B. G. Malkiel, and Y. Xu (2001). Have individual stocks become more volatile? an empirical exploration of idiosyncratic risk. *The Journal of Finance 56*(1), 1–43.

Cao, C., T. Simin, and J. Zhao (2008). Can growth options explain the trend in idiosyncratic risk? *The Review of Financial Studies 21*(6), 2599–2633.

Chaboud, A., B. Chiquoine, E. Hjalarsson, and C. Vega (2009). Rise of the machines: Algorithmic trading in the foreign exchange market. *FRB International Finance Discussion Paper No. 980*.

Chen, C. W., T. C. Chiang, and M. K. So (2003). Asymmetrical reaction to US stock-return news: Evidence from major stock markets based on a double-threshold model. *Journal of Economics and Business 55*(5–6), 487–502.

Chowdhry, B. and V. Nanda (1991). Multimarket trading and market liquidity. *The Review of Financial Studies 4*(3), 483–511.

Chuliá, H., M. Martens, and D. van Dijk (2010). Asymmetric effects of federal funds target rate changes on S&P100 stock returns, volatilities and correlations. *Journal of Banking and Finance 34*(4), 834–839.

Chun, H., J.-W. Kim, J. Lee, and R. Morck (2004). Patterns of comovement: The role of information technology in the U.S. economy. *NBER Working Paper*.

De Melo, G. and S. Siersdorfer (2007). Multilingual text classification using ontologies. In C. Nédellec and C. Rouveirol (Eds.), *Advances in Information Retrieval*, Volume 4425 of *Lecture Notes in Computer Science*, pp. 541–548. Amati, Giambattista and Carpineto, Claudio and Romano, Giovanni.

Debole, F. and F. Sebastiani (2005). An analysis of the relative hardness of Reuters-21578 subsets. *Journal of the American Society for Information Science and Technology 56*(6), 584–596.

Degryse, H. (2009). Competition between financial markets in Europe: What can be expected from MiFID? *Financial Markets and Portfolio Management 23*(1), 93–103.

Durnev, A., R. Morck, and B. Yeung (2004). Value-enhancing capital budgeting and firm-specific stock return variation. *The Journal of Finance 59*(1), 65–105.

Durnev, A., R. Morck, B. Yeung, and P. Zarowin (2003). Does greater firm-specific return variation mean more or less informed stock pricing? *Journal of Accounting Research 41*(5), 797–836.

Ederington, L. H. and J. H. Lee (1993). How markets process information: News releases and volatility. *The Journal of Finance 48*(4), 1161–1191.

Ellsberg, D. (1961). Risk, ambiguity, and the savage axioms. *The Quarterly Journal of Economics 75*(4), 643–669.

Epstein, L. G. and M. Schneider (2008). Ambiguity, information quality, and asset pricing. *The Journal of Finance 63*(1), 197–228.

Epstein, L. G. and M. Schneider (2010). Ambiguity and asset markets. *NBER Working Paper*.

Evans, M. D. D. and R. K. Lyons (2008). How is macro news transmitted to exchange rates. *Journal of Financial Economics 88*(1), 26–50.

Fang, L. and J. Peress (2009). Media coverage and the cross-section of stock returns. *The Journal of Finance 64*(5), 2023–2052.

Fink, J., K. Fink, G. Grullon, and J. Weston (2006). Firm age and fluctuations in idiosyncratic risk. *Working Paper*.

Fleming, M. J. and E. M. Remolona (1999). Price formation and liquidity in the U.S. Treasury market: The response to public information. *The Journal of Finance 54*(5), 1901–1915.

Foucault, T. and A. J. Menkveld (2008). Competition for order flow and smart order routing systems. *The Journal of Finance 63*(1), 119–158.

French, K. R. and R. Roll (1986). Stock return variances: The arrival of information and the reaction of traders. *Journal of Financial Economics 17*(1), 5–26.

Gagliardini, P., P. Porchia, and F. Trojani (2009). Ambiguity aversion and the term structure of interest rates. *The Review of Financial Studies 22*(10), 4157–4188.

Glosten, L. and P. Milgrom (1985). Bid, ask and transaction prices in a specialist market with heterogeneously informed traders. *Journal of Financial Economics 14*(1), 71–100.

Goldstein, M. A. and K. A. Kavajecz (2000). Eights, sixteenths, and market depth: changes in tick size and liquidity provision on the NYSE. *Journal of Financial Economics 56*(1), 125–149.

Goldstein, M. A. and K. A. Kavajecz (2004). Trading strategies during circuit breakers and extreme market movements. *Journal of Financial Markets 7*(3), 301–333.

Goldstein, M. A., A. V. Shkilko, B. F. Van Ness, and R. A. Van Ness (2008). Competition in the market for NASDAQ securities. *Journal of Financial Markets 11*(2), 113–143.

Green, T. C. (2004). Economic news and the impact of trading on bond prices. *The Journal of Finance 59*(3), 1201–1233.

Groß-Klußmann, A. and N. Hautsch (2011). When machines read the news: Using automated text analytics to quantify high frequency news-impled market reactions. *Journal of Empirical Finance 18*(2), 321–340.

Guo, H. and R. Savickas (2008). Average idiosyncratic volatility in G7 countries. *The Review of Financial Studies 21*(3), 1259–1296.

Hamao, Y., J. Mei, and Y. Xu (2003). Idiosyncratic risk and the creative destruction in japan. *NBER Working Paper*.

Hameed, A., R. Morck, J. Shen, and B. Yeung (2010). Information, analysts, and stock return comovement. *NBER Working Paper*.

Hansen, P. and A. Lunde (2005). A realized variance for the whole day based on intermittent high-frequency data. *Journal of Financial Econometrics 3*(4), 525–554.

Harris, L. E. (1994). Minimum price variations, discrete bid-ask spreads, and quotation sizes. *The Review of Financial Studies 7*(1), 149–178.

Harris, M. and A. Raviv (1993). Differences of opinion make a horse race. *The Review of Financial Studies 6*(3), 473–506.

Hasbrouck, J. (1991a). Measuring the information content of stock trades. *The Journal of Finance 46*(1), 179–207.

Hasbrouck, J. (1991b). The summary informativeness of stock trades: An econometric analysis. *The Review of Financial Studies 4*(3), 571–595.

Hasbrouck, J. (1995). One security, many markets: Determining the contributions to price discovery. *The Journal of Finance 50*(4), 1175–1199.

Höchstötter, M., R. Riordan, and A. Storkenmaier (2011). International stock market comovement and news. *Working Paper*.

Hendershott, T., C. M. Jones, and A. J. Menkveld (2011). Does algorithmic trading improve liquidity? *The Journal of Finance*. forthcoming.

Hendershott, T. and R. Riordan (2009). Algorithmic trading and information. *Working Paper*.

Hess, D., A. Kempf, and M. Malinowska (2008). Liquidity provision in periods of high information flow. *Working Paper*.

Huang, R. D. (2002). The quality of ecn and nasdaq market maker quotes. *The Journal of Finance 57*(3), 1285–1319.

Hutton, A. P., A. J. Marcus, and H. Tehranian (2009). Opaque financial reports, R^2, and crash risk. *Journal of Financial Economics 94*(1), 67–86.

International Telecommunication Union (2009). Measuring the information society - the ICT development index. *White Paper*.

Irvine, P. J. and J. Pontiff (2009). Idiosyncratic return volatility, cash flows, and product market competition. *The Review of Financial Studies 22*(3), 1149–1177.

Jin, L. and S. C. Myers (2006). R^2 around the world: New theory and new tests. *Journal of Financial Economics 79*(2), 257–292.

Joachims, T. (1998). Text categorization with support vector machines: Learning with many relevant features. In C. Nédellec and C. Rouveirol (Eds.), *Machine Learning: ECML-98*, Volume 1398 of *Lecture Notes in Computer Science*, pp. 137–142. Springer Berlin / Heidelberg.

Jones, C. M. and M. L. Lipson (2001). Sixteenths: direct evidence on institutional execution costs. *Journal of Financial Economics 59*(2), 253–278.

Kandel, E. and N. D. Pearson (1995). Differential interpretation of public signals and trade in speculative markets. *Journal of Political Economy 103*(4), 831–872.

Karolyi, G. A., K.-H. Lee, and M. A. van Dijk (2009). Commonality in returns, liquidity, and turnover around the world. *Working Paper*.

Khandaker, S. and R. Heaney (2009). Do emerging markets have higher stock synchronicity? the international evidence. *Journal of Business and Policy Research 4*(1), 79–98.

Kim, O. and R. E. Verrecchia (1991). Market reactions to anticipated announcements. *Journal of Financial Economics 30*(2), 273–309.

Kim, O. and R. E. Verrecchia (1994). Market liquidity and volume around earnings announcements. *Journal of Accounting and Economics 17*(1–2), 41–67.

Klar, J. and I. van den Bongard (2008). Determinants of the bid-ask spread and the role of designated sponsors: Evidence for Xetra. *Working Paper*.

Krinsky, I. and J. Lee (1996). Earnings announcements and the components of the bid-ask spread. *The Journal of Finance 51*(4), 1523–1535.

Kyle, A. S. (1985). Continuous auctions and insider trading. *Econometrica 53*(6), 1315–1335.

La Porta, R., F. Lopez-de Silanes, and A. Shleifer (1998). Law and finance. *Journal of Political Economy 106*(6), 1113–1155.

La Porta, R., F. Lopez-de-Silanes, A. Shleifer, and R. Vishny (2000). Investor protection and corporate governance. *Journal of Financial Economics 58*(1–2), 3–27.

Lee, C. and M. Ready (1991). Inferring trade direction from intraday data. *The Journal of Finance 46*(2), 733–746.

Leippold, M., F. Trojani, and P. Vanini (2008). Differences of opinion make a horse race. *The Review of Financial Studies 21*(6), 2567–2597.

Leopold, E. and J. Kindermann (2002). Text categorization with support vector machines. how to represent texts in input space? *Machine Learning 46*(1), 423–444.

Lewis, D. D., Y. Yang, T. G. Rose, and F. Li (2004). RCV1: A new benchmark collection for text categorization research. *Journal of Machine Learning Research 5*, 361–397.

Li, K., R. Morck, F. Yang, and B. Yeung (2004). Firm-specific variation and openness in emerging markets. *The Review of Economics and Statistics 86*(3), 658–669.

Liu, P., S. D. Smith, and A. A. Syed (1990). Stock price reactions to the wall street journal's securities recommendations. *Journal of Financial and Quantitative Analysis 25*(3), 399–410.

Madhavan, A. (2000). Market microstructure: A survey. *Journal of Financial Markets 3*(3), 205–258.

Madhavan, A., M. Richardson, and M. Roomans (1997). Why do security prices change? a transaction-level analysis of NYSE stocks. *The Review of Financial Studies 10*(4), 1035–1064.

Mendelson, H. (1987). Consolidation, fragmentation, and market performance. *Journal of Financial and Quantitative Analysis 22*(2), 189–207.

Mitchell, M. L. and J. H. Mulherin (1994). The impact of public information on the stock market. *The Journal of Finance 49*(3), 923–950.

Morck, R., B. Yeung, and W. Yu (2000). The information content of stock markets: Why do emerging markets have synchronous stock price movements. *Journal of Financial Economics 58*(1–2), 215–260.

Morse, D. (1981). Price and trading volume reaction surrounding earnings announcements: A closer examination. *Journal of Accounting Research 19*(2), 374–383.

Newey, W. K. and K. D. West (1987). A simple, positive semi-definite, heteroskedasticity and autocorrelation consistent covariance matrix. *Econometrica 55*(3), 703–708.

Niederhoffer, V. (1971). The analysis of world events and stock prices. *The Journal of Business 44*(2), 193–219.

Niessen, A. (2007). Media coverage and macroeconomic information processing. *SFB 649 Discussion Paper 2007-011.*

Pagano, M. (1989). Trading volume and asset liquidity. *Quarterly Journal of Economics 104*(2), 255–274.

Patell, J. M. and M. A. Wolfson (1982). Good news, bad news, and the intraday timing of corporate disclosures. *The Accounting Review 57*(3), 509–527.

Petersen, M. A. (2009). Estimating standard errors in finance panel data sets: Comparing approaches. *The Review of Financial Studies 22*(1), 435–480.

Piotroski, J. D. and B. T. Roulstone (2004). The influence of analysts, institutional investors, and insiders on the incorporation of market, industry, and firm-specific information into stock prices. *The Accounting Review 79*(4), 1119–1151.

Ranaldo, A. (2006). Intraday market dynamics around public information arrivals. *Swiss National Bank Working Paper.*

Read, D. (1999). *The Power of News: The History of Reuters* (2 ed.). Oxford: Oxford University Press.

Riordan, R., A. Storkenmaier, and M. Wagener (2010a). Fragmentation, competition and market quality: A post-mifid analysis. *Working Paper.*

Riordan, R., A. Storkenmaier, and M. Wagener (2010b). Public information arrival: Price discovery and liquidity in electronic limit order markets. *Working Paper.*

Roll, R. (1988). R^2. *The Journal of Finance 43*(3), 541–566.

Ronis, D. L. and E. R. Lipinski (1985). Value and uncertainty as weighting factors in impression formation. *Journal of Experimental Social Psychology 21*, 47–60.

Ryan, P. and R. J. Taffler (2007). Are economically significant stock returns and trading volumes driven by firm-specific news releases. *Journal of Business Finance & Accounting 31*(1), 49–82.

Soroka, S. N. (2006). Good news and bad news: Asymmetric responses to economic information. *The Journal of Politics 68*(2), 372–385.

Stock, J. H. and M. W. Watson (1988). Testing for common trends. *Journal of the American Statistical Association 83*(404), 1097–1107.

Storkenmaier, A., R. Riordan, C. Weinhardt, and R. Studer (2010). The impact of economic news on information and liquidity in electronic futures trading. In T. Dreier, J. Krämer, R. Studer, and C. Weinhardt (Eds.), *Information Management and Market Engineering: Vol. II. Studies on eOrganisation and Market Engineering*, pp. 37–54. KIT Scientific Publishing.

Storkenmaier, A., M. Wagener, and C. Weinhardt (2010). Public information in fragmented markets. *Working Paper*.

Tetlock, P. C. (2007). Giving content to investor sentiment: The role of media in the stock market. *The Journal of Finance 62*(3), 1139–1167.

Tetlock, P. C. (2008). All the news that's fit to reprint: Do investors react to stale information. *Working Paper*.

Tetlock, P. C., S. A. Macskassy, and M. Saar-Tsechansky (2008). More than words: Quantifying language to measure firms' fundamentals. *The Journal of Finance 63*(3), 1427–1467.

Thompson, R. B., C. Olson, and R. Dietrich (1987). Attributes of news about firms: An analysis of firm-specific news reported in the wall street journal index. *Journal of Accounting Research 25*(2), 245–274.

Thompson, S. B. (2011). Simple formulas for standard errors that cluster by both firm and time. *Journal of Financial Economics 99*(1), 1–10.

Thomson Reuters (2008a). Reuters Newsscope Sentiment Engine: Guide to sample data and system overview. *Thomson Reuters White Paper*.

Thomson Reuters (2008b). Reuters Newsscope Sentiment Engine: Output image and file format. *Thomson Reuters White Paper*.

Tong, S. and D. Koller (2001). Support vector machine active learning with applications to text classification. *Journal of Machine Learning Research* 2, 45–66.

Treynor, J. (1995). The only game in town (reprint). *Financial Analysts Journal 51*(1), 81–83.

Veldkamp, L. L. (2005). Slow boom, sudden crash. *Journal of Economic Theory 124*(2), 230–257.

Veldkamp, L. L. (2006). Information markets and the comovement of asset prices. *Review of Economic Studies 73*(3), 823–845.

Veronesi, P. (1999). Stock market overreaction to bad news in good times: A rational expectations equilibrium model. *The Review of Financial Studies 12*(5), 975–1007.

White, H. (1980). A heteroskedasticity-consistent covariance matrix estimator and a direct test for heteroskedasticity. *Econometrica 48*(4), 817–838.

Willard, K. L., T. W. Guinnane, and H. S. Rosen (1996). Turning points in the civil war: Views from the greenback market. *The American Economic Review 86*(4), 1001–1018.

Wurgler, J. (2000). Financial markets and the allocation of capital. *Journal of Financial Economics 58*(1–2), 187–214.